MY CHOIR JOURNEY

Brian E. Davies

To Linda,

with best wishes,

Brian Davies

Published by

Llyfrau Cambria Books, Wales, United Kingdom.

Cambria Books is an imprint of

Cambria Publishing Ltd.

Discover our other books at: www.cambriabooks.co.uk

For all my choir friends,
past and present

Books by Brian E. Davies

Mumbles & Gower Pubs (2006 & 2018)

Wales – A Walk Through Time:
> Flat Holm to Brecon
>
> Brecon to Harlech
>
> Harlech to Cemaes Bay

Mumbles & Gower Through Time

A-Z of Mumbles & Gower

Front Cover Picture

The Morriston Orpheus Choir at the Taipei National Concert Hall in Taiwan

CONTENTS

FOREWORD

As choirs seek to rebuild membership following the pandemic, this book is essential recruitment reading.

It tells, with warmth, gratitude and affection, of the joys of comradeship in song. On international tours, bonds are strengthened not only between choir members but also with audiences across the globe. Music is what governments define as soft power, an ambassadorial mission which trancends distance, language and politics.

My early experiences, further west in the then-industrial hub of Llanelli, were not dissimilar to those of Brian: the chapel and eisteddfod backgrounds, the sturdy, foundational impact of four-part singing of hymns and anthems, the enormous influence of enlightened, disciplined but kind teachers. So, too, my own later experiences, accompanying Welsh choirs on organ and piano in far-flung corners of the globe or leading the BBC National Orchestra of Wales on its many international tours. At post-concert receptions hosted by the Welsh societies of American, Canadian, Australian cities, by the orchestras of the same countries, Eastern Europe or Japan, I have discovered a common humanity of kindred spirits bonded by the civilising power of music. The same experience shines through Brian's book.

Closer to home, with Morriston grandparents and, later, my younger brother, Alun, as Morriston Orpheus organist, the international touring and recording successes of the Choir were certainly not lost upon me; neither are my memories of Ivor Sims, Eurfryn John and Alwyn Humphreys. So too, the experiences of playing at massed male choral festivals at the Royal Albert Hall over a 45-year period. From the eyrie of the organ console, I've sensed that those huge audiences are my musically-extended Welsh family!

1

Congratulations, Brian, on committing your illuminating memories to print in such a readable and entertaining way. I thoroughly commend your book, confident that its pages will bring as many warming smiles to the faces of readers as they did to mine.

Huw Tregelles Williams, OBE, FRCO. President, Welsh Association of Male Choirs, former Head of Music, BBC Wales.

INTRO

On 14 March 1995, as we lined up backstage at the Sydney Opera House, my fellow top tenor, Tecwyn, turned to me, warmly shook my hand and wished me the best of luck. I said the same to him. Our choir then entered the stage to a tremendous ovation from the audience packed into the great auditorium, many of them standing and cheering. After the Australian National Anthem, our conductor faced the choir and said, 'Give them Hell!' before we launched into an impassioned rendering of *Men of Harlech* in Welsh. It brought the house down!

This is a story about the joy of singing in a choir and travelling the world. More specifically, it is about a life singing in three Welsh male choirs, one of them internationally acclaimed, and latterly, singing in a high-quality a cappella choir. My story includes what goes on behind the scenes and occasionally delves into the murky world of choir politics. Inevitably, it includes a personal view of the unfortunate 'split' that took place in the Morriston Orpheus Choir in 2007.

My story relates many incidents that occurred over the years, some of them hilarious. I sometimes refer to a drinking culture and this gives rise to many of the stories (and contributed to some of the camaraderie and fun). The book is mostly written in chronological order and, besides relating my own choir memories, provides a commentary on some of the golden years of Welsh male choral singing.

I start with my early days, singing in chapel as a boy in the Welsh valleys. Little did I know that I would end up singing at the Sydney Opera House, Carnegie Hall and many other world-class venues. Much of my story describes choir tours to various parts of the world and I am aware of the maxim that 'what goes on tour, stays on tour'. I have therefore been selective and hope I haven't embarrassed anyone.

My story is about a choral life that left little time for other hobbies. It was family, work and choir, not always in that order of priority, and I am eternally grateful to my wife Mari and my family for the tolerance and support that allowed me to follow my choir journey.

Many of the people featured in my story have sadly passed away and I would like to pay my respects to them all, and to their loved ones. They are now singing in the great celestial choir in the sky. One day, hopefully not too soon, I will join them - if I pass the audition!

Brian E. Davies

August 2023

1 - THE GARN

It all began at Bethel, in the small Welsh mining village of Garndiffaith. I returned to the Eastern Valley of Gwent at the age of eight, and the priority was to re-enrol in Garndiffaith Junior School, closely followed by Sunday School at Bethel Primitive Methodist. There were four or five thriving chapels in the village, but Bethel was chosen for a simple reason. It was the nearest.

My father and I moved in with my grandmother and my auntie's family. The semi-detached council house at Lower Ty Gwyn was a vast improvement on the tiny gas-lit, white-washed cottage where we'd all previously lived. This had been in a row appropriately called Davies's Court, which was lower down on the Garn. These dilapidated cottages were demolished soon afterwards.

Going to chapel meant singing, either in the choir or, if you were one of the chosen few, singing solo. As well as learning about the scriptures and the evils of drink, the children were meticulously prepared for the big event of the year, the Chapel Anniversary. The village chapels held their anniversaries on consecutive Sundays in the spring, each trying to outdo the other with their parades through the streets. We were all treated to a new outfit for the occasion and, although the chapel services and concerts were the main events, there was also the Anniversary tea to look forward to, a small reward for the hard work in rehearsals.

The singers were fine-tuned under the direction of strict conductors who coaxed us into trying to reach perfection. The chapel would be packed for the performances, and I remember the nervousness waiting to sing. As a budding boy soprano, I always worried about the high notes, although I was usually capable of reaching them. Some children gave recitations of poetry that were beautifully articulated, the result of elocution lessons and many hours of practice. Everybody was encouraged to take part and the Anniversary services were a real community occasion.

The seeds of music were sown at home when I was a small child. My Auntie May sang oratorios with the choir at Noddfa Chapel in Abersychan and my father raised a few eyebrows as a boy when he sang *Carolina Moon* in the chapel eisteddfod. My father often regaled me with stories of the operas and the great tenors and baritones. I remember him telling me about Gigli and Björling and about arias like *Che Gelida Manina* from La Bohème. Another favourite was the *Prologue* from Pagliacci sung by legendary baritone, Tito Gobbi. He saved enough money to buy a Phillips radiogram, together with some records, and would proudly invite his friends around to listen to his collection. I remember one evening sitting through a recording of La Bohème (I was devastated at the time because I wanted to listen to 'Journey into Space' on the radio!). On Christmas Day, the *Hallelujah Chorus* was always played and on Easter Sunday, it was the *Easter Hymn* from Cavalleria Rusticana. Such was the musical background of my childhood. It was a working-class community, but people had an appreciation of music. Concerts were performed in the valley's chapels and singing came naturally. The village's male voice choir was the well-known Garndiffaith Gleemen, conducted by Horace Carter, a friend of my father. The choir won many prizes.

My singing in chapel must have been reasonable because it was recommended that I should have my 'voice trained'. This was an expensive option: half-a-crown for an hour of voice tuition. My father opted to pay for weekly lessons so, aged about ten, I started singing lessons with Madame Violet Branch-Davies (popularly known as Madame Branch). The lessons were all about breathing and phrasing, as well as singing scales and other vocal exercises; but correct breathing was emphasised over and over. The places to breathe were marked with a pencil tick on my music scores; woe betide me if I breathed anywhere else!

Thus, I was introduced to songs like *O for the Wings of a Dove,* and *Where'er You Walk*. I still remember the words of these songs that were rehearsed over and over. Eventually, I was deemed ready to compete in Eisteddfod competitions. My first competition was the local Garndiffaith Eisteddfod. The 'prelims' (preliminary heats) were held in the local school with the finals in the Workmen's Hall in front of a large audience. I went to the prelims where the test piece was *The Rising of the Lark* which I hated because of its tricky high notes. I was extremely nervous and failed to pass the prelims. At least I was spared the nerve-wracking experience of singing in the finals! My confidence gradually grew, but there was another boy soprano around the circuit, I think his name was Cledwyn. He was also a pupil of Madame Branch and was more experienced (and better) than me. My best result was second place at Tredegar Eisteddfod where the test piece was *How Beautiful Are the Feet* from Handel's Messiah (Cledwyn came first). My prize for coming second was a little purse containing a two-shilling piece.

The most rewarding part of my time as a boy soprano was singing in a little concert party and performing to local audiences. We rehearsed around the piano in someone's parlour on Sunday evenings after chapel. My favourite piece was *Art Thou Troubled*, another Handel song that has always remained in my heart. At around this time, there was a well-known girls' choir in the valley called the 'Silver Songsters'. There was also the young Janet Price from Abersychan who went on to become a highly regarded and sophisticated soprano and teacher. The world-famous soprano, Dame Gwyneth Jones also came from Pontnewynydd in our valley and achieved great fame in the opera houses of the world. I'll never forget Dame Gwyneth's 'homecoming' concert held in Pontypool years later. There was a huge symphony orchestra accompanying Dame Gwyneth and her wonderful voice soared above the orchestra as she sang *Isolde's Liebestod* and other great arias.

I left the Garn School to go to West Monmouthshire Grammar School for Boys, down the valley in Pontypool. Eventually my voice broke, and my singing was put on hold. The next logical step was piano lessons, but we couldn't afford a piano! Unfortunately, the grammar school's music lessons were a bit limited; I was given a recorder but when I played it out of turn it was snatched away from me. I felt excluded but the music master wouldn't relent; I must have really upset him. Eventually he gave me an old violin to keep me quiet! I was required to practise at home but felt a fool carrying a violin case home on the bus to the Garn. I was afraid the local boys would throw stones at me! I soon gave it up. My singing at this time was restricted to croaking hymns in Assembly.

The experience that had a profound effect on me was a concert by the Garndiffaith Gleemen at the Workmen's Hall; this was their annual Remembrance Day concert. My cousin was in the choir, and I remember him and the other choristers sipping a small glass of sherry at the Garn Workmen's Club before the concert to warm up their vocal cords (my father was unable to join the choir due to shortness of breath, a condition exacerbated by his war service, during which he took part in the Normandy campaign). I was about thirteen at the time and sat on my own in the audience. I enjoyed the choir's opening items and listened to the guest soloists, but it was when the choir sang *By Babylon's Wave* that it happened. This was my first hearing of the piece, and it began very quietly, conveying a sense of foreboding:

'Here by Babylon's wave, though heathen hands have bound us,
Though afar from our land, the pains of death surround us'

The hushed theme continued until suddenly the choir changed to fortissimo, crying:

'Woe unto thee! Babylon mighty city, for the day of thy fall is nigh,

For thee no hope, For thee no pity, though loud thy wail riseth on high ... ... '

I was electrified. The hairs on the back of my neck stood up and I was tingling all over. The anthem continued to its great climax of *'Be woe! Be woe! Be woe!'* with the first tenors excelling at the end. It was unforgettable and I was hooked. The concert ended with Horace Carter's own arrangement of Tosti's *Goodbye,* and I prayed that one day I would be up there singing in the choir. I didn't know then that I would end up singing *By Babylon's Wave* and all the other great male voice 'warhorses' many times and that my choir journey would take me all around the world.

2 - CWMBRAN EARLY YEARS

During my teenage years, the memory of the Garndiffaith choir stayed with me, despite the attractions of rock and roll. When I was (almost) old enough to drink, my father took me to one of his favourite haunts, the Twyn-y-Ffrwd public house, near Abersychan. On Sunday evenings there was always great singing in the lounge-bar, with landlady Gwyneth at the piano and some of the Garndiffaith Gleemen joining in. I thought this was brilliant and it encouraged me further.

By this time, I'd moved down the valley, left school, and started work. I was initially based in Cwmbran and later in Cardiff. I went to college and passed exams and took my driving test and failed. The latter is important because when I returned to work in Cwmbran, I had some driving lessons with Cwmbran School of Motoring. The instructor was Bill Fry, who happened to be a member of Cwmbran Male Voice Choir. I expressed an interest and before I knew it, my driving instructor was driving me to a rehearsal. After a chat with the musical director, Clifford Jones, I was placed in the first tenors. The choristers alongside me listened to my efforts and at the end of the rehearsal, I was accepted into the choir. Bill shook my hand in congratulation and politely asked 'do you take a drink?'. When I replied in the affirmative (despite my chapel upbringing), I was promptly taken to a drinking club in Old Cwmbran. There I met several other choristers and proceeded to drink numerous pints of beer. It seemed that this was another initiation test! Next morning, I realised the social side was almost as important as the music; 'work hard, play hard' was the order of the day. Thus began seventeen happy years singing with the top tenors of Cwmbran, with many great friendships and experiences. I passed my driving test shortly afterwards.

Cwmbran (translation 'Valley of the Crow') is a modern town in the Eastern Valley, about five miles north of Newport, and is overlooked by the high Twm Barlwm hillfort and the mountain ridge of Mynydd Maen. Cwmbran Male Voice Choir was formed in 1964, a few years before I joined, and was about sixty or seventy strong at that time. The choir had its roots in Upper Cwmbran, one of the oldest parts of the town, overlooking the valley, and with a history of mining like my home village of Garndiffaith. There was a strong choral tradition there, stretching back to the beginning of the 20th century.

A male voice choir consists of four main parts: First (Top) Tenor, Second Tenor, First Bass (Baritone) and Second (Bottom) Bass. When I joined Cwmbran, it was a young choir, and although there was a wide spectrum of ages, there were a lot of members in their twenties and thirties. I remember with clarity some of the items we were practising at that first night of rehearsal: there was *O Praise the Lord with One Consent*, an anthem by Handel, *The Recognition of Land* by Grieg, and the Welsh hymn *Llanfair* arranged by Mansel Thomas. I'll never forget the joy of learning the top tenor lines and joining harmony with the other parts.

I was soon kitted out with a choir tie and a smart blazer badge. I had to buy my own black blazer and grey slacks; black shoes and socks completed the outfit. Later, we were provided with dinner suits and a red velvet dickie-bow! I was given a folder containing the current repertoire and encouraged to 'do my homework'. I settled into the routine of rehearsals every Monday and Thursday and a life that left little time for other hobbies. I was in the choir before I was married and, luckily, my new wife, Mari, allowed me to continue my singing. I made friends with the other choristers and was formally introduced to the Queen: not Her Majesty, but the Queen public house in Upper Cwmbran, a favourite watering hole for 'after practice'. The choir's connection with Upper Cwmbran was strong: some of the choristers had previously belonged to the old Upper Cwmbran Male Voice Choir that rehearsed at Upper Cwmbran School. The Queen crowd included Graham Bowkett,

Ron Pitt, Ivor Maggs, Eric Edwards and John Harris (aka Boxer). The latter was well-named as he was handy with his fists. On one occasion, following an eisteddfod competition, we were in a chip shop getting supplies before the long journey home. One of the local yobbos started taking the mickey out of our 'monkey suits' and Boxer floored him with a single blow. He and his mates soon scarpered. Boxer was a good companion to have around in times of trouble. He was also a great second tenor.

I was also friendly with Peter Johns, the choir's hard-working secretary, and Don Price, a fellow top tenor. Our conversations and arguments after practice were invariably about choir business, with a bit of politics and rugby thrown in. One of our drinking companions was a member of a rival choir. His surname was Knight, and we reckoned he didn't have much of a voice. Behind his back, we called him 'Silent Knight'! We also had a bottom bass in our choir that no-one had ever heard a sound from. He was called 'Whispering Smith'.

Cwmbran MVC conductor Clifford Jones was a brilliant musician and formed a great team with accompanist, Lucy Clark, and assistant conductor, Harold Richards. Cliff was keen on 'contemporary' music as well as the traditional repertoire and we tackled works by Kodaly and William Mathias as well as Welsh hymns, spirituals and classical pieces. We sang many of the great works of the Welsh male choir repertoire, including *Crossing the Plain*, *Castilla*, *The Spartan Heroes*, *By Babylon's Wave*, *The Martyrs of the Arena* (with its great ending) and the greatest of them all *Nidaros* by Daniel Protheroe. It was thrilling to sing these pieces, particularly as a top tenor.

The first concert I performed in was at the Maesyrhiw Country Club, a popular local venue. My father and his friends turned up to support me and gave me their critical opinion. Another memorable early performance was at Rodney Parade, Newport, when we entertained the All Blacks rugby team and their supporters in the Newport clubhouse after their game against Monmouthshire. I still have the official supporters' tie, given to me afterwards.

The highlight of the year was the choir's Annual Concert, held at Llantarnam School Hall. The venue later changed to the Congress Theatre and, later still, to the Cwmbran Leisure Centre, a larger venue. Guest artistes at the 'Annual' were well-known names from the world of opera, and the concerts would always be sold out. I remember Maryetta Midgley, Maria Moll, Helen Field and the bass Forbes Robinson singing with us as well as the valley's own Janet Price and many Welsh National Opera principals.

I remember one London-based tenor called Tom Swift who thrilled the audience with his high C's. He decided to stay in Cwmbran overnight and joined us at the Queen Inn after the concert. Tom enjoyed himself so much that he stayed on next day for the Sunday lunchtime session before catching his train back to London!

Some of us regularly went to performances of the Welsh National Opera. The first opera I attended was in Bristol, a WNO performance of *Carmen* at the Hippodrome. We booked a box overlooking the stage and thoroughly enjoyed ourselves. I remember throwing flowers down onto the stage at the end, towards Janet Coster who gave a great performance as Carmen.

We also attended the Proms at the Royal Albert Hall, including a performance of Beethoven's *Choral Fantasia*. Peter and I dressed up for the occasion, donning our tuxedos and feeling pleased with ourselves. When we arrived at the Albert Hall, the stewards promptly directed us to the rear of the stage: because of our attire they assumed we were part of the London Symphony Chorus! We quickly realised the mistake and found our proper seats in the audience but after the show we decided to keep up the pretence, basking in the glow of admiring concertgoers! I didn't know then that I would perform at the Albert Hall many times in the future.

Another early opera experience was a first visit to Covent Garden. I was in London for a conference, and playing at Covent Garden was *Boris Godunov* by Mussorgsky, with the great Bulgarian bass, Boris Christoff, singing the title role. My colleague and I turned up, naively hoping to buy tickets at the box office, but, of course, the performance was sold out. We hung around waiting for possible returns, when suddenly an American gentleman offered us two spare tickets. The prices were astronomical, so we reluctantly declined, but finally, when the last bell sounded, he gave us the tickets at a much lower price. We accompanied him to the Front Circle to see Boris Christoff from the best seats in the house.

The first time Mari came with me to the opera, we were joined by a couple of choir friends. The *Barber of Seville* was fully booked, so I bought tickets for *Simon Boccanegra* instead, hoping for the best. Halfway through the opera, I turned to my companions to whisper a comment and noticed they were all fast asleep. Including Mari. Obviously not a good choice! It nearly put Mari off opera for good. It wasn't until we saw *La Traviata* in Verona sometime later that she switched on again. Happily, we have enjoyed many operas together since. One of our highlights was *Falstaff* at Covent Garden with Welsh stars Bryn Terfel, Rebecca Evans and Robert Tear. I made sure that everybody near us in the audience knew we were Welsh!

As well as the choir's 'Annual Celebrity Concert' there were numerous charity concerts at chapels, churches and concert halls with occasional 'away' trips to England. I remember a concert at the Swan Theatre in Worcester and another memorable concert at the Central Hall in Coventry. We received a kind invitation to visit Coventry Welsh Rugby Club after the concert, where some of the city's Welsh exiles were looking forward to some good 'afterglow' singing. A strict instruction was issued to everyone to get back onto the buses immediately after the concert so we could make a quick getaway to the rugby club. Inevitably, some choristers ignored this and headed for the nearest pub; the rest of us were sitting on the buses, waiting and complaining. By the time we rounded up the errant choristers, it was too late to go to the rugby club. The jolly pubgoers were not in the least bit sorry, singing their heads off on the trip home while the rest of us tried to get some sleep.

We regularly entered Eisteddfod competitions, including the local Cwmbran Eisteddfod which, improbably, was held in the works canteen of the Girling brake factory. The test piece at the 1970 Cwmbran Eisteddfod was *The Dong*, an arrangement by Harold Noble of Edward Lear's poem, sung unaccompanied. I remember the ominous opening lines: *'When awful darkness and silence reign, Over the great Gromboolian plain ...'* and the final climactic cry: *'The Dong! The Dong! The Dong with the luminous nose!'* Nonsense of course but a fiendishly difficult sing. We didn't win. We gained some success at the Bristol Eisteddfod, however, which was held in the University building at the top of the hill. We celebrated in good style at the Mauretania Hotel just down the road.

Another regular competition was at Kington in Herefordshire. This was always running late, sometimes by several hours, so it was touch and go whether we could finish singing and sprint to the pub before closing time. We usually performed well but I can't remember us winning at Kington; I think we came second several times. This was also the result when we competed at the Hereford Music Festival. This was held at the Shire Hall, which has splendid acoustics, and we gave a creditable performance of *Recognition of Land* by Grieg, a lengthy Scandinavian cantata with a fairly high degree of difficulty. To our disappointment and amazement, we were beaten by Hereford Police Choir with their rendition of *Yellow Bird (up high in banana tree)*. The adjudicators must have wanted to keep on the right side of the law! On this occasion, 'entertainment value' seemed to be given higher marks than 'musical quality', a lesson heeded for the future. Our choir rehearsed *Yellow Bird* very soon afterwards!

Once, we ventured to the wilds of West Wales to compete at the Crosshands Eisteddfod, held in the Miners' Public Hall. The competition was again won by the local choir, but undeterred, we headed for the local rugby club to drown our sorrows. This was Cefneithin Rugby Club, proudly associated with Barry John and many other famous Welsh internationals. This was the early seventies and Gareth Edwards, and Barry John were our heroes. We were keen to visit Barry John's home rugby club and to see the memorabilia on display, but they wouldn't let us in; the club was packed out with eisteddfod goers and competitors. We crept around the back to see if there was another way in, but no luck. However, there was a window open! A couple of us climbed in and joined the merry throng; it had to be done. Not long afterwards, one of our baritones, Eric Edwards, became the proud father of a baby boy. The baby was christened Gareth Barry John Edwards! (when he grew up, he became the landlord of the Queen Inn in Upper Cwmbran!).

Another competition we entered was the Morriston Eisteddfod, held in the magnificent Tabernacle Chapel, considered to be the non-conformist cathedral of Wales. Little did I know that this great building was to feature prominently in my future choral career.

One of the major competitions we regularly entered was the South Wales Miners' Eisteddfod at the Grand Pavilion in Porthcawl. The event was notorious for running late and it was sometimes after midnight when we took the stage. On one occasion, the test piece was *Songs from Karad* by Kodaly, and we were under strict instructions not to partake of alcohol before our performance. We endured hours of waiting in a nearby hotel sipping lemonade and spitting feathers. It didn't help that the opening lines of the piece were: *'Pretty hostess, drink to my health, fill my flagon, fill it higher ...'*. It was also very noticeable that members of a rival choir, also in the hotel, were drinking beer as if there was no tomorrow! They were entering into the spirit of the piece before going on stage and, of course, they won the competition hands down. We came nowhere, and by the time we left the stage, all the pubs were closed. So much for abstinence.

Then there was the Annual Choir Dinner-Dance. These events were extremely popular in the 1970s and were formal affairs with everybody in their finery and with a guest speaker and speeches from the choir officers and musical director. This was an opportunity to thank everybody for their hard work and especially the ladies for their support. I remember one Dinner-Dance at the Chase Hotel, Ross-on-Wye. I had organised the event on this occasion and agonised over everything from booking the band to looking after the guest speaker and was in such a state of anxiety that I could hardly eat my dinner. But being the event organiser had its compensations. Mari and I had booked a room for the night (at our own expense) and the hotel manager kindly gave us the 'four-poster room'. He proudly told us that a well-known political leader slept in the bed the previous night. He didn't say with whom!

Cwmbran Male Choir (we dropped 'Voice' from our title at some stage) was much like a family, with an active ladies' committee. The ladies raised substantial funds for the choir by organising dances, fetes, social evenings etc. Those ladies who wanted to follow the choir usually travelled on the choir buses to 'away' concerts. This was not a problem as there were always two buses, with enough spare seats for supporters. For certain events, a 'choir only' trip would be deemed appropriate.

Finally, there was the Annual General Meeting. I've left this solemn event until last because choir politics is a tortuous affair, especially Welsh male voice choir politics. The choir AGM was mostly a back-slapping occasion, thanking everybody, with repeated applause. People were elected to the offices of chairman, secretary, treasurer, transport officer, etc, and for each of these there was usually only one candidate who had been arm-twisted into standing. Then there was the committee for which there were occasionally one or two more candidates than needed, necessitating an election. But it was 'Any Other Business' that was sometimes the most contentious, with choristers able to raise issues that were bugging them. On one occasion, the chairman was trying to explain away a particular cock-up. His explanation delicately avoided naming the guilty party, but this didn't satisfy one of the basses who kept springing to his feet and loudly insisting: 'Mr Chairman, somebody *must* be blamed!!'

After I'd been in the choir for a few years, I naively decided to stand for committee. I had an optimistic, but misguided idea that I could somehow 'make a difference'. What a fallacy. I came bottom of the poll with just 19 votes (out of a choir of 70 plus); most of these were my drinking mates. I was the only candidate not elected, by a large margin. The next worst candidate had over 40 votes! I was devastated by this. I thought I was universally popular and widely respected. How wrong I was. I thought I'd better do some serious soul-searching. After pondering my possible weak points, I wondered whether my habit of going for a pint before rehearsal with my top tenor pal, Tony Williams, may have something to do with it. We would usually stroll into rehearsal very late, often mid-song. Apparently, some choristers resented this and considered me a part-timer. This view spread through the choir when I had the audacity to stand for committee. Suitably chastened, I decided to change my ways (a bit).

3 - KINDRED SPIRITS

Soon after joining Cwmbran Male Choir, I was back in Cardiff to complete my final year at the University of Wales Institute of Science & Technology. One of my fellow students at UWIST was Des Downes, a fellow trainee engineer. We soon discovered we had much in common, including a love of singing and rugby (and beer). How I managed to get through that year unscathed and pass my finals remains a mystery to me. Particularly as Mari and I were married in the middle of it!

There was a certain day of the week that was our singing and drinking day. After our first lecture finished at eleven o'clock, we skipped the next session because the lecturer 'taught' advanced electrical engineering in a totally baffling way. We were gaining nothing by attending these lectures, so most of us avoided them (apart from a few dedicated Chinese students). With the afternoon also clear of lectures, we were free for the rest of the day. We would hop across to the Woodville Inn just in time for open tap and stay there until they kicked us out at afternoon closing time. By this time, many pints of Hancock's Home Brew had been imbibed and our singing voices were well and truly lubricated. My repertoire of songs had increased due to my choir membership and the Welsh-speaking Des, from Tumble in West Wales, had a great knowledge of Welsh hymns and folksongs. He also had a great voice and later became an extremely popular and successful member of several prominent Welsh choirs, becoming fondly known as 'Desarotti' due to his fine tenor voice (and similar appearance to the great man). Des also acquired another nickname while playing prop for Newport Saracens rugby team. At the time, American football was popular on TV and there was a famous player known as 'The Refrigerator'. Inevitably, Des became 'The Tumble Dryer'!

19

This was a time of strict licensing hours, but after leaving the Woodville Inn, we knew where we could continue our drinking. The 'Club' was in a sleazy back street and contained a motley crowd of hard drinkers and students. We were encouraged to sing and soon discovered that we could perform on the stage and receive payment! Six checks was the fee, each check exchangeable at the bar for one pint of beer! So, there we were, indulging two of our great loves, singing and drinking, free of charge all afternoon. We shared the platform at the club with all manner of performers, including a guy playing the saw (using a violin bow) and someone else playing the spoons. All playing for their beer. It was uproarious. Des was a friend for life.

Not long after this I met Barry. There was a rugby international in Cardiff and as usual, a gang of us were singing after the match in the Borough Arms in St Mary Street. There was always a great reunion of friends from all over Wales who got together at every international to sing and to celebrate another great Welsh victory (it was the 1970s). I was standing on a table, trying to conduct the gathered throng, when I spotted this character resplendent in a dragon shirt right at the centre of things and singing his heart out - the inimitable Barry Page. Next thing I knew he was standing on the table, singing *Delilah*. He was introduced and I discovered that Barry was a fellow trainee and had just returned from Voluntary Service Overseas in Ghana. Barry soon joined me in Cwmbran Male Choir, and I had found another friend for life. We shared much that follows in the Cwmbran story.

One of our escapades came at the Pontrhydfendigaid eisteddfod in Cardiganshire. Pontrhydfendigaid is a small village a long way from everywhere, but it has an exceptionally large pavilion that hosts a prestigious annual eisteddfod. The Cwmbran choir made the long journey there to compete in the male-voice choir competition. I don't remember what we sang, but we performed well without winning. Unbowed by this disappointment, we headed for the nearest alehouse. Pontrhydfendigaid boasts two public houses, the Red Lion and the Black Lion. I'm not sure which of these two creatures we communed with, but a good singsong was enjoyed in the bar before the choir transport officer shouted the dreaded words 'everybody out, the bus is leaving in five minutes!' This was the cue for one last song, the draining of glasses, and a visit to the gents' toilets before the long trip home. Now, most gents' toilets have brilliant acoustics, with their shiny tiled walls and confined space. It was the tradition to sing the ending of *The Martyrs of the Arena* in the toilet before leaving. We belted out *'O Living God, to Thee our Souls are Soaring, and Death is the Dawning of Endless Light!!'*, a truly magnificent ending for the top tenors, the sound of which reverberated around the walls of the toilet and left us with a great glow of satisfaction. Tony, Barry and I (all top tenors) congratulated each other before the light truly dawned upon us. We were alone. Everybody else had gone. We rushed out of the pub and down the road only to see our bus pulling away. We ran after it, sure in the belief that they were only teasing us, until the tail-lights disappeared in the distance. They had purposely left us behind!

Our predicament quickly dawned on us. Pontrhydfendigaid is truly the back of beyond, about 85 miles from Cwmbran and right out in the sticks. There we were, at midnight, on a Saturday night, standing forlornly at the side of the road. We started to walk! Then we burst out laughing at the futility of it. Then we decided to try to thumb a lift. Amazingly a car soon stopped. It was an eisteddfod-goer seemingly bemused by the sight of three lonely choristers, still in their blazers, trudging along the dark and winding road. We were offered a lift to Tregaron. Wow! This was only about six miles away and also in the wilderness, but it was in the right direction. We gratefully accepted. Arriving at Tregaron we saw an apparition! It was a choir bus, apparently stopped for a 'comfort break'! But it wasn't our bus - it was a choir bus from Llanelli. We approached the peeing choristers and begged a lift. After some discussion they agreed to take us as far as Llanwrda, a place I'd never heard of, but also in the right direction.

At Llanwrda, in the early hours, we waved goodbye to our new-found friends from Llanelli, who turned off in the other direction. We started to walk towards Llandovery, aiming to thumb another lift. But there was no traffic. It was very cold and started to rain. We had no raincoats. We turned up the collars of our blazers and trudged on for miles, eventually reaching the outskirts of Llandovery. Then a van passed us and hesitantly stopped, some distance down the road. We quickly raced to the van before the driver could change his mind. It was a farmer taking some sheep to market. I quickly jumped in next to the farmer and Tony and Barry clambered into the back with the sheep. It was obviously smelly, dirty and uncomfortable in the back and I thought I'd got the best of the deal. Until I realised the farmer smelt worse than the sheep! Especially with the heater on. But it was wonderful. The farmer took us all the way to Brecon. We were now only thirty-odd miles from home, but it was four in the morning. We stood in the rain outside the barracks in Brecon pondering our next move. There was a bus depot opposite and there was an empty bus outside, parked up for the night. It looked very tempting. It was one of those buses with rubber buffers on the doors and we managed to prise the doors open enough to squeeze through and into the bus. We had at least found some shelter and we lay on the seats and covered ourselves with newspapers and tried to get warm and go to sleep. Eventually it got light, and the rain stopped so we freed ourselves from our temporary home and started walking again, slowly and painfully. There was still little traffic, and we walked all the way to Bwlch, about eight more miles, before we managed to thumb a lift. This took us to Abergavenny. We were now within striking distance of home, and I phoned my father-in-law from a call box. He came up from Cwmbran to collect us. We were home in time for breakfast but severely unhappy at the vindictive choir officials who had abandoned us on purpose. All three of us immediately resigned from the choir.

The following week we each received a phone call from Clifford Jones, the choir conductor, imploring us to return. He had not been involved in the heinous act and wanted us to come back. It was only his personal intervention that persuaded us to return. When everyone heard the tale of our return journey, it became part of choir folklore. The few guilty choir officials sniggered but we came out of it better than they did. The BBC made a TV programme about the Cwmbran choir shortly afterwards, during which Barry and I were interviewed about the Pontrhydfendigaid episode. Our story was broadcast to the nation on television.

My stock seemed to rise a bit afterwards and I started taking the choir more seriously. I was even elected to the committee. When Peter got married and moved to Caerphilly, I took over as secretary. Peter was a hard act to follow but I soon discovered that the secretary had considerable influence. I was able to get involved in arranging concerts at lots of interesting venues, many of them new to the choir.

Sometime after I became the secretary, there was serious upheaval in the Cwmbran Male Choir. There was a major disagreement over the appointment of the accompanist. The conductor wanted to change the accompanist by bringing back someone who had previously played for the choir. Some of the officers and members wanted to retain the existing accompanist, with whom they were personally friendly. There was an unholy row, typical of choir politics, with the upshot that the chairman and treasurer resigned from the choir. The conductor also tendered his resignation. Our stalwart deputy conductor, Harold Richards manfully filled the breach, but the choir was in crisis.

As secretary, I was the only officer remaining and had to assume the chairman's role and address the choir at rehearsal, trying to be fair to both sides, which was difficult. It was decided to hold a vote on whether to accept the conductor's resignation and after a debate, the vote was taken. By a narrow majority, the choir voted, albeit reluctantly and certainly very sadly, to accept the conductor's resignation. I had the difficult task of informing him, a task made much easier by the gentlemanly and dignified way he accepted the outcome. I was personally very sad, particularly after receiving Cliff's support in the Pontrhydfendigaid affair. I had enjoyed ten years under his expert musicianship, and it seemed like the end of an era.

4 - WEINLAND

One of the Cwmbran choristers was Kurt Kenzler, a German ex-prisoner of war who stayed in Wales after the war and married a Welsh girl. On one of his business trips back to Germany, he met members of a male choir in Bad Langenbrücken, a spa village near Bruchsal in the state of Baden-Württemberg. The village sits in an attractive wine-growing region referred to as 'Weinland' in a popular song. The German choir, named 'Mannesgesangverein Eintracht Bad Langenbrücken', was interested in making an exchange visit to Wales. Thus began a great adventure and the start of some wonderful trips and friendships.

Cwmbran choir had never been abroad (apart from forays across Offa's Dyke) and in 1972, a tour to West Germany seemed an ambitious undertaking. However, the choir made the decision to go and began raising funds. We collected tons of old newspapers to sell for newsprint and did a 10-mile sponsored walk along the Monmouthshire & Brecon Canal, stopping to sing on the way and collecting with buckets. People were incredibly generous.

Peter Johns and I visited British Airways in Cardiff and fixed the choir's flight from Heathrow to Frankfurt, where people from the German choir were to meet us and transport us to Bad Langenbrücken for our stay of three nights. We would be hosted by choir families, and we provided details of our party members so that a suitable 'match' could be made. The proposed trip caught the imagination more widely and the *South Wales Argus* keenly followed our progress. Their reporter joined us on the tour and the newspaper provided coverage throughout.

On the day of departure there was a buzz of excitement on the coaches taking the choir and supporters to Heathrow Airport.

Unfortunately, Heathrow was fogbound, and our flight was delayed. We were stuck in the departure lounge for hours, so some of us decided to have a few drinks and do a bit of singing (to keep the voices in trim).

We eventually ascended the aircraft steps and took off in high spirits (with Barry singing *Nearer my God to Thee*!). The plane trip was marvellous, the drinks were free and everything in the world was wonderful. When we reached Frankfurt, the coaches were waiting, and our German hosts greeted us warmly. We loaded our suitcases onto the buses and discovered crates of beer in the luggage compartment. This was for us to drink on our journey down the autobahn. What a welcome! We travelled south marvelling at the countryside and when we arrived at Bad Langenbrücken, the whole village was waiting, despite our delay. There was bunting everywhere, and the band was playing. A reception was held at the Kraichgauhalle (village hall), where there were welcome speeches and both choirs sang. The beer and wine flowed freely. Eventually we were partnered with host families.

With typical German efficiency, choristers had been matched according to age and occupation. I was introduced to Gerd Gerstman: we were almost exactly the same age (he was born just one day after me) and we were both electrical engineers (he worked at Phillipsburg Nuclear Power Station). He took me home to meet his mother, father and sister, and I slurred my hellos. He showed me my bedroom and said we needed to get straight back to the Kraichgauhalle for another party in our honour. I dumped my suitcase and was whisked away.

The rest of the evening was a blur. The Kraichgauhalle had been transformed and we were now seated at long tables, being served with large quantities of food, beer and wine. There was an oompah band playing. Soon everybody was dancing. Talk about making friends! I was grabbed by a lady of a certain age who crushed me to her ample bosom and virtually carried me around the dance floor. When the music stopped, I tried to escape. No chance. She held me even tighter until the music started again. I was staring pleadingly into her grinning face, inches from mine. She had gold teeth! Then to my relief, the drinking songs started. We returned to our tables and tried to sing along. We soon got the hang of it. I remember singing 'Ein Prosit, Ein Prosit, Der Gemütlichkeit!' while we raised our glasses high in the air. We started off sitting down, then we all stood up and continued drinking and singing. Then we stood on our chairs and did the same. Finally, everybody was standing on the tables, kicking bottles and glasses over, linking arms, embracing, dancing, singing and drinking. What a party! What a day!

I woke up lying on a sofa in a strange room, with a woman looking down at me and trying to cover my naked form with a blanket. Realisation quickly dawned. The woman was Frau Gerstman, Gerd's mother. I must have stumbled into the wrong room during the night in my stupor. I croaked the only thing in German I could think of: 'Wieveil uhr ist es?'. She answered 'Sieben' in a serious voice and left me. When the coast was clear I crept to my bedroom but couldn't sleep any more. How was I going to apologise? How was I going to face the family?

When I plucked up enough courage, I went downstairs and sheepishly entered the kitchen. The entire family, including aunties and uncles, was seated around a beautifully laid breakfast table. It was Sunday morning and there was a large cake in the centre of the table, the traditional 'Sonntag Köche'. All eyes turned to me. Then they all started laughing and shaking my hand, saying something about being careful not to mix wine and beer together. To my profound relief, I was welcomed to the table. Thus ended my first night in a foreign land.

I returned to my room and changed into my choir uniform. We were to sing during morning Mass at the Catholic church. It was a beautiful church, with lovely acoustics, and we sang the Handel anthem *O Praise the Lord with One Consent* and some beautiful Welsh hymns. The Langenbrücken choir also sang, *a cappella*, as always. It was very moving and the bonding between the two choirs was already evident. This was cemented further when both choirs marched from the church to the war memorial in the village cemetery where prayers were said and both choirs sang again. I was moved to tears. In a spontaneous gesture we took off our choir ties and handed them to our German counterparts. They returned the gesture as we shook hands and embraced. The war was still fresh in the minds of the older choristers on both sides, who had once fought against each other. It was a poignant moment and a clear reminder of the folly of war.

Afterwards, some of us were taken to the vineyards on the slopes overlooking the village. Some of the German choir members belonged to the local wine co-operative and we were entertained by one of them at his 'wine cabin'. We enjoyed a barbecue and tasted the delicious white wine. I remember wandering out among the vines, reflecting, and literally drinking in the true atmosphere of the 'Weinland'.

The main concert of the tour was held at the Kraichgauhalle on the Sunday night, with both choirs performing. We sang *Weinland* in German, both choirs together, with arms linked, swaying from side to side. It was a lovely evening and afterwards we spilled out into the gardens, socialising and meeting many of the choir families.

The following day, there was a full itinerary. In the morning we visited the local fabrics factory where high quality material was being woven into beautiful patterns. We were then taken to the magical university town of Heidelberg where we sang at the magnificent castle overlooking the town and the River Neckar.

In the evening there was a farewell party at the Kraichgauhalle. By this time warm friendships had been made and there was much talk about the German choir's return visit to Cwmbran. When our coaches left the following morning, there were many handshakes, embraces and kisses and lots of tears. It's amazing how much

28

camaraderie can be established in such a short time. The friendships would last for many years.

I made sure I bought Mari a nice present. It was a cuckoo clock, purchased from Heini, a choir member and the local clockmaker. I managed to get it home in one piece and it remains in perfect working order some fifty-odd years later, much to the delight of our grandchildren.

In due course, the Langenbrücken choir and their supporters visited Cwmbran. They were met at Heathrow and taken to Windsor for lunch and a tour of the castle. They crossed the Severn Bridge into Wales and for many of them, this was their first visit to the UK. We arranged concerts and tours to local places of interest: the Eastern Valley of Gwent and modern town of Cwmbran were obviously very different from their 'Weinland' but we provided them with a completely new experience. It was difficult to replicate the German parties, but we certainly matched their hospitality. Gerd and fellow chorister Manfred (a butcher) stayed with Mari and I in Pontypool and they made a great fuss of our little daughter, Lucy. The farewells were again tearful.

The link between the two communities was strengthened by civic representation. Our local Mayor had travelled with us and met the Burger Meister at the German end; this was repeated on the return visit. Eventually, Cwmbran became formally twinned with the town of Bruchsal, very close to Langenbrücken. Our choir was proud to have made a positive contribution to the twinning.

Our second trip to Langenbrücken was in 1975. This time our party was larger as more partners and supporters were invited. Mari couldn't come because of our (by now) two small children but kindly agreed to allow my non-chorister pal, Ken Williams, to travel as my wife! This wasn't as bad as one of our other choristers, who left his wife at home and took his girlfriend! (this caused a bit

29

of controversy). A special deal was done with British Airways to charter our own Boeing 707 aircraft for the 150 or so choir and supporters.

Ken and I stayed with Gerd and family and another enjoyable programme of concerts and events was laid on. We stayed for five nights and had more time to explore this beautiful part of Germany. We performed at the Bundesgartenschau (Federal Garden Show) in the city of Mannheim, at the confluence of the Rhine and Neckar rivers. This magnificent festival is held biennially in different cities throughout Germany. We sang on a floating stage on a lake in the Luisenpark, quite an experience.

On a free day, Gerd took Ken and I across the Rhine into France, my first visit to the country (the difference in the pace of life was noticeable). The choir was also taken on a tour of the Neckar valley before visiting the scenic Mümmelsee lake, deep in the forest. We took boats out on the lake and had a fine old time before visiting the lakeside bar. It was here that I was introduced to the delights of Kirschwasser. This is an exceptionally fine schnapps, made from morello cherries and it certainly had a 'wow' factor. I should mention here that my friend Gerd kept a refrigerator in his bedroom, and had schnapps in the freezer compartment, together with special glasses. He was in the habit of taking a shot of ice-cold schnapps first thing in the morning to wake him up. I tried it and it worked a treat! Gerd's family made their own schnapps, mainly from Mirabelle plums, and had barrels of it in their well-stocked wine cellar. Gerd's father, Herbert, was an incredibly resourceful individual who could turn his hand to anything. His large garden, with its array of fruit and vegetables, was a sight to behold.

The farewell party was again held in the Kraichgauhalle, with much eating, drinking and dancing. I remember one of our choristers, much the worse for wear, trying to eat a huge Frankfurter. He was yelping with pain as he kept eating his own fingers as he tried to eat the giant sausage!

My final visit to Langenbrücken with the Cwmbran choir was in 1980. I recall visiting the beautiful palace at Bruchsal and suppressing an urge to burst into song, inspired by the splendour of the place; we also visited the lovely spa town of Baden-Baden. Another memory of the trip, apart from the formal concerts, was a specially arranged visit to the Hoepfner Brewery in Karlsruhe. The choir was invited into a great beer hall where we sat at long tables and watched a film about the brewery. Soon, large bowls of pretzels were provided followed by trolleys of beer in special glasses, wheeled in by ladies in traditional costume. The beer was delicious, and the pretzels were salty, so we drank more beer. We soon broke into song as the beer flowed. Everybody was blissfully happy, particularly our hosts who really appreciated our singing (despite its gradually deteriorating quality). And we got to keep the glasses.

When the German choir made their third visit to Wales in 1982, we invited Gerd's mother, Irma, and father, Herbert, to stay with us. This was a great adventure for them, and they were delightful, interacting with Mari and our children despite their complete lack of English. Their sign language was hilarious. As well as the arranged concerts and social events we took them around to see some local beauty spots including the Black Mountains and Cefn Onn Gardens. They were very appreciative of our homeland or 'heimat' as Herbert called it.

Around this period, the Garndiffaith Gleemen formed an association with a male choir in the village of Wiesloch, home of the Winzerkeller Wiesloch vineyards and quite near to Bad Langenbrücken. Barry and I were invited to travel to Germany with the Gleemen to help celebrate the 110th anniversary of the Wiesloch choir. The Gleemen were conducted by a friend of mine,

Gethin Banfield, and my cousin, David, was a choir member. We travelled by coach and ferry, staying overnight at Valkenburg (Netherlands) on the way out, and at Ostend on our return. Barry and I were made very welcome, staying with a delightful German family.

A vast marquee had been erected in Wiesloch for the occasion of the anniversary (the Germans are the world's experts at erecting huge marquees) and it was like a whole village under one roof. This was HQ for the duration of the trip, with concerts by both choirs and numerous festivities including the usual dancing, eating and drinking. There are male choirs in almost every village and town in Germany, and every anniversary is celebrated with great enthusiasm. It's almost like a continuous party, with these great marquees moving from place to place like a military operation. One of the highlights of the occasion was a performance by the US Forces Band from a nearby army base. They were fantastic, playing Glenn Miller classics, jazz and blues and marching through the crowd and even on the tables.

While we were at Wiesloch, Barry and I visited our friends in Langenbrücken. We decided to go by train, and having bought the tickets, I asked the stationmaster the time of the train. He held up two fingers and answered 'zwei bier', pointing to the station bar. Thinking he'd misunderstood my German, I asked again, pointing at my watch. 'Zwei bier' he insisted. Then the light dawned. There was time for us to drink two beers before the train was due. He was spot on!

The friendship with Gerd continued for years and he came over to visit us independently. Our family also stayed with his family in Bad Langenbrücken when we were holidaying in Europe and we visited the thermal spa baths to bathe in the buoyant waters, which delighted our children. In due time, I moved to Swansea with my job, and left the Cwmbran choir, joining the Morriston Orpheus. We stayed in contact with Gerd, and on our joint fortieth birthdays, he drove over from Germany to stay with us in Mumbles for a couple of weeks. It was his birthday the day after mine and we arranged a joint celebration at the Valley Hotel in Bishopston. Gerd brought over two barrels of special German beer and we invited Barry and some of my new friends from the Orpheus to join the party. The singing was going well on my birthday when at midnight it became Gerd's birthday, a special moment.

I settled into my new life in Swansea, and Gerd and I corresponded for several more years. The Cwmbran Male Choir's association with the Langenbrücken choir continued to prosper, and it was a proud moment when the Langenbrücken choir came over to participate in the 1,000 voices Albert Hall Festival in 1995. The two choirs celebrated forty years of harmony in 2012, and contacts continue.

The town of Cwmbran's twinning with Bruchsal also continued to thrive, with many cultural and sporting exchanges over the years, making an important contribution to international understanding and co-operation.

5 - A NEW ERA

After the departure of Clifford Jones, the Cwmbran choir set about finding a new conductor and adverts were placed in the *South Wales Argus* and *Western Mail* to attract the best candidates. After auditions, the choir appointed Huw Davies who, at the time, was the deputy conductor of Blaenavon Male Choir and the Cwmbran Baroque Singers. Huw arrived at an exciting time for the choir, becoming a popular musical director. I continued my work as secretary and enjoyed a good relationship with Huw. The choir's accompanist at this time was Thelma Cantello, later succeeded by Meurig Jones, a proud North Walian. The choir's president was the popular Pat Lanigan who was a great supporter. The choir continued its busy concert schedule, both locally and across the border, and chorister numbers were steadily increasing.

Over the years, we organised a series of exchange visits with other choirs, including the Silver Ring Choir of Bath, where we enjoyed singing at the Assembly Rooms, a beautiful Georgian concert venue. A similar exchange was arranged with Reading Phoenix Choir and, closer to home, we arranged exchanges with Newport Male Voice Choir and the Gwent Elizabethan Singers.

Another successful exchange was with Côr Meibion Maelgwn of Llandudno, conducted by Davy Jones. When I was attending a conference at Llandudno, I met one of the members who was a local police officer. He invited me to the choir's rehearsal which was conducted entirely in Welsh and hugely enjoyable. After practice we went to Conway Yacht Club for refreshments and afterwards, I was given a police escort back to my hotel!

Other exchanges included Stevenage Male Voice Choir, Wolverhampton Orpheus Male Choir and Warley Male Voice

Choir from the West Midlands. We also had several exchanges with the Casterbridge Singers of Dorchester (named after the location in Thomas Hardy's novels). These exchanges helped us to perform at new venues including the Central Hall in Birmingham and the historic Corn Exchange in Dorchester. In Stevenage, we sang at a theatre, but I mostly remember Barry's impromptu stand-up performance at the afterglow. He's a brilliant comic and I was convulsed with laughter even though I'd heard most of the jokes before.

On the way back from one of these trips, our coach stopped at the roadside for a much-needed comfort stop. Everybody disembarked and lined up in the dark alongside the bus and started peeing. The steam was rising when, suddenly, floodlights came on! There was a house right next to us, unseen in the dark, and the outside lights had been switched on. Two terrified-looking ladies were staring at us from their window! We couldn't stop peeing and we couldn't hide. Talk about being caught in the act! At least there was safety in numbers. We all had to finish, no choice. Some were quicker than others. One or two of the slowest gave the ladies a smile and a wave before clambering back onto the bus. Hopefully, they didn't see the large 'Cwmbran Male Choir' sign at the back of the bus as we accelerated away!

Particularly enjoyable were the exchanges with Côr Meibion Aberafan, with whom a great rapport was established. The concerts always ended with the two choirs on stage and the experience of over 150 male voices singing together was amazing. At one of our joint concerts at the Congress Theatre in Cwmbran, the audience was so enthusiastic that we sung the whole of the 13-minute *Nidaros* again as an encore! This must have been a first. In my contacts with Aberafan, I met some of the officials of the Welsh Association of Male Choirs, an organisation that I was destined to become closely involved with, but more of that later.

Among the UK concerts that I remember from those times was one at the King's Hall, Derby after which we were entertained at the Rolls Royce Club. We also gave a series of concerts at Soundwell Parish Church in Bristol. The afterglows were always held at the local British Legion club and were among the most enjoyable I can remember. We also undertook a series of concerts in the delightful village of Winchcombe, in the Cotswolds. These concerts were to raise funds for the local cottage hospital and were held in the parish church, with afterglows at the village hall. During one of our visits to Winchcombe, we were given a guided tour of nearby Sudeley Castle, by kind permission of the owner.

Before the first of these Winchcombe concerts, a little planning was required, so our choir chairman and I made a visit to meet the concert organisers. We met the vicar and inspected the church before meeting the main organiser, who was the local paper mill owner. We visited his lovely house and played croquet on the lawn with the vicar and our host (the game was surprisingly hard fought). We were then entertained to a delightful afternoon tea. When the tea was being poured, our host asked if we would prefer Indian or Chinese. Our esteemed chairman promptly replied, 'I'll have a drop of Indian for a change'. I nearly choked on my cucumber sandwich! I soon stopped smiling, however, because when the home-made barley wine was produced, I was refused any because I was driving.

Another concert was at Oxford Town Hall, a lovely venue, where I sang a short solo in *Goin' Home*, a choir arrangement from the 'New World' symphony. The afterglow was in a large room at the hall where there was a minstrel gallery: perfect for Barry. He gave another virtuoso performance that had everybody in stitches. It was one of those evenings that you didn't want to end. We had to be dragged onto the buses.

One of our St David's Day concerts was at the Royal Festival Hall in London, where we joined forces with Cwmbach Male Choir and the BBC Concert Orchestra. The concert was conducted by Owain Arwel Hughes and the compere was the legendary Cliff

Morgan. The Wales v Scotland rugby international was taking place while we were rehearsing, and Cliff kept us updated on the score. Wales won, which gave our concert performance some extra *hwyl*! I remember the programme included the fine Welsh hymn tune *Moab* and the concert was broadcast live on BBC radio and overseas. After the concert, our choir was invited to join a private party on board the *Tattershall Castle*, a paddle steamer moored in the Thames. It was a fine night as we mingled with the other guests before singing on the open deck and having a great afterglow. Passers-by on the embankment were stopping to listen.

Trips to London always involved refreshment stops at one of the M4 Services. On one early trip we stopped at breakfast-time. They were advertising a 'special breakfast' with 'double' everything for only £4.00. We all joined the long self-service queue and waited patiently. Most of us just wanted coffee, but Dennis decided he wanted the special breakfast. When he eventually got to the front of the queue, he ordered the special, but with only one egg. The server told him it only came with two eggs. Dennis insisted on one egg. The server said that if he wanted the special, he must have two: after all, he didn't have to eat the second egg. But Dennis was adamant, he didn't want the second egg on his plate. The argument went back and forth for ages. It was like a pantomime. Yes, I can! No, you can't! The queue was growing longer. People were getting impatient and complaining loudly. Dennis was going red in the face. Finally, a compromise was reached. Dennis could have a smaller breakfast with one egg. It cost him £5.00.

Another weekend trip took us to Cornwall, where we were guests of the Polperro Fishermen's Choir. We were able to explore the picturesque little fishing village and a couple of drinks in the Three Pilchards went down very well before the show. Mari came with me, and we stayed overnight at the Holiday Inn in Plymouth. Mari happened to share the lift with Rolf Harris, who was also staying at the hotel. He was extremely affable (little did she know!). On our way back, we performed a concert in Exeter to round off a pleasant weekend. There were other concerts at the Towngate Theatre in Basildon and in Ealing, London. After the rehearsal at Ealing, we headed for the nearest pub for a pre-concert tipple. It turned out to be an Irish pub and there was a collecting box for the IRA on the bar! I quickly ordered a pint of Guinness.

On another occasion we were invited to give an after-dinner performance at the Grosvenor House Hotel in Park Lane, London. Very swanky. The event was the annual bash of the British Amusement Catering Trade Association. We travelled up to London and hung around for hours in a side room while the guests enjoyed their lavish banquet under the chandeliers of the Great Room (we had to make do with a sandwich and a can of beer). Before our spot, the Band of the Welsh Guards entertained the guests, marching up and down the dance floor. Very impressive. Eventually, very late into the night, we were called to the stage to perform the finale. We had to wake up some of the boys! By this time our audience was well away and cheered us to the roof. Little did they know we were all knackered. But we gave a good performance. Afterwards, we couldn't mingle with the happy punters, or even have a drink. It was straight back on the buses for the tedious trip back up the M4.

The choir performed with several other well-known bands over the years and had a happy association with our friends in the Cwmbran Band. It was always tricky getting the balance right for any joint items. The bands could blast you off the stage if they got too carried away! In 1979, the Cwmbran Male Choir recorded its first album. We combined with the famous Lewis Merthyr Band and produced an LP entitled 'Voices and Brass - A Winter Celebration'. The recording was made at the Congress Theatre by Pye Records and was released in time for Christmas, another notable achievement for the choir.

6 - MASSED CHOIR FESTIVALS

It was with some pleasure that the Cwmbran choir received the news that a 'Monmouthshire Massed Male Choir' festival was to be organised and all the male-voice choirs in the county would be invited. The idea was the brainchild of one of our choristers, Bryan Taylor, together with colleagues from other Monmouthshire choirs, and eleven choirs agreed to take part. The big event took place in the steel town of Ebbw Vale and the Leisure Centre was the venue, with concerts on three consecutive nights in October 1973. The concerts were a huge success, with the celebrated BBC musical director Rae Jenkins taking the baton, and John Samuel and Gareth Williams as accompanists. Soloists were Michael Rippon (baritone) and Kenneth Bowen (tenor) and the choir programme included classics such as *Spartan Heroes* and *Martyrs of the Arena*. All three nights were sold out and the event was recorded for posterity by EMI Records. Incredibly, it was the first massed male choir to sing in Wales for over fifty years.

At the end of the final night's performance, still energised by the great finale of *Nidaros*, some of us decided to celebrate by visiting a certain night club. The only slight problem was that the club was a couple of valleys away. Our driver (my friend, Ken) decided to take the direct route 'over the top' following mountain roads. As we were travelling through the blackness, we suddenly saw a car ahead with its headlights pointing to the sky. The car had hit a sheep and flipped right over! It had happened just a moment earlier and fortunately, no-one was seriously hurt. We stopped and gave assistance until proper help arrived. Then we carried on to the night club and celebrated in style.

The success of the Monmouthshire Massed Male Choir was the inspiration for another event in 1975 when the Torfaen Massed Male Choirs performed at Pontypool Leisure Centre. Six local choirs joined forces and were conducted by Alun John. The event was so successful, it was repeated three years later.

At around this time, Cwmbran choir became an active member of the Welsh Association of Male Choirs, and I was asked to become a member of the Association's executive committee. Danny Williams of the famous Treorci Male Choir was my mentor: he thought the Association could do with some younger blood! Danny was a real character with a bass voice as deep as the ocean.

The Association soon began organising annual 'One Thousand Voices' festivals at the Royal Albert Hall. These events were open to all member choirs and enabled them to enjoy the thrill of singing in a great massed choir, to audiences of around 5,000 people. Leading up to these big events in London there were regional massed choir concerts held in various parts of South Wales, with full-scale concerts at the Afan Lido in Port Talbot televised by HTV Wales. Cwmbran Male Choir took part in many of these festivals and hosted one of the regional concerts in Cwmbran where I remember being conducted by John Haydn Davies, conductor emeritus of Treorci Male Choir; it was an honour to sing under his baton.

There was also a BBC TV recording of the massed choir at St David's Cathedral in Pembrokeshire. This was recorded in the middle of winter, and I have never been so cold in my life. We were on stage for hours and hours, and all the cathedral doors were wide open to allow the many cables to be connected to the production units outside. An icy wind blew straight through the cathedral, freezing us to the bone. Much later, we were taken to a hotel and given hot soup to warm us up. But we were still chilled. I couldn't even face a cold beer! It was reckoned afterwards that the event may have killed off several elderly choristers! I never got to see the TV programme.

There was a much more pleasant event later in the year when the massed choir gave a performance at Oystermouth Castle in aid of the Ryan Davies Memorial Fund. (Ryan was the well-known Welsh comedian, actor, singer, and songwriter who tragically died in 1977 at the age of 40.) The concert was organised by Mike Evans, Ryan's former manager, and the concert was staged outdoors on the banks of the castle, which provided a spectacular backdrop. In between rehearsals I was able to make my first acquaintance with the White Rose Inn in Mumbles in the company of my friend Gethin Banfield, conductor of the Garndiffaith Gleemen.

The show was also taken to the Colston Hall in Bristol for four years running to help celebrate the Bristol Wine Festival. Several local English male choirs were invited to join us on stage and the individual choir conductors took turns to conduct items. I remember our own conductor, Huw Davies, conducting majestically, drawing every ounce from the 500 singers on stage. I heard a chorister near me, from a local choir, whose own conductor's turn was next, mutter under his breath 'follow that!'. It was a great compliment for Huw. There was always time to sample the delights of Bristol's watering holes and a regular favourite was the historic 'Llandoger Trow' pub, just a short sprint from the Colston Hall.

The Association also provided a massed choir to participate in the centenary celebrations of the Welsh Rugby Union at the National Stadium in Cardiff in July 1980. We entertained a large gathering from around the world who had come to Wales to help celebrate the momentous occasion.

The trips to the Albert Hall were always looked forward to with great anticipation. Cwmbran choir performed in the Association's first Albert Hall festival in 1978, when the massed choir was conducted by Owain Arwel Hughes. Subsequent festivals were conducted by Alun John and accompanists included Bryan Davies of Ferndale at the piano and Huw Tregelles Williams playing the

Albert Hall organ. The Cwmbran choir took part again the following year when the event was broadcast live on BBC Radio with the inimitable Alun Williams giving the commentary. Several festivals were recorded by Mike Evans for Black Mountain Records.

The weekends in London were always eventful. On one occasion, the Association used a London agent to block-book hotel rooms for all the choirs and supporters thereby obtaining favourable rates. The Cwmbran choir and its many supporters were allocated to the Regent Palace Hotel, located centrally near Soho and Piccadilly Circus. I informed the agent that our party would be about 200 strong and the agent provisionally booked 50 double rooms and 100 single rooms. When the final list of names was completed, it was clear the party comprised mostly couples, and we would require mostly double rooms. The final rooming list was sent to the agent in good time, but they apparently did not inform the hotel of the room changes. When we arrived at the hotel, there were not enough double rooms available, only single rooms. Chaos ensued. The lobby of the hotel was full of 200 confused people, and it was worse than Piccadilly Circus outside. I was going around all the happily married couples asking for volunteers to split up. Many agreed with great delight! Some agreed reluctantly. Others point blank refused to be separated from their loved ones. In the end it was all sorted out amicably, but there was much night-time tiptoeing along corridors! That was not the end of the matter, however. Two single rooms were much more expensive than one double and the hotel had been paid in advance by the agent. Our choir refused to pay the difference and it transpired that there were numerous other choirs affected by similar cock-ups at other hotels. The total costs involved were frightening. A legal wrangle ensued between the agent and the Association that took years to be sorted out.

One of our favourite stopping places en route to London was the

Royal Oak pub in a village in Berkshire, where a warm welcome was always guaranteed. A few songs would also be well received. On one choir rugby trip we visited the pub, and the wartime flying hero, Douglas Bader, was in the bar. Barry entered with his giant leek and bobble hat and Douglas Bader said, "You don't look a bit like Max Boyce!". Barry responded, "And you don't look a bit like Kenneth More!" (Kenneth More played Douglas Bader in the great film 'Reach for the Sky.')

For trips to the Albert Hall, the policy was for the four coaches carrying choir and supporters to travel in convoy in case of breakdown, and we would stick to the M4 motorway. On one occasion, however, a few of us made a last-minute decision to leave the motorway and divert our 'choristers only' bus to the Royal Oak for lunch, leaving the other three buses in the convoy. The inevitable happened. Unknown to our happy throng at the pub, one of the other buses broke down on the motorway. They were stuck on the hard shoulder while we were carousing at the Royal Oak blissfully unaware of their plight (no mobile phones). When we eventually caught up with them on the motorway, the sight of our happy, smiling, semi-inebriated faces did not go down well with those who were stranded. Their anger increased when several of our group relieved themselves along the side of their stricken bus! Suitably chastened, we loaded the women, children and elderly onto our bus and sent them onward while we waited for a relief bus to arrive. It was the least we could do.

I hugely enjoyed helping in the organisation of these Albert Hall festivals and making the annual pilgrimage to London. Most of the audience were family and friends, as well as Welsh exiles from far and wide, and it was great that Mari could be in the audience to see me singing on the stage of the Albert Hall.

For the first festival, I was given the job of catering officer. It was my task to organise the feeding of around a thousand hungry choristers and to do it in a very tight time slot between the rehearsal and the performance. Fortunately for me, the excellent catering facilities at Imperial College were handily placed to the rear of the Albert Hall and it was just a question of getting everybody off stage and directing them through the Stage Doors and down the steps to the road behind the Hall, and then along to Imperial College. Simple?

Our stage manager was the indefatigable Layton Watkins who, with his clipboard and commanding presence, worked miracles getting everybody on and off stage. Unfortunately, the route from the stage to the dressing rooms and the Stage Door was anything but straightforward. The multitude of corridors above and below the Albert Hall stage includes a series of concentric circles at different levels around the great hall, with stairways running up and down between them. Once you lose your bearings in one of these circular passageways, you can wander around and around without ever finding your way out. You end up doing lap after lap of the Albert Hall, often running into a vortex of choristers rushing the other way. I have heard stories of choristers being lost there and never being seen again! There was one elderly chorister who became so completely lost and confused that he burst into tears before someone took him gently by the hand and led him to safety.

The other problem is that choristers are like sheep. They follow the man in front. All you need is one idiot to wander off in the wrong direction, and everybody will blindly follow. It took all of Layton's stentorian shouting and cajoling and the superhuman efforts of the choir marshals to direct (most of) the choristers to Imperial College for their dinner. Once we got them there, the professionalism of the College's catering staff took over. I did the catering job for two festivals. It was enough.

I then took over from Danny Williams as the publicity officer for the Association and my duties included dealing with the press and our sponsors. My other important task was to arrange the production and printing of the Albert Hall festival programmes. These programmes were designed to be souvenirs, containing pictures and information about the choirs taking part, as well as conductors, accompanists and solo artistes. Added to this were advertisements and various articles as well as the programme of music to be performed. The compilation of all this material was a nightmare. There were always twenty to thirty choirs taking part and each of them were required to send me (1) a photograph of their choir (2) a write-up about their choir (3) a photo and write-up of their conductor (4) a photo and write-up of their accompanist/s and (5) any adverts. Only five things for each choir but the total number of items ran into hundreds.

Of the five items I needed from each choir, I would sometimes receive one, or perhaps two or maybe even three (if I were lucky); rarely four, never five and frequently none. This despite many letters and phone calls (no texts or emails then). Even threats that their choir pic or their beloved conductor's mug shot would be missing from the glossy programme did not seem to bother them. My patient printer, Dick Harper of Brynymor Press in Swansea was creating a masterpiece with great gaps where there should be smiling faces. As the great day approached, and my pleading became more frantic, bits and pieces would arrive in the post until finally the presses had to run. The printing of the several thousand programmes was a major operation, especially as it was being done against the clock. We then had to transport them to the Albert Hall where they had to be delivered into the safe hands of the 'Programme Supervisor'. Once there, they were carefully counted and distributed to the large army of official programme sellers. This was big business, with the programmes selling at several pounds each, and the cash receipts had to be assiduously checked to the satisfaction of our treasurer, before the Albert Hall took their cut. I wonder how many of these historic documents have survived: I still have a few to remind me of the agonies I spent trying to get them done on time.

For the third 'One Thousand Voices' Festival at the Royal Albert

Hall, we were honoured by the presence of our Patron, His Royal Highness, The Prince of Wales. There was a fair bit of security involved and we had to provide a list of the officers of the Association who were to be presented to HRH. I presume this was so they could run security checks on us to verify that we were not dangerous criminals or potential terrorists. There was a pukka pre-concert reception laid on and we were lined up in good time to receive our royal guest. The line-up was in alphabetical order, and I was the first in line because my name was Davies. The second in line was called Evans, but he was very keen to be first, so I agreed to swap places. When the Prince arrived and was introduced, he just shook hands with my friend and immediately moved on to me for a proper chat (it doesn't always pay to be first!). We shook hands and he asked me about my choir then, with a laugh, asked whether we practised in the pub! I was a bit nonplussed and tried to be serious, stating that we had a proper rehearsal room. Seemingly disappointed at this, he moved on down the line. After the reception, the officers of the Association joined the Prince in the royal box for the show and, of course, the massed choir gave a terrific performance, worthy of royalty.

Barry and I continued to attend the Albert Hall concerts each year, even after our direct involvement was over. The Fridays were spent touring the pubs of Soho and the Saturdays enjoying the concerts and afterglows. We ended one evening by gate-crashing a private black-tie reception at the Royal Lancaster Hotel. We were suitably attired, so mingled easily, helping ourselves to canapes and drinks. We started chatting to the guests and very soon Barry was telling his jokes. The quiet hum of polite conversation started changing to gentle giggles, then chuckles, then loud guffaws of laughter as Barry got into his stride, eventually standing on a table and entertaining the crowd. There was complete uproar and when Barry was finally allowed to finish, there was wild applause. There was a sad ending, however. When we were leaving, Barry discovered somebody had nicked his prized cashmere overcoat!

7 - FESTIVAL INTERCELTIQUE, BRITTANY

For ten magical days every August, the city of Lorient in Brittany hosts a great Celtic gathering: the Festival Interceltique de Lorient. All the Celtic nations and regions are represented including Wales, Scotland, Ireland, the Isle of Man, Cornwall, Brittany and Galicia from northern Spain. There are thousands of singers, dancers, musicians, pipe bands, folk groups and craftspeople as well as sports men and women performing and competing. Vast crowds, in the hundreds of thousands, attend every year. Each Celtic country and region displays the best of its culture and the atmosphere in the city is fantastic. Cwmbran Male Choir was delighted to be selected to represent Wales at the 1979 festival and it was unforgettable.

A small group of us went over in an advance party to check out the accommodation and arrangements. We were accompanied by some other members of the Welsh contingent including Siân James (a fine young singer and harpist), a Welsh folk dancing group and some members of the Welsh golf and bridge teams. We travelled by Brittany Ferries from Plymouth to Roscoff, and the sea was very choppy, but we didn't care!

We arrived in Lorient in the evening, and I was staggered by the scale of the event. There were radio stations and TV studios specially installed for the festival and a PA system was operating throughout the city. Our accommodation was in university halls of residence with men and women segregated in separate buildings. The dormitory facilities were basic in the extreme: twenty to a room and cold showers, with hole-in-the-ground toilets. But it was fine. Our meals were provided in a great hall at the Palais des Congrès near the harbour, where there was organised chaos. They were catering for over a thousand performers at a time, but the food was good with plenty of wine to wash it down. The vast dining hall was the best place to interact with fellow Celts and to compare languages and cultures. On the first day we established HQ at a bar called 'Le Maryland', and Le Patron, Michel, was delighted to welcome us. The bar was the place to be during our off-duty periods.

The coaches carrying the bulk of our choir and supporters arrived at the Palais des Congrès the following evening after a long journey and another rough channel crossing. They were tired and hungry and totally unprepared for the great melee that greeted them. It was dinner time and the Palais des Congrès resembled a cross between Waterloo station and feeding time at the zoo. After a day spent happily touring the bars of Lorient, I was desperately trying to organise things for the choir party. And failing. I told them how wonderful it all was. Nobody believed me. The Mayor and the Chairman of the Council were with our party and must have wondered what the hell they were getting into. I was getting stick from everyone. I promised them that everything would be alright in the morning. They still didn't believe me. They booed and cursed me, accused me of being drunk. But within twenty-four hours they were happy. It was true. It really was wonderful. As long as you entered into the spirit. And everybody did. In spades.

We got a taxi to take the Mayor's party to their hotel. We somehow got everybody fed and installed in their dormitories (with wives separated from husbands). They were unhappy at first but soon realised it was a bit of a laugh. The next morning, they were all feeling better, the sun was shining, and the festival atmosphere was everywhere. The colour and spectacle were all-embracing. It was as if magic dust had been sprinkled on everyone. People were smiling at me; some even shook my hand or patted me on the back. They were ready for the fray: a busy concert schedule, and some serious partying.

My pal, Barry, arrived by train and was already in the mood. He had got everybody laughing and singing on the train. Truly. They all tumbled out onto the station platform where I met him. He was smartly dressed in a choir blazer and tie but was wearing a huge rubber foot. Like the ones clowns wear. He was limping along complaining 'I've got a bad foot!'. It was hilarious. He stationed himself in an empty glass police sentry box, outside the police station. He was standing to attention with a serious look on his face but wearing his foot. People passing by were collapsing in stitches.

The opening concert was held in a packed stadium. We had the honour of opening the ceremony and sang in the centre of the field. With Huw expertly conducting, we sang *Oes gaf'r eto* (Counting the Goats) and *Down among the Dead Men* (a Drinking Song). Our singing was broadcast on the PA throughout the city, and we were cheered wildly by the thousands of spectators present. We continued singing to great applause, before marching off to line up at the side of the pitch. This was the cue for the grand entrance of the Red Hackle Pipe Band from Glasgow. They marched up and down the pitch with their bagpipes and drums, and were a sight to behold, with the pipe major in front throwing his 'stick' high in the air. They turned around at the far side of the pitch and marched back towards us. As they got closer, my knees started to knock. They were a fearsome sight. They seemed unstoppable. I was in the front row of the choir, and they were bearing down on us. They were seemingly going to march straight through us! Then, when we could see the whites of their eyes, they turned about with military precision. The pipe major had a twinkle in his eye when we shared a beer in the Maryland afterwards.

The Maryland was our regular meeting place after concerts and during off duty periods. It was open all night as were most bars during the festival. Some of the Red Hackle boys also frequented the place and we built up a good rapport. The afterglow singing was an important part of the festival and people would flock to the

49

bar once we started up. There was a lot of banter and I remember a group of locals in the bar making good-natured but disparaging remarks about Welsh rugby. This was a mistake. We challenged them to a scrummaging contest and three of our beefy choristers packed down against their three biggest. It was Wales versus France, in the bar. At the call of 'now!' both front rows started to push against each other. After a few minutes and much grunting, slowly, inexorably, the French started to back-pedal. Their backward movement became a rush as they were pushed out through the open doors and through the outdoor seating area, scattering tables and chairs. They were pushed right across the road and ended up in the hedge in total disarray. It was a wipe-out. The Welsh were victorious. The French bought the beer.

For our next engagement, we sang in a Mass at Lorient's modern cathedral. We were joined by a wonderful choir and musicians from Galicia, the Celtic province in north-west Spain. They were dressed in colourful traditional costume and had their own instrumentalists, including bagpipes and drums. Their musical standard was high, and it was a privilege to share the stage with them. We sang the Breton National Anthem together in the Breton language. The tune is the same as the Welsh National Anthem, but with Breton words. It starts: *'Ni Breizizh na galon, karomp hon gwir fro'* (Brittany of my heart etc). The Bretons are fiercely proud of their Celtic culture.

We encountered a few 'difficulties' during the Festival but (nearly) all were overcome with good grace. One of the problems was the loud snoring of one of the choristers in our dormitory. This was thunderous, like a volcanic eruption. It was driving mad those who misguidedly wanted to sleep. There were two solutions: (a) stay in the Maryland all night: it was about a kilometre away and outside the snore zone, or (b) remove the snorer. This was achieved quite effectively by waiting until he was asleep, then wheeling his bed out of the dormitory. The bed containing the sleeping snorer was wheeled as far away as possible, right along the landing, to be left at the top of the stairs. The dormitory doors were then firmly

50

closed, and this helped some of the boys to get a bit of kip.

The highlight of the festival was on Sunday, when there was the magnificent 'Great Parade' through the streets of Lorient. Many thousands of spectators lined the route, standing up to ten deep on each side. The total attendance was estimated at around a quarter of a million! The colourful two-mile procession included all the performers from the festival and many Breton bagadou (bands) in traditional dress with their bagpipes, bombards and drums. These represented the villages and towns of Brittany and their ladies and children had particularly beautiful costumes. Then there were the choirs and folk dancers from all the various countries as well as pipe bands from Scotland and Ireland. The Cwmbran choir proudly marched in the procession, stopping every so often to give a short performance to the cheering crowds. The experience lives long in the memory.

The procession finally ended at the Palais des Congrès and afterwards we fought our way through the huge crowds to reach the Maryland for some well-earned refreshment. The pipe major of the Red Hackle band had beaten us to it and was halfway through his pint. But his nose was squashed all over his face. During the procession he had thrown his 'stick' up so high in the air that he missed it on the way down and the knob-end hit him right on the nose! Painful. He was bloodied but unbowed.

Our Mayor was delighted with the warmth of the welcome and asked our liaison officer to select a special restaurant for a celebratory lunch. He invited the local dignitaries and our choir officers, and we assembled at 'La Muette' (The Seagull), a wonderful beach-side restaurant and a paradise for seafood. The meal was superb. After starting with Coquailles St Jaques (scallops) we had a great seafood platter. There were oysters, several kinds of crabs, langoustines and all manner of other shellfish, some of them very tiny, all served with a delicious sauce and some exquisite dry white wine. Then there was fresh peach

51

Melba. I've described the menu because it was one of the finest meals of my life. It was a concert-free day, so we stayed at the restaurant all afternoon and savoured every mouthful.

In the middle of the week, we took part in a combined concert with the Galician choir and a Breton folk group, again at the cathedral which was packed with many standing. Another of our concerts was in the fishing village of Plouhinec, some way outside Lorient. The venue was a huge twelfth century church and there was only an old harmonium for our accompanist. There was also a complete absence of any seats for the audience, so we feared the worst.

At the rehearsal, our accompanist, Meurig, tried out the harmonium. He pumped the pedals and it wheezed and emitted clouds of dust and a thin, weedy, sound. It was pronounced unfit for service, so we sang *a cappella*. Fortunately, the acoustics were excellent. The audience started filing in, in their hundreds. The church was soon packed, and they were all standing. We gave a full concert programme, unaccompanied, and the audience stood throughout and applauded enthusiastically. It was a late concert and went on until after midnight. After several encores and the anthems, we headed for a Breton fishermen's bar across the road for one of the best afterglows ever. When we arrived, Le Patron played a loud recording of the Toreador's Song from Carmen over the bar's loudspeakers to welcome us. The singing soon started. Whenever there was a lull in the singing, he gave another blast of the Toreador's Song and we all cheered and joined in. This happened many times. It was raucous. Hours later, as dawn was breaking, we reluctantly boarded the buses with Carmen still ringing in our ears.

Our final performance was again in the stadium, another spectacular highlight. This time we performed with the Irish pipe bands and dancers and as we all joined together for the finale, singing *Auld Lang Syne*, there wasn't a dry eye in the place. Late that night, there was an incredible music event going on at the Port du Peche (Fishermen's Port). All along the front of the port there were stages set up with different bands and performers playing. There were huge crowds thronging the port, and it was great fun moving from stage to stage, enjoying the music and dancing in the street. What a festival ending! Barry summed it up later when he said it had been 'ten days of sunshine, happiness and friendship'. We were all sorry to leave Lorient. I vowed to return but didn't realise how soon it would be.

When the choirs were selected for the following year, I was given the opportunity of returning as one of the official delegation. There were two Welsh male choirs selected this time, from Glynneath and Maesteg. They performed together for some of the concerts and separately for others. The accommodation was again in the university dormitories, but this time there was an improvement: we were only ten to a room. I attended as many concerts as I could, supporting both choirs. There was one concert in a lovely church, with the two choirs combined, and I remember them singing *Ar Hyd y Nos* so beautifully and movingly they made me feel proud to be Welsh. Another joint concert was given at the main concert hall at the Palais des Congrès. This time I sang with the choirs on stage, and it was great to be performing at the festival again. The Maryland was again colonised and there was some mighty afterglow singing. People would crowd around the outside area of the bar, listening and applauding. Bottles of wine and beer would appear at our tables to keep us going.

Because the Maryland was quite a distance from our accommodation, some of the boys sought out another bar, much closer, which was very handy for a quick one. In more ways than one, it transpired. It had some very friendly ladies perched on stools at the bar and we quickly realised it was a knocking shop. Undeterred, we carried on drinking, determined to be sociable. We were made very welcome indeed. Soon we were singing. One of the girls started to do her party trick. She could balance pints on her head. If you ordered a beer, she would deliver it to your table on her head. No hands. Every time she did this there were loud cheers. We kept ordering pints and kept on cheering and singing. Of course, nobody succumbed to temptation, but it may have been the only time Welsh hymns were sung in a brothel!

The local beach at Larmor Plage was a popular location for people to spend any free time. The itinerary for the choirs was constantly changing, but we were promised that one of the days would be completely free. On this day, almost everybody made their way to the beach, which was a couple of kilometres away. I was sat in the Maryland with a couple of the boys, contemplating going to the beach myself, when one of the festival organisers rushed up to me and said that the Welsh choir was required to sing at the radio studio in an hour's time. This performance would be broadcast on French radio. He was serious. But everybody was scattered, mainly at the beach. We couldn't contact them (no mobile phones). More importantly, the conductors and music staff were nowhere to be found. We put out a message on the city's PA system, combed the bars and desperately gathered as many choristers as we could find. We found about twenty or thirty. But still no conductor. Thus, I found myself conducting the Welsh choir on French radio. Or to be more accurate, waving my arms whilst trying to stop the boys laughing. We quickly shaped up, however, and managed a creditable performance of *Cytgan y Morwyr* (The Sailor's Chorus). Should have been 'The Drunken Sailor's Chorus'! But the producer was delighted. I was in a cold sweat as we headed back to the Maryland.

I returned to Lorient a few years later with Mari and the children when we were camping in Brittany. But it wasn't festival time, and it wasn't quite the same. I had been fortunate to attend two of the great early years of the festival. Since then, it has continued to go from strength to strength and the Festival Interceltique de Lorient remains one of the greatest cultural events in Europe.

My earliest choir photograph: Cwmbran Male Choir pictured at Griffithstown Baptist Church in 1971.

Relaxing with Tony Williams (left) and Ralph Powell (right) after an early Cwmbran performance.

56

Singing together with our German friends outside the Kraichgauhalle in Bad Langenbrücken in 1972.

An informal performance at Schloss Heidelberg (Heidelberg Castle) with Clifford Jones conducting. Jackets and ties seem to be the order of the day, apart from the 'scruff' in the middle!

57

The floating stage on the lake in the Luisenpark, Mannheim, on which the Cwmbran choir performed at the Bundesgartenschau (Federal Garden Show) in 1975 (Alfred Ziethen Verlag, Sinthern).

Singing at the beautiful Catholic church in Bad Langenbrücken in 1980, with Huw Davies conducting.

Our family stayed in Bad Langenbrücken with our German friends whilst holidaying in Europe. Left to right: Gerd Gerstmann, Phil, Lucy, Gerd's father Herbert, and Mari.

Huw Davies conducting the Cwmbran Male Choir at the Annual Celebrity Concert at Cwmbran Stadium in 1978.

Part of the Grand Parade in Lorient, Brittany, at the Interceltic Festival in 1979. The colourful two-mile procession was watched by around a quarter of a million people.

The Cwmbran Male Choir pictured in Cwmbran town centre in 1982.

Officers of the Welsh Association of Male Choirs at the Choir of the Year Final at St David's Hall in 1982. Left to right: Vivian Fisher (President), Brian E. Davies, Glaslyn Evans, Glyn (Bach) Jones, Mervyn Downes, John Poole (Chairman) and Sir Alf Gooding (Sponsor, Catnic Ltd).

61

Cwmbran Male Choir on stage at St David's Hall in Cardiff in the Final of the 1982 Choir of the Year Competition, Gareth Whitcombe conducting.

California here we come! The Cwmbran choir pictured with the car raffled to raise funds for the tour.

San Francisco City Hall, where the Cwmbran choir sang after being welcomed by the city's Mayor. The choir sang on the grand staircase under the great dome (Wikimedia Commons Bernard Spragg NZ).

Four tenors, a lady, and a gun! Sierra Nevada, California, 1983. The other three tenors are Charlie Skyrme, Don Price, and Colin Foster with the gun.

Impromptu singing at the Santa Clara Mission, California, 1983.

The Crystal Cathedral, Garden Grove, Los Angeles. This is the largest glass building in the world and Cwmbran Male Choir was the first Welsh choir to sing there (Wikimedia Commons Wattewyl).

8 - CHOIR OF THE YEAR COMPETITION

During my time with the executive of the Welsh Association of Male Choirs, I was actively involved in organising a new Choir of the Year Competition. This was open to all member choirs and was different from the usual eisteddfod format: male choirs of any size could enter and sing their own choice of music in a twenty-minute programme. Marks were allocated for musical quality, variety of content, entertainment value and presentation. This encouraged choirs to perform a wide range of music and enabled the smaller choirs to pit themselves against the big guns. Welsh Brewers kindly agreed to be our first sponsors and I remember a convivial meeting with their publicity manager at a Cardiff pub to set it all up.

The competition immediately became successful, with around twenty choirs entering in the first year. Regional heats were held, with the six best choirs qualifying for the Grand Final. As the competition developed, choirs from both South and North Wales took part, as well as affiliate members from outside Wales. The first final in 1978 was held in the Rhondda Valley Leisure Centre, with Dunvant Male Choir as worthy winners. In 1979, the final was held at Barry Memorial Hall, and was broadcast on BBC television, then in 1980, the final was held in Pontypool Leisure Centre. Cwmbran Male Choir participated in 1979 and were successful in the heat at Blaenavon but were unfortunately knocked out in the semi-final in Swansea.

After three successful years, the sponsorship of Welsh Brewers ended but we were able to find a new sponsor in Catnic Limited of Caerphilly. The stature of the event was raised several notches by the decision to stage the 1982 final at the newly opened St David's Hall in Cardiff. This magnificent concert hall opened in August

1982, and our Grand Final was one of the first major events to be held there. It was great to liaise with Catnic, led by prominent Welsh businessman and entrepreneur, Sir Alf Gooding. He was generous in his support, and I was able to work closely with Ed Carey, his public relations guru. The excitement increased for me personally when the Cwmbran choir succeeded in reaching the final.

On the big night, I had a busy time working behind the scenes while also singing with my own choir. The final was a complete sell-out, with 2,000 people packed into St David's Hall to listen to the six choirs. The event was compered by Alun Williams of the BBC. Our distinguished panel of adjudicators gave proper priority to musical quality, but the other factors were also important. The winner received the 'Choir of the Year' trophy and £1,000 and the worthy winner on the night was Risca Male Choir from Gwent. Cwmbran gave a spirited performance, but the overall standard was extremely high. My disappointment at Cwmbran not winning was offset by the success of the event itself. I remember standing on stage at the end while everybody sang the National Anthem. In the front row of the audience, Ed Carey gave me the thumbs up. The sponsors were happy!

I remained involved in organising the Choir of the Year competition for several more years as the event's prestige continued to grow. The list of adjudicators resembled a 'who's who' of music and included the great bass-baritone Sir Geraint Evans and the conductor of Morriston Orpheus, Alwyn Humphreys. Winners included Froncysyllte from North Wales and in 1984, Bolsterstone Male Choir from Sheffield took away the trophy (at least their conductor was Welsh!). Two days after the final they managed to drop the crystal rose bowl trophy at a publicity event in Sheffield and it was smashed to pieces. I quipped at the time that they'd made sure the trophy would never come back to Wales! Happily, a replacement was soon provided.

In the meantime, one of the more memorable Cwmbran choir bookings was an invitation from the local Saunders Valve company (courtesy of John Charles, one of our choristers) to entertain some of its American corporate guests. The guests were being treated to a 'medieval banquet' at an exclusive country house hotel near Abergavenny and the choir was asked to be the surprise after-dinner entertainment. Around sixty choristers went to the hotel and kept well out of sight before assembling quietly behind a large screen at one end of the oak-panelled dining hall. The company's top brass and their important American guests were dining on the other side of the screen, being served by flunkeys in powdered wigs. At the conclusion of the dinner, the company's head honcho made a speech, welcoming the visitors to Wales and proudly extolling the 'Land of Song'. On cue, the choir started humming *Myfanwy* behind the screen which was gradually withdrawn as we became louder. The effect was tremendous, and the Americans were gobsmacked. We then gave a performance of Welsh songs before mingling with the guests and continuing with some afterglow singing. I chatted to one of the Americans, who praised the quality of the singing. He also praised the quality of the beer, which surprised me somewhat because he had a cinnamon stick in his pint! The company was delighted, and I hope it secured the business deal. They may not have been so delighted with the bar bill: there was a free bar all night and the boys shamelessly took full advantage. Eventually, after a great party, we staggered onto the buses.

In the summer of 1981, the choir performed at the Greenbelt Festival, at Odell Castle in Bedfordshire. This major open-air festival of arts, faith and music has grown from a mainly Christian music festival into a more inclusive event attracting over 20,000 people. We sang on a specially constructed stage, and I guess it was the closest we got to singing at Glastonbury.

68

Later in 1981, the choir had another change of conductor when Huw Davies decided to leave after five years of successful service. This time around, we sought the advice of Glynne Jones, Director of Music for Gwent County, and conductor of the Pendyrus Male Choir. This led to the appointment of Gareth Whitcombe, a talented young musician, who was head of music at a local comprehensive school. Gareth's appointment heralded a further period of success for the choir.

This was a 'golden' period for choirs in the valley and in Cwmbran alone, there were several thriving male choirs as well as mixed choirs. A Cwmbran Choral Festival was held in 1981 featuring the local choirs, and Cwmbran Male Choir achieved a notable success at the competition.

Shortly after Gareth's appointment, I stood down as secretary, having done the job for six or seven years. My professional career was moving forward, and I had other priorities. I was officially thanked for my hard work by the chairman in his speech at the annual dinner. He qualified his remarks by commenting that I didn't suffer fools gladly! But I always tried to make things happen.

In April 1983, Barry and I had a completely different experience when we attended the Sainsbury's Choral Festival at the Royal Albert Hall. The event included a public performance of Carl Orff's *Carmina Burana* and I thoroughly enjoyed singing this exciting work in one of my few experiences of singing in a mixed choir.

In August 1983, the Cwmbran choir recorded its second album at the Brangwyn Hall in Swansea for Sain Records. The LP was called 'Echoes of the Valleys' with Gareth Whitcombe conducting and accompanists Meurig Jones and Derek Parry. The album included *The Crusaders* and *Italian Salad* with solo tenor parts by Gwilym Leek and yours truly (although Gwilym did most of it).

Meanwhile, in the Association, the idea of taking a massed male choir to America became a major topic of discussion. It quickly became obvious that the ethos of whole choirs participating, as at the Albert Hall, would not be possible. Those individuals who could afford the considerable cost would go on the trip, leaving their less well-off choir colleagues behind. There was also the thorny issue of joint rehearsals, and there was a fear that all this would have a detrimental effect on our member choirs, a view I subscribed to. There was, of course, an opposite view among some members of the executive committee and inevitably a breakaway occurred. This eventually led to the formation of Côr Meibion De Cymru (South Wales Male Choir) that recruited many of its members from existing choirs and toured America, subsequently carrying out various other overseas tours.

At around this time there was also a controversy about a Welsh male choir visiting South Africa. It was the era of apartheid, and the South African organisers were making strenuous efforts to recruit a Welsh choir to tour their country. The choir that eventually went on this 'generously funded' trip to South Africa consisted of members of numerous different choirs. It was dubbed the 'Jones Choir', possibly to ensure the anonymity of those who decided to go. I wanted no part of it. I was approached personally several times, including once after the Choir of the Year finals in Cardiff. I was attending a reception at the Park Hotel with our sponsors when a certain gentleman approached me. I gave him short shrift and he left me alone. I was then telephoned at my office, and I again explained very clearly that I was not interested. I still strongly believe that the tour was ill-advised, and I am glad that I refused to take part in it.

9 - CALIFORNIA DREAMING

Cwmbran Male Choir occasionally hosted touring groups from overseas, and among these were the California Girls' Choir and the River Falls Band from Wisconsin. Then in 1980, the choir hosted the Santa Clara Chorale, a choir from the San Jose region, south of San Francisco. This visit included a successful concert in Cwmbran and a mayoral reception, and the Californians really appreciated the warm welcome. They invited our choir to make a return visit, offering to host us for part of a proposed tour. The idea of touring California fired our imagination, and it was a challenge we readily embraced.

This would be a 'choir only' tour because of the high costs, and to help raise the funds required, we decided to raffle a car. A local motor dealer loaned us a car to display at events where we could sell raffle tickets: these included concerts, carnivals and agricultural shows, and a promotion at Abergavenny on market day. We invited other choirs, bands and even rugby and football clubs to participate and many did. Once we sold enough tickets to cover the cost of the car, we were in profit. It took a lot of management and hard work, but we eventually raised a large part of the tour cost. The winning ticket was drawn at the choir's pre-tour concert, with the car displayed in front of the stage.

There were other fund-raising activities: the Treorci and Pontarddulais Male Choirs generously gave sell-out concerts in Cwmbran; we did a sponsored window-clean when 1,000 windows were cleaned for the senior citizens of Cwmbran! We even did a sponsored 'sing-a-thon', taking over the Congress Theatre and singing all day. Behind the scenes, the choir's officers and committee were working hard on logistics, making contacts, fixing concerts. Barry contacted Welsh societies in San Francisco and Los Angeles who were extremely helpful. We featured in the American

Welsh language newspaper *Ninnau*. People over there were looking forward to our visit; we would be ambassadors for Wales.

The tour was finally arranged, with a fantastic two-week itinerary. A glossy tour brochure was produced with a foreword by the Prince of Wales. Gareth prepared a repertoire including Welsh hymns and folksongs, opera choruses, songs from the shows and, of course, *The Battle Hymn of the Republic*. In the meantime, I started a new job in Swansea, and although it was difficult suddenly heading off to California, the dream became a reality. It would be my first visit to the USA.

On 21 September 1983, seventy-five members of Cwmbran Male Choir, plus music staff, departed Heathrow for Boston en route to San Francisco. Our guest soloist was the lovely Siân James, who had been such a success at the Interceltic Festival in Lorient. Siân, with her harp and Welsh costume, was much loved by choir and audiences alike. At Boston we had a few hours between flights so some of us escaped the airport and found a convivial bar where we said hello to America in song. On reaching San Francisco, our hosts from the Santa Clara Chorale met us with a warm welcome. It was late at night as we were whisked off to various homes. Four of us (all first tenors) were hosted by Chorale member, Suzy, who loaded us into her big Mercedes.

The tour took off next day and our feet didn't touch the ground. We were taken into San Francisco and crossed over Oakland Bridge to Treasure Island where I stood on the beach and gazed at Alcatraz prison out in the bay. We went downtown to St Mary's Cathedral where we gave a short recital before an official engagement at City Hall. Here, we were welcomed by Dianne Feinstein, the Mayor of San Francisco (the city's first female mayor, who later became the longest-serving female US senator, and who sadly recently passed away, aged 90).

We were also met by the famous Welsh tenor, Ryland Davies,

who was performing at San Francisco Opera. We sang from the grand staircase in the magnificent foyer of City Hall, a location frequently featured in Hollywood films. All this before lunch. We then had a couple of hours free, so Barry and I visited the waterfront and had lunch at Fisherman's Wharf.

Our concert that evening was at the historic Santa Clara Mission, dating from 1777, one of the twenty-one Spanish missions in California. The Mission is at the heart of Santa Clara University and is the home church of the Santa Clara Chorale. We shared the stage in a memorable concert in beautiful surroundings. Afterwards there was an afterglow arranged at a hotel in San Jose. Most of the choir went there by coach, but our group travelled in two cars. I was invited to drive the Mercedes, and was instructed to follow the car in front, driven by Suzy. The inevitable happened. We stopped at a red light, and I lost the car in front. Unfortunately, I didn't know the way! My fellow first tenor, Charlie, was with me and neither of us knew where the hotel was, or its name. I drove around and around San Jose, looking for a hotel with our buses outside. At one stage I tried to drive up a freeway slip road the wrong way and was stopped by the police. I explained my predicament and the bemused cop turned me around and sent me on my way. We drove around for ages until we eventually spotted a hotel with a coach outside. The choir were all getting on it! The afterglow was over. Suzy was mightily relieved to see us (and the Mercedes). I was to have another escapade with the Merc the following day.

Next day, Suzy took us up to the Sierra Nevada mountains to see the awesome giant redwood trees. We visited a client of hers, an elderly lady, who lived alone in a timber cabin, high up in the redwood forest. She was an incredible character who regaled us with stories, sitting on her porch. She had a loaded shotgun on her lap! I was a bit nervous, but she made us four Welshmen very welcome.

I was invited to drive the Merc back down the mountain. It was a steep descent with switchback bends, and I was quite enjoying myself. Until the brakes failed! I was pumping the brake pedal, but nothing happened. We were going around the bends faster and faster. I tried to keep the car on the road as I searched for the handbrake. I remembered it was in the dashboard and you had to pull it out. I reached a straight bit of road and pulled it out as hard as I could. It took us an age to stop. We were all shaken but ok. I lifted the bonnet and discovered there was no brake fluid: it had all leaked out. Suzy had the car serviced the day before our visit, but the brake system had not been sealed properly. Extremely dangerous. We limped home very slowly using the handbrake. Suzy went to the garage and blitzed them, and got the car fixed. I did not drive it again.

Our evening concert was in the McKenna Theatre at San Francisco State University, organised by the Welsh American Society of Northern California. We had a great reception and at the afterglow, there were crates of Felinfoel beer for us, specially imported from Llanelli! There was more singing and meeting with Welsh exiles, many of whom were experiencing the *hiraeth* (longing for home). It was very emotional. But our day wasn't finished. After the afterglow a few of us were taken to the fabulous Fairmont Hotel, high up on Nob Hill. We ascended the hotel's high tower on the external glass elevator up to the revolving Crown Room at the top. What a view! There we sat, sipping our drinks at midnight, watching the myriad lights of 'The City by the Bay' unfold beneath us.

Our final day in the Bay area was spent seeing more of the sights, including the Golden Gate Bridge. I drove another (different) car up some of San Francisco's very steep hills and down Lombard Street, the famous crooked street with hairpin turns. Later in the day, the four of us were invited to Suzy's boss's place for a 'gourmet dinner'. His house was palatial with a swimming pool and tennis courts etc. We enjoyed the facilities before getting ready for dinner. When we entered the huge dining room there was a concert pianist playing on a grand piano. A team of French chefs had been brought in and there were about sixty guests. But we were the guests of honour! We were applauded in and were seated at circular tables of ten, each of us at a different table.

The meal was lovely, and the wine was flowing. The conversation was lively, and we were treated with great courtesy. Towards the end of the meal our host stood up and made a short speech welcoming us. Then he surprised us by inviting us to sing! Unexpected as this was, how could we refuse? The four of us joined together in some Welsh songs by the piano. Our hosts were delighted. What a memorable final night in the Bay! The following morning, we said our goodbyes and began the long drive southwards along the Pacific Coast Highway towards LA.

The route is one of the world's great scenic drives and we passed through Santa Cruz to reach Monterey for our first stop. We then visited Carmel and Pebble Beach and saw the famous Lone Cypress out on the point. Later we stopped at a highway services for a short break. I was staggered to see a gun shop, right next to the cafeteria. The array of lethal weaponry on display was enough to supply a small army. It told me a lot about guns in America. I found it extremely depressing.

We continued along the Pacific coast, marvelling at the views, and on to San Simeon, about halfway between San Francisco and LA. This was the location for a short mid-tour break of two nights with no official concerts. We stayed in an attractive motel alongside San Simeon Bay, where the Pacific rollers were crashing in. There was an outdoor pool, a bar and restaurant and we were able to chill and unwind. One of the boys had his guitar so we could sit by the pool and enjoy some relaxed singing. By this time, the choir had acquired a groupie who followed us everywhere and regularly supplied us with packs of Budweiser beer. He was extremely popular.

On our first evening in the bar, we sang some songs which the locals seemed to enjoy. We also drank the bar dry. The following morning, we woke up to see a giant truck delivering replenishments. They didn't intend to run out on our second night!

After an enlivening walk along the beach, some of us went to Hearst Castle, high up in the San Simeon State Park. This magnificent hilltop mansion was built for William Randolph Hearst, the newspaper and media magnate, and includes many art treasures from across the world. One of the highlights is the fabulous Neptune Pool, with its elaborate statuary and wonderful views. The pool's centrepiece is the façade of a Roman temple, specially imported from Europe. In the heyday of the 1920s and '30s, Hearst entertained many A-list personalities here, including Charlie Chaplin and Bob Hope, as well as Franklin Roosevelt and Winston Churchill. I found the opulence a bit over the top.

In the afternoon, we staged 'This is your Life' for Barry. This hilarious event culminated with him being ceremonially thrown into the motel pool. For the evening in the bar, it was agreed that everybody in the choir should give a solo item. The word had got around and when we assembled, the bar was packed with local people, including the Sheriff. One after another, the choristers stood up and performed to great cheering and laughter. It went on for hours. After the choir finally finished off with *The Star-Spangled Banner*, the Sheriff made a speech. He said he'd never had so much fun with his pants on!

Next morning, one of the choristers felt unwell. He was peeing green! We diverted to the nearest town to find a doctor. The town was called Cambria, which has obvious Welsh connotations. Whilst waiting for him, we wandered around and came to a house with a plaque proclaiming it to be Cambria's oldest building. The lady of the house was in the yard feeding the raccoons and made us very welcome. We had a long chat and gave her a copy of our tour brochure as a keepsake. The sick chorister was soon given the all-clear but was advised to refrain from drinking alcohol for a week. Poor dab. He got no sympathy whatsoever. We continued our journey south towards LA.

We passed through San Luis Obispo to our lunch stop at Santa Barbara. I was captivated by this beautiful place lying between the mountains and the Pacific Ocean. Most of the choir visited an 'All You Can Eat' restaurant (I felt sorry for the proprietors). I contented myself with a snack while I wandered around taking in the scenery. I was sorry to leave Santa Barbara.

Our route continued through Ventura and Malibu to Santa Monica. Here we turned inland to drive along Sunset Boulevard, through Beverley Hills and Hollywood. Magical places. We skirted downtown LA and followed the Santa Ana Freeway to our destination at Anaheim, home of Disneyland and our base for the following week. Our motel had excellent facilities and was within walking distance of Disneyland, where we were due to perform the next day. Our itinerary also included a series of concerts organised by the Welsh American Society of Southern California, led by passionate Welshman, Donald Davies. There were also several 'tourist' things arranged.

The performance in Disneyland was quite an experience. We gave a concert on a central stage in the 'Happiest Place on Earth', entertaining the large crowds. Afterwards, we were given lunch and then had a free run of the place. We tried all the rides: the one I remember most is Space Mountain. It was exhilarating. In the evening we visited a music club. Some of our choristers performed on the stage and got paid for it!

The following day it was Universal Studios in Hollywood. We saw many stage-sets, including the Bates Motel from Alfred Hitchcock's film 'Psycho' but I guess the highlight was 'Jaws'. Crossing a lagoon in a small boat, this great shark with wide open jaws suddenly leapt out of the water and rocked the boat violently.

It was scary even though you knew it was only made of plastic. Later, we walked along Hollywood's 'Walk of Fame' with its star names. Barry and I then visited the Hollywood Bowl and 'took the stage'. Pity there were only tourists there to see us.

Afterwards we travelled to the city of Pasadena for a big concert. The large audience included many Welsh exiles, and a favourite concert item was *Take Me Home*, an atmospheric piece reminiscent of mining days in Wales. We returned to Anaheim for the late evening, to a handy hotel bar, near our motel, which became our HQ for the week.

On Sunday morning we sang at the Crystal Cathedral in Garden Grove. This is the largest glass building in the world and holds almost three thousand people. It was completed just three years before our visit, and we were the first Welsh choir to perform there. The cathedral was packed full and there were another couple of thousand people in the parking lot, where the service was relayed live. We sang at the opening of the service, which was televised live to fourteen countries, including Australia and New Zealand. The celebrated Reverend Schuller was leading the service and each Sunday there was a famous personality presented from the pulpit. On this occasion, the guest was Hollywood star, Efrem Zimbalist Junior. At a certain point in the service, the whole side of the cathedral opened wide, seemingly at the press of a button, allowing the sunshine to flood in. It was spectacular, pure showbiz. After the service, a group of us were invited to a barbecue, where we socialised with our Californian friends. The welcome and generosity were outstanding.

Our performances in the Los Angeles area were gathering large numbers of followers and the evening concert at a modern church in Orange County was packed. We had another warm welcome at one of the most enjoyable concerts of the tour.

Next morning, we visited Knott's Berry Farm, a theme park with some well-known rollercoasters. The two most frightening were 'The Corkscrew' and 'Montezooma's Revenge'. We went on the Corkscrew, which twisted violently in a double upside-down loop at high speed. Afterwards I staggered around trying to let my insides settle down. Montezooma's Revenge was surely out of the question, its name was enough to put you off. But we were egging each other on and a few of us were stupid enough to be persuaded. It was a giant vertical loop-the-loop. They strapped you in as if you were taking off in the space shuttle. Then you were taken up a high vertical track. It stopped at the top with you facing the sky. They left you there trembling, then suddenly dropped you down vertically, backwards. You then looped the loop at high speed before going up another high vertical track. Again, they held you at the top, this time facing straight down to the ground far below. Then they dropped you again. You were going so fast at the bottom that you looped the loop again, the other way round. Then you came, mercifully, to a halt. We were like quivering jellies. A special lunch had been arranged for us at the theme park. Aunt Mary's famous chicken dinner followed by home-made apple pie. I wasn't hungry.

In the afternoon we enjoyed some much-needed relaxation by the motel pool. By this time most of the choir were sporting cowboy hats and our resident groupie was keeping us supplied with Budweiser. There was a large jacuzzi alongside the swimming pool, and we decided to see if we could fit the whole choir in it. By squeezing in tight, and sitting or standing on each other's shoulders, we managed to get everybody in, including Siân, our lovely young soloist, in her bikini! It was hilarious. Sadly, I can't find the photographs.

The final concert of the tour was in Fullerton, another satellite city of LA. This was in Eastside Presbyterian Church, which was more like a theatre. I noticed a familiar face entering the theatre and incredibly, it was the lady we met briefly in Cambria! The one with the raccoons. She had travelled over two hundred miles down to LA to see us perform. We made a huge fuss of her.

Late that night we went back to Disneyland and had drinks at a themed waterside bar that looked like a Chinese lagoon, complete with 'willow pattern' bridges and sailing junks. Then we went to one of the swish Disney hotels where there was a brilliant jazz band playing. We drank margheritas and enjoyed the jazz until the early hours.

The final event of the tour was a farewell party at the house of Donald Davies, the chairman of the Welsh Society. Donald, resplendent in his red blazer with the three feathers, had been a great supporter and organiser for the tour. His house was a grand affair up in the Hollywood hills. The choir sung at the poolside and speeches were made and it was a fitting ending to a wonderful tour. On the way back to the motel, we visited a bar high up in the hills for a final nightcap. The view from here was spectacular. The whole of Los Angeles was laid out before us with millions of twinkling lights, like the view from where ET's spaceship landed!

The next morning, we said our final farewells and departed LAX on our direct flight to Heathrow. I returned home wearing my cowboy hat and laden with gifts from Disneyland for Mari and the children. In the future, I would travel across the world many times on choir tours. But I still look back on the tour of California as one of the most magical. Barry called it 'The Tour of Smiles'.

I continued singing with Cwmbran Male Choir until December 1983, when my family moved to our new home in Mumbles. Before this, there were several more concerts, including another one at the Assembly Rooms in Bath. After my last rehearsal, a crowd of us went up to the old Bush Inn in Upper Cwmbran, high above the town; the landlord at the time was Nigel, one of our choristers. The lounge bar at the Bush was like a cosy front room with sofas and armchairs and, of course, a piano. We gathered around the piano, with Connie playing, and sang until very late. My last concert with Cwmbran was at Weston-Super-Mare a couple of days later. After the concert, Barry and I went to a nearby bar and reminisced. It seemed like the end of a long chapter.

I enjoyed seventeen memorable years singing with Cwmbran Male Choir and was delighted when the choir honoured me with Life Membership. They presented me with an engraved carriage clock that still has pride of place on my writing desk.

10 - NANCY INTERNATIONAL CHORAL FESTIVAL

When I accepted my new job in Swansea, my family and I had to come to terms with uprooting and leaving behind all our friends and family in the Eastern Valley. However, Mari and the children soon realised we were moving to a very special place.

While I was staying over in Swansea before moving house, I had a phone call from Dunvant Male Choir, inviting me to a rehearsal. I was collected from my hotel and taken to their rehearsal in Gowerton, where there were well over 100 choristers present. Their singing was tremendous (they'd recently won the National Eisteddfod and Choir of the Year competitions) and I was made very welcome. After the rehearsal, I was taken to the 'Found Out' pub for a drink. There I met the choir's musical director and officers and was enjoying a convivial chat until I knocked my pint over. What a mess! (first impressions and all that).

A short time later, I called in the Valley Hotel in Bishopston and got chatting to a chap called Gareth at the bar. He introduced me to Harold Rowe, a member of the famous Morriston Orpheus Choir. The meeting was to change my life. Harold soon took me to a rehearsal, and I was hooked. I'd seen the Orpheus in concert previously and been very impressed. Now I had a chance to join this great choir.

We moved to our new home in Mumbles just before Christmas 1983, and on 8 January 1984, I joined the Orpheus. Our rehearsals were held at the old Calfaria Chapel in Morriston, a building owned by the choir. I had a voice test with Alwyn Humphreys, the musical director, which seemed to go well, and after the committee approved my application, I joined the first tenor section.

I soon realised this was a very different outfit from Cwmbran. Everything seemed more 'professional', and the Welsh language was much more in evidence. A good proportion of the choir members were Welsh speakers, as were all the music staff, including deputy conductor, Huw Rees, accompanist, Mair Wyn Jones and organist, Clive Williams. Everybody in the choir seemed to have a good voice and there was a much busier concert programme as well as regular recordings and media commitments.

The choir had a blazer uniform as well as dress suits complete with frilly shirt fronts and a red velvet dickie-bow. The latter ensemble clipped on and, frankly, looked a bit naff. This was later changed to a simple black bow tie which was much classier. The two buses travelling to away concerts were for choristers only and there was a 'dry bus' and a 'wet bus'. The 'dry bus' usually returned home an hour after the concert finished and the 'wet bus' stayed on until the afterglow ended (i.e., when the bar closed). I was usually to be found on the 'wet bus'.

I already knew some of the choir's repertoire and was able to get up to speed fairly quickly. The first concert I attended was at Llansamlet Church, where I sat in the audience; I was allowed on stage at the following concert in Abergavenny, which was a great thrill. A week later, I took the stage at St David's Hall in Cardiff where we sang with Helen Field, Dennis O'Neill and Delme Bryn Jones.

When I joined the Orpheus, the choir held two major 'home' concerts each year: the Annual Celebrity Concert was held at Tabernacle Chapel in Morriston, with the list of guest celebrities like a 'who's who' of opera. The second concert, the 'MOCSA' Concert, was held at the Brangwyn Hall in Swansea, organised by the Morriston Orpheus Choir Subscribers' Association. The subscribers are a supporters' club for the Orpheus, consisting of hundreds of members, from all corners of the globe. The MOCSA committee also organised the choir's 'Young Welsh Singer of the

Year' competition and the concert provided a stage for the winner. The MOCSA concert also featured a well-known celebrity and in my first year this was the singer, Iris Williams (the previous year was The Spinners). The MOCSA competition has showcased and helped to launch many notable Welsh singers over the years, including Rebecca Evans, Kathryn Jenkins and Bryn Terfel.

The choir's programme of 25 to 30 engagements a year meant a concert about once a fortnight as well as rehearsals every Sunday and Wednesday. Many concerts were in Wales but there were regular trips over the border. There were also album recordings and TV appearances.

In addition, there was a 'choir within a choir'. A smaller group known as the Calfaria Singers undertook engagements at venues where the full choir was not required. These included performances at clubs, weddings, birthdays etc. Deputy Conductor, Huw Rees usually took the baton for these and there would normally be about 20 or 30 singers.

There was always something happening. In Chatham in Kent, we sang at a packed theatre. Unfortunately, one of the choristers became ill while we were singing and threw up on stage! We were quietly singing *Myfanwy* at the time, and I heard the tell-tale 'splashing' noise coming from the second tenors. Choristers were shuffling quickly out of range but carried on singing as the poor sick chorister was led away. But the smell lingered, made worse by the heat of the theatre lights. An exclusion zone developed in the middle of the second tenors, but the show went on until the interval when there was a clean-up operation behind the closed curtains. The sick chorister soon recovered, and we were all able to laugh about it at our overnight hotel stop.

We also made the long trip to Barton-on-Humber, near to the famous Humber Bridge. We stayed at a hotel in Scunthorpe and at the afterglow, a surprise 'This is your Life' was staged for choir secretary, Royston Pugh (a real character), and his wife Olive, a valued choir administrator. On the way back home, by invitation, there was a singing stop at Rugeley Workmen's Club in Staffordshire.

Other early engagements included the official opening of the Taliesin Arts Centre at Swansea University in June 1984, where the choir performed in the company of Sir Geraint Evans. There was also an appearance at the Trellech Festival near Monmouth, held in the beautiful church of St Nicholas. I was delighted that my friends Barry, Ken and Des were able to come up from Cwmbran for the concert.

One of the final concerts each year was at St David's Hall in Cardiff, a Christmas Concert to raise funds for Leukaemia Research. This was always a complete sell-out, and we appeared every year with a top Brass Band and a junior choir, usually the BTM (Bedwas, Trethomas & Machen) Band and a brilliant children's choir from Ceredigion. A celebrity Father Christmas always made an appearance. Just before Christmas, a smaller group of us would sing at Ty Olwen Hospice at Morriston Hospital, to bring some cheer to the patients there.

I continued my role as the publicity officer for the Welsh Association of Male Choirs for a couple more years. There were the continuing Albert Hall festivals and Choir of the Year competitions, and I still enjoyed the buzz of being involved, but soon realised that the commitments were becoming too heavy. I eventually decided to stand down from the Association's executive committee, but I was pleased that my fellow Cwmbran chorister, Ivor Maggs, had joined the executive committee, and would eventually become chairman of the Association. If I'm honest, I'd had more than enough of committee work, and it was great to be singing without having any other responsibilities.

During 1985, the Golden Jubilee of the Morriston Orpheus Choir was celebrated. The choir was formed in 1935 by the legendary Ivor Sims, as a breakaway from the Morriston United Choir, and had achieved great things in its fifty years. The choir won the Chief Male Voice Choir crown at the National Eisteddfod of Wales on seven occasions and achieved a worldwide reputation through its overseas tours, broadcasts and recordings. It performed for Her Majesty The Queen in the Royal Command Performance at the London Palladium and sang to the royal family and many heads of state at the celebrations in Hyde Park for the wedding of the Prince and Princess of Wales. It also performed for the Pope on his historic visit to Wales.

The jubilee celebrations included a grand dinner at the Brangwyn Hall, attended by numerous celebrities and dignitaries. There was also a series of major concerts at venues including the Royal Festival Hall, the Royal Albert Hall and Birmingham Town Hall. There were two overseas tours during the year: the first one took the choir to the International Choral Festival at Nancy in France, with concerts en route in Brittany and Chartres Cathedral. The second tour was to West Berlin to take part in a series of Grand Military Concerts at the Waldbühne amphitheatre.

One of the albums recorded in the year, *You'll Never Walk Alone*, won the prestigious Music Retailers Award for the 'Best Choral Record of 1985'. The presentation was made to Alwyn Humphreys and choir officers by Rt Hon Edward Heath MP at a glittering ceremony at the Café Royale in London. By 1985, the choir membership was well over a hundred.

The tour to France started with a concert at the Royal Festival Hall in London. Our programme included a medley of Second World War songs marking the fortieth anniversary of the end of World War Two. Immediately after the concert, we continued to Folkestone, for an overnight stop before our channel crossing to Boulogne. Then followed a long coach journey through Normandy and Brittany to our first destination at St Briac-sur-Mer. It was a tedious journey, but for Dai it was bliss.

Dai bought a very large bottle of whisky in Duty Free and happily consumed it during the coach journey. All of it. The choir was late arriving at St Briac, so we went directly to a civic reception laid on in our honour. By this stage, Dai was comatose, and it was difficult to wake him. We couldn't leave him on the bus, so he was carried off (unfortunately, he couldn't stand). There was nowhere to hide him, so we had to take him into the civic reception. We filed into the municipal hall supporting Dai vertically between two other choristers. We hoped nobody would notice him. Luckily, there were long tables laid out for a meal, so we sat him down and propped him up, with a minder on each side. He continued sleeping.

The tables were laden with charcuterie, salad and carafes of wine. We tucked in, ensuring we always put some food on Dai's plate. This was gradually eaten by his minders, giving the impression that Dai was participating. The choir soon polished off everything, but it was only the first course! More food soon arrived: delicious chicken and vegetables. Then other courses kept coming. The carafes of wine were replenished as fast as we could drink them. The feasting and drinking went on for hours. After the meal and warm speeches of welcome, the two minders, by now very shaky themselves, carried the still comatose Dai back out vertically. It just looked like three men staggering behind one another. Poor Dai was completely oblivious to the whole thing and hadn't eaten a crumb. He probably woke up next morning wondering what planet he was on.

The following day, there was a 'friendship' visit to St Malo Rugby Club. The concert in the night was in the church of St Briac and was due to start at 9.00pm. But the church was empty. Everybody was outside chatting and socialising but casually started wandering in when they realised the choir was ready. Eventually, the church was packed, and we proceeded to much applause. This became another late night and was the second of our two nights in St Briac-sur-Mer. The visit had been arranged by a Breton choir supporter who was a keen MOCSA member, and the welcome had been fulsome. We waved our fond goodbyes early next morning.

There now followed another long trip across country to Chartres where we were due to sing at the cathedral. The organisers arranged a splendid lunch at a restaurant in Chartres, before our afternoon performance. The experience of singing in the great cathedral was uplifting and memorable.

From Chartres we continued to Paris for an overnight stop. We were billeted in a hostel on the outskirts. Unfortunately, there was a curfew at 9.00pm, so we hurried to the nearest bar before returning to the hostel early, feeling very deprived. It was my first visit to Paris, and I wanted to see the sights, but the hostel gates were securely locked. So, five of us, including Dudley Williams, hatched an escape plan. We bribed the security guard! He unlocked the gates and organised a taxi, which took us on a magical tour of Paris by night. Then Dudley asked the taxi driver to take us to the Pigalle and he dropped us off outside the Moulin Rouge. We went into the bar across the street, the one frequented by the dancers from the show. Some of the showgirls were in the bar and one of them turned around, looking surprised, and said 'Hello Dudley!' I was gobsmacked. We had an extremely happy time at the Pigalle and returned to the hostel many hours later. Nobody in the choir knew about our escapade. We got back in time for breakfast and caught up with our sleep on the onward coach journey to Nancy.

The city of Nancy was the location for the 1985 biennial International Choral Festival and was our home for the following week. Nancy is a beautiful city in the province of Lorraine and provided a great setting. The Place Stanislas square in the centre with its magnificent buildings, fountains and golden gates has been ascribed as a UNESCO World Heritage Site.

The choir was accommodated by volunteer families and on arrival, Peter Davies and I were introduced to our hosts. We were taken to their home and shown our room. It featured a double bed. Because both of us were called Davies, they assumed we were brothers and wouldn't mind sleeping together! Mealtimes were interesting. We were introduced to an aperitif called Suze, and the meals seemed to be deconstructed. The various elements were served as separate courses. For example, one of the courses was just peas. Occasionally a small amount of meat would appear. And a small glass of wine, served with an explanation of the grape variety, vineyard and vintage. The kindness was much appreciated.

The festival featured choirs from all around the world, with concerts at venues throughout the city. There was no official competition, although a competitive edge soon developed. In our first concert, we were up against the Bulgarian State Male Choir and a choir from the United States. We were a little apprehensive, particularly about the Bulgarians, knowing their reputation. They were in full evening dress, with white-tie and tails, and sang *a cappella* in typical Eastern European style. The Americans were also pretty good and when we took the stage, we had it all to do. We needn't have worried. We brought the house down. Our choice of programme and the 'hwyl' of our singing carried the day. There was a great buzz afterwards.

We shared the stage with numerous other international choirs at concert halls and theatres throughout the city. On the Sunday, all the choirs packed into the cathedral and sang a specially composed Mass. There were also informal events, street parades and open-air performances. There were about thirty choirs taking part in the festival and, inevitably, a pecking order emerged. The goal was to be one of the two or three choirs invited to perform in the festival's closing concert held on an open-air stage in the central city square with an audience of thousands.

The popularity of the Orpheus was building, and it soon became clear that we would be in the grand finale with a wonderful youth choir from Riga in Latvia (then part of the Soviet Union). They performed in colourful national costume, and it was felt that they were the most popular choir of the festival, with the Orpheus a close second. It was a great occasion sharing the stage with them.

The following day all the choirs enjoyed a final lunchtime party in a great hall. The impromptu singing from table to table was very moving. Each choir sang their own country's traditional songs and there were some poignant moments. The Iron Curtain didn't exist in Nancy and the barriers were well and truly broken down. It was a privilege for us to add a Welsh flavour to the occasion, and there were tears shed that day.

We returned to Nancy two years later but there was a busy period before then. The Orpheus travelled the length and breadth of Wales and England singing in events and music festivals, including those at Chichester, Chelsea, Hungerford and Llandrindod Wells. We sang the opening concert of the National Eisteddfod in Fishguard (which was televised), performed in Bristol on St David's Day and at the Poole Arts Centre.

One of the interesting things we did was a BBC TV recording for a programme called 'Don't Break Your Heart', about healthy eating. We were filmed singing *Food, Glorious Food* in Tesco's while dodging around behind the fruit & vegetable stalls, popping out from behind melons and cauliflowers!

In the meantime, I was roped in to help organise the MOCSA Concert and managed to secure the services of Don Estelle (of 'It Ain't Half Hot Mum!' fame) with a great band called The City Lights. They proved to be an excellent combination to accompany the choir and the winner of the Young Welsh Singer of the Year competition. This was the last MOCSA concert using this format. Henceforth, the entire final of the Young Singer Competition would be held as part of the concert, negating the need for a 'star name'. This proved a popular move.

The choir was invited back to Nancy for the 1987 International Choral Festival, the only choir invited to return. Some of us travelled by train, staying overnight in Boulogne. My friend Steve Kember and I stayed with another family and one evening, we were invited to a 'mirabella party'. The main feature was a special kind of potent spirit made from mirabella plums - a bit like German schnapps. I needn't say more!

The Orpheus was conducted on this tour by deputy conductor, Huw Rees and he and the choir were given a great welcome. Our fellow participants at the opening concert were the Moscow Students' Choir and a choir from Colombia. Our programme included a lively spiritual called *I'm Gonna Walk* which raised the roof. We performed in about six concerts in total and again took part in the final concert in Place Stanislas square, together with the Moscow Students' Choir and a brilliant choir from Zagreb (then in Yugoslavia). It was another colourful and memorable ending to the festival.

We missed the final gathering of choirs next day, having been separately booked for a concert for the British Council in Épinal, some 50 miles south of Nancy. This was an enjoyable theatre concert, but somehow lacked the excitement of the festival. Nevertheless, we again carried fond memories of Nancy on the train journey home.

11 - BERLIN BANDANZA

The 1985 choir tour to Berlin was organised by the British military and followed two previous Orpheus visits. We travelled to Berlin by coach and, because I was due to attend a conference in the UK towards the end of the tour, a flight back was arranged for me. The organisers requested a choir of fifty voices and happily the required number was able to make the trip.

On the long outward journey, I followed our progress across Europe with a map, trying to work out distances and times of arrival. I think this was when I acquired my choir nickname 'Brian the Brain' (unknown to me at the time). We had an overnight stop at the Stornoway Barracks of the Royal Regiment of Wales at Lemgo, near Hamelin, and were well looked after. We visited the attractive town of Hamelin next morning and I went in a rather classy shop with Tony Madge. I spotted a nice item for Mari and in my best German, I enquired the price: *'Wieviel kostet das?'* I asked, showing off to Tony. On being told the (extortionate) price, I exploded *'How much??'* (in English). Tony fell about laughing, and soon told the rest of the choir. From then on, whenever choristers were told the price of anything, they would all shout *'How much??'*. My only purchase was a cheap plastic badge which said, *'I'm following the Pied Piper'*. I wore it for the rest of the tour.

We continued to the border crossing at Helmstedt, where things got serious. We were now crossing the Iron Curtain into communist East Germany at Checkpoint Alpha. The security checks were stringent before we were allowed to enter the autobahn corridor to West Berlin. The first things I noticed were the watchtowers in no-man's-land. We followed the autobahn corridor for 110 miles and were not allowed to stop. Finally, we reached the Checkpoint Bravo crossing point into West Berlin at Dreilinden. After more security checks we were allowed to re-enter 'the West'. West Berlin was effectively an island in the middle of East Germany surrounded by the Berlin Wall and was split into British, American and French sectors. The Russian sector of East Berlin was on the other side of the wall, accessed by the infamous Checkpoint Charlie, a pleasure we would experience later.

We were to be accommodated at Spandau Barracks, right next door to Spandau Jail, the prison housing the Nazi prisoner, Rudolf Hess. On arrival, tired and hungry, we were led to a huge barrack block where we climbed several steep flights of stairs to our billet. This was an echoing dormitory with many beds and very little else. The showers and toilets were a route march away. The place was depressing and basic. It may have been (just about) acceptable for squaddies but was totally unsuitable for the choir. We were sure that Rudolf Hess was considerably more comfortable in Spandau Jail! We refused to stay there, did a smart about-turn and marched out of the building. While we waited for the bigwigs to decide what to do, we were fed in the mess. A high-ranking army officer soon arrived and inspected the quarters. After a conflab, we were relocated to RAF Gatow. What a difference! It was like a hotel. No more than four to a room and en suite facilities. The food was excellent and the icing on the cake was the corporals' mess. Here the drinks were ridiculously cheap and there was even a Happy Hour! The corporals' mess became HQ, with occasional forays to the sergeants' and officers' messes. We were made welcome in all three and performed 'social' concerts in each.

We were soon hard at work rehearsing for the main event, a series of Grand Military Concerts at the Waldbühne, a huge outdoor amphitheatre near the Olympic Stadium. This was a gigantic undertaking featuring over five hundred military bandsmen, with the Orpheus playing a prominent role. The Waldbühne seats over 22,000 people and a great stage was erected to accommodate the musicians, with the choir positioned in the centre. The lighting and sound systems were brilliant, and it was like taking part in a rock festival. The choir sang with the bands in a programme of rousing British music including *Rule Britannia* and *Land of Hope and Glory*. We also sang in Welsh, Scottish and Irish sections, including folk songs and *God Bless the Prince of Wales*. For this item, Alwyn conducted the whole ensemble with great panache. There were marching displays in the arena by British, American and French military bands, including the Royal Marines (who were the best), and performances by Berliners, including children. It was a spectacular show for the huge audience who waved their lighted candles in the dark, a great sight. The finale was a performance of Tchaikovsky's *1812 Overture* by 500 bandsmen and the Orpheus singing in Russian. The ending featured the cannons of the Royal Horse Artillery exploding, the bells ringing, and a spectacular display of pyrotechnics. Wow! Little did anyone know that some of the Orpheus were wearing their pyjamas under their dress suits to keep out the cold!

The show was repeated for three nights running, but there was ample opportunity to socialise and enjoy the many other (liberal) attractions of Berlin (my lips are sealed!).

On one of the days, the military authorities arranged for the choir to visit East Berlin. This entailed crossing through Checkpoint Charlie to the other side of the Berlin Wall. We travelled on a British military bus accompanied by an army officer and were warned to be well-behaved at the crossing. Unsmiling East German border guards entered the bus and scrutinised our papers as well as meticulously examining all around and underneath the bus. It was a bit unnerving. We toured parts of East Berlin including viewing the cathedral and State Opera House as we travelled along Unter den Linden. There were many Red Army soldiers around, but they had two arms and two legs like the rest of us. I believe the main reason our visit was allowed, was for us to visit the Russian War Memorial in East Berlin. This vast memorial and cemetery for 5,000 of the 80,000 Soviet soldiers who fell in the Battle of Berlin in 1945, was an awe-inspiring place. But it was with a sense of relief that we returned through Checkpoint Charlie.

On our last night in Berlin, we had a humdinger of a party in the corporals' mess. I was due to be picked up by an RAF driver at the crack of dawn to be taken to Tegel airport for my arranged flight, so I didn't expect much sleep. Before going to the mess, I carefully turned Harold's mattress and bedding upside down so that he would have extreme difficulty getting into bed later. When we staggered back in the early hours, the rest of us in the room were in stitches watching Harold's performance trying to get into bed. Chuckling to myself, I crawled into bed having set my alarm clock for 4.30 a.m. to be ready for my lift to the airport. But Harold had planned his revenge. I was woken up being violently shaken. My driver had arrived, and I was missing from the rendezvous point. Harold had deviously changed the time on my alarm clock, and I'd slept well past the allotted time. There were minutes to spare before my flight and I hadn't even finished packing! I grabbed all my gear and rushed down to the car where an anxious-looking airman was waiting. Mumbling my apologies and cursing Harold to high heaven, we drove off at high speed to Tegel airport where I caught my flight by the skin of my teeth.

The rest of the choir returned in leisurely fashion by coach. They again stayed overnight with the Royal Regiment of Wales at Lemgo, where they gave a concert for the troops. They had a great night, and a fabulous spread was laid on for them.

Another tour to Berlin took place five years later and is described later in this chapter.

In the meantime, in 1987, the choir performed at a gala tribute to the singer Matt Monro who'd sadly died in 1985. Known as 'The Man with the Golden Voice', Matt Monro was one of the most popular entertainers of the 1960s and '70s and the Orpheus had recorded its own tribute, a trilogy of his songs brilliantly arranged by Alwyn, featuring *Portrait of my Love*, *Softly as I Leave You* and *Walk Away*. We were invited by Matt Monro's widow to take part in the glittering tribute event, held in the Great Room of the Grosvenor House Hotel in London. There was a galaxy of stars present; everybody from the world of British show business was there. The master of ceremonies was Bob Monkhouse and performers included Petula Clark. The Orpheus was given the honour of closing the show and our finale included the *Trilogy* and a special arrangement of *Born Free*. It was a spectacular night to remember.

There was also a short tour to Cornwall, with concerts at Truro and Redruth and we performed a concert in Anglesey, on Alwyn's home patch. We also took part in the centenary celebrations of the St John's Ambulance Brigade, a major event held in Hyde Park in London. There were nearly 170,000 people attending and we were privileged to sing to Her Majesty The Queen and other royals, accompanied by the Band of the Grenadier Guards.

In the summer of 1987, six of us were invited to sing with the Dyfed Choir for a special recording of Mahler's Second Symphony (The Resurrection). The recording was on an impressive scale, conducted by Gilbert Kaplan, a wealthy American and celebrated Mahler enthusiast. We joined forces with The Ardwyn Singers, BBC Welsh Chorus, Cardiff Polyphonic Choir, London Symphony Chorus and the London Symphony Orchestra for the recording. Soloists were Benite Valente (Soprano) and Maureen Forrester (Contralto). Choir rehearsals were held at Welsh National Opera HQ in Cardiff, under chorus master John Hugh Thomas, and the full recording took place at St David's Hall (Kaplan wanted the recording to be made in Wales, including the finest Welsh voices). The great choir had the opportunity to excel itself in the magnificent final movement of the symphony with its dramatic ending. It must have cost a fortune to produce, but it was worth it. The recording received the highest praise from leading music critics and reached number one in the UK classical album charts, staying there for many weeks. All the performers were presented with a special facsimile copy of the first page of Mahler's original score, which Kaplan owned.

The Orpheus continued its busy programme, including the City of London Festival held at the Broadgate Circle, a modern open-air amphitheatre in the heart of the Square Mile. After rehearsal, we sought refreshment in a nearby bar. While we were complaining about the price of the beer, a crowd of loud city types burst in and ordered jeroboams of champagne. Goodness knows what they cost, but these clowns didn't drink the champagne, they just squirted it at each other! The concert was great, however, the city audience refusing to allow the choir to leave the stage.

At around this time, I contacted my old friends in Cwmbran to help me arrange an Orpheus concert at Cwmbran Leisure Centre to help raise funds for our forthcoming American tour. I was in Cwmbran early on the evening of the concert, anxiously waiting for the Orpheus to arrive, but by the concert start time, only one choir coach had arrived. The hall was packed with over 600 people, but we only had half a choir! I had an urgent discussion with Alwyn, and he lined up the 'half choir' to check the balance of voices. He was happy, so we started the concert with half of the Orpheus. We completed most of the first half of the concert before the second bus arrived (after having broken down). The boys had changed into their concert dress on the bus and 'quickly' joined us on stage. Imagine the spectacle. The concert became a triumph, however. I was told our rendering of *By Babylon's Wave* was especially memorable. One lady audience member remarked 'it wasn't just a concert; it was an experience'. We raised a substantial amount for our trip, and it was great to be among my Cwmbran friends again.

In 1989, the Orpheus ventured into the world of pop music. Mike Peters, of The Alarm, invited us to participate in a recording of an evocative song he'd written called *A New South Wales*. The song was a hit, reaching the Top Thirty and winning a silver disc. This led us to a TV recording at HTV in Cardiff followed by an appearance on the 'Wogan Show' at the BBC in London. This was a brilliant event with a studio audience and with Joanna Lumley hosting the show (Wogan was away). Our fellow guests were Harry Secombe and Spike Milligan, who were hilarious. There followed an appearance at The Alarm's sell-out concert at St David's Hall, at which the choir were cheered like rock stars. A year later there was a recording with the group T'pau at Rockfield Studios in Monmouth.

In between these happy events, there was a much sadder, devastating occasion when the Provisional IRA attacked the Deal Barracks of H.M. Royal Marines in Kent. A time bomb was exploded on 22 September 1989, killing eleven marines from the Royal Marines Band Service and seriously wounding another twenty-one. The Orpheus had a long-established relationship with the Royal Marines Band and happened to be giving a concert in Kent the week following the atrocity. On the Sunday morning, we diverted to the Deal Barracks to pay our respects and sang at the Barracks gates before singing *Cwm Rhondda* and *Gwahoddiad* at a special memorial service in the Barracks Chapel. It was a sombre and moving occasion.

The tour to Berlin in September 1990 started with a visit to West Sussex for a formal concert at the Arundel Festival and a more relaxed affair at Chichester Police Club. The choir stayed in

Worthing and while we were there, Bill and I visited an excellent local hostelry. When the landlord learned about the choir, he asked if 'a few of the boys' could come on the Sunday lunchtime for a sing, offering a free pint as an incentive. I had a quiet word with a few choristers and told them to keep it to themselves but of course, the word spread like wildfire. When I got to the pub on the Sunday it was crammed with about fifty Orpheus choristers all expecting a free pint. The landlord couldn't oblige everybody, but we had a good sing anyway.

I should mention here that Bill Kenny, my room-mate on this trip, had joined the Orpheus earlier in the year. He heard a group of us singing at Christmastime in my local pub, following which I introduced him to the choir. Bill hailed from Merseyside and was part of the 'Mersey Beat' in the Sixties. He had recorded with a group called the Black Knights and appeared on the same bill as the Beatles. He also played at the Star Club in Hamburg and featured in the film *Ferry Across the Mersey* with Gerry and the Pacemakers. He became a great friend and companion and shared in many of my later choir experiences.

From Worthing, the choir proceeded directly to Luton Airport for our flight to RAF Gatow in Berlin. This time we staye d at the Edinburgh House hotel, where the military normally accommodate their officers. The food and accommodation were superb, and all paid for. The drinks at the bar cost just one deutschmark (about 25p).

We were in Berlin for the 'Bandanza', billed as 'The Great Berlin Band Show'. This was again held at the Waldbühne arena, and the extravaganza featured over six hundred performers. The line-up included the Massed Bands of the British Forces, Fanfare Trumpeters, Pipes and Corps of Drums, Morriston Orpheus Choir and Children's Choirs from East and West Berlin. There were two days of rehearsals before three shows on consecutive nights. Each show featured a 'star' performer: firstly Liza Stansfield, then Leo

Sayer and on the final night, Cliff Richard. It was an experience sharing the stage (and the lift in our hotel) with Cliff!

On the second night, part of the canopy high up on the staging caught fire! (despite the rain). We were watching helplessly from the stage when one of the riggers rapidly scaled the huge structure and managed to put out the fire before it got a real hold – a brave man. A serious catastrophe was narrowly avoided.

The main theme of the Bandanza was a musical journey around the British Isles, and the Orpheus contribution included *Jupiter* from *The Planets*, *Rule Britannia* and *The Londonderry Air* as well as *Dafydd y Garreg Wen, Men of Harlech*, and *Ar Hyd y Nos*. The Grand Finale featured *Zadok the Priest* and *The Royal Fireworks*. Rockets and mortars were fired from behind the stage while full-sized cannons blasted out either side. All this to the accompaniment of a spectacular display of lasers and fireworks. Finally, a lone piper played *Highland Cathedral* high above the stage before the massed Pipes and Drums ended with *Auld Lang Syne*.

The final show was attended by the Princess Royal and at the end, the officer commanding personally thanked the choir. He said our country should be proud of us. The 'Berlin Bandanza' was recorded for posterity and the album sleeve records that 'the performances took place in conditions of almost non-stop wind and rain, but the Berlin audiences not only came but remained for the whole very wet evenings. Their marvellous spirit and enthusiasm inspired everyone concerned with the performances'. Amen to that.

We were celebrating in the hotel bar after the final show when I started chatting to one of the crew. I said how impressed I'd been by the lasers, not so much by the fireworks. He turned out to be the head fireworks man! In my embarrassment, I made a noble gesture and bought him a drink. It cost me one deutschmark.

In between the rehearsals and performances, Bill and I explored

Berlin. The Berlin Wall had recently come down and I obtained some bits to take home. After Checkpoint Charlie in 1985, I found it strange being able to wander freely across to East Berlin through the Brandenburg Gate. Walking along Unter Den Linden was strangely unnerving. I took a photograph of the cathedral but inadvertently also took the picture of a man on a bicycle. He leapt off his bike and angrily tried to grab my camera (memories of the Stasi were obviously still raw). I still have his photograph! Bill and I carried on to ascend the Berlin TV Tower, constructed by the GDR administration in the 1960s as a symbol of East Berlin. The tower was the tallest building in Germany with its distinctive sphere modelled on the 'Sputnik' satellite. It dwarfs the radio tower in West Berlin, but we ascended both.

The choir's final engagement in Berlin was at Montgomery Barracks where we entertained the Royal Welch Fusiliers. They returned the compliment with a brilliant marching and drumming display and honoured the choir by presenting us with 'The Flash'. This is the name given to the five overlapping black ribbons uniquely worn by the Royal Welch on the back of the collar and dates back over two hundred years to when soldiers wore pigtails. It's said that the enemy never saw The Flash because the Regiment never retreated.

Before leaving Berlin, the choir had official photographs taken at the Reichstag and at the Russian War Memorial. Mari told Roy Noble live on Radio Wales about my trip and sent him a piece of the Berlin Wall. He was delighted.

12 - CANADA AND THE USA

The first long-haul major tour I undertook with the Orpheus was to Canada and the United States in the spring of 1989. The Orpheus had made two successful tours to North America in the 1970s and after the second of these, their conductor, Lyn Harry, stayed on in Canada. He formed the Hamilton Orpheus Choir, which later became the Canadian Orpheus, and our tour was organised by one of their members, Dr Wally Landers. Our guest artistes were Welsh sopranos Rebecca Evans and Glenys Roberts and musical director, Alwyn Humphreys, was supported by accompanist Mair Wyn Jones and organist Alun Tregelles Williams. Our tour doctor was the popular Julian Bihari, an ear, nose, and throat specialist who dispensed large quantities of 'Swansea Mix' (boiled sweets from Swansea market) to keep our throats lubricated. They worked a treat.

Our 105 choristers took off from Gatwick, bound for Hamilton, Ontario, where our Canadian friends welcomed us. Harold and I met our host, Ray Williams, a Welsh exile and keen choir and rugby man, and we slept the first night in Ray's comfortable basement. Next morning, we were on the road, headed for the city of London, Ontario.

We stayed on the campus of the University of Western Ontario for a couple of days and our first concert was at Althouse College concert hall, with a good audience well-supported by the local Welsh Society. Next morning, there was a trip to the beach resort of Grand Bend, on the shores of Lake Huron. It was a beautiful day, and we had an opportunity to swim in the Great Lake and relax. In the evening the Welsh Society organised a buffet and social evening in our honour.

This was to prove somewhat embarrassing as the Welsh Society expected us to sing for our supper. But the choir was under strict instructions from the musical director not to indulge in any 'afterglow' singing (to protect our voices for the long tour). So, the choir wives and supporters started singing instead, conducted by one of the choristers, which caused an unseemly scene. Next morning a choir meeting was held in the University hall which became known as the 'four square' meeting.

The choir chairman, Huw Madoc-Jones, took the stage and made an impassioned speech, saying he stood 'four square' behind the musical director. The choir was urged to behave professionally, particularly as the concert itinerary was to become increasingly demanding. The choristers listened attentively and agreed wholeheartedly with the sentiments expressed, with a unanimous show of hands. We pledged to observe the off-stage singing embargo for the duration of the tour.

Next stop was the city of Utica in New York State, and we crossed the Canada/USA border at the Peace Bridge near Buffalo. At Utica, we were again billeted on a university campus and some of us escaped to find a nearby bar called the Village Tavern. This was a splendid place with a circular island bar with stools all around it. Choir members formed a happy circle, and we soon discovered it was cheaper to buy the beer in pitchers. A gang of us returned to the bar the following night after our concert at Whitesboro High School. This time the (forbidden) singing started, encouraged by the barman who supplied numerous free pitchers of beer. We were attracting plenty of punters and he was happy. This carried on until the early hours when somebody suggested we go to an all-night diner for breakfast. I ended up in a car with some of our new-found friends and we drove to a roadhouse called 'Breakfast at Tiffany's' where a crowd had gathered. We gave a mini concert in the restaurant, including the USA, Canadian and Welsh National Anthems. Then we had corned beef hash for breakfast before returning to our billet for a brief sleep. Then we were on the road again.

Back across the Canadian border to the beautiful city of Kingston, located where the St Lawrence River flows out of Lake Ontario. Harold and I were hosted by an ex-pat Texan lady and the first evening was spent at the Toucan pub near the waterfront. We were later invited back to someone's house where we played a crazy Texan tequila game. We all sat around a circular table in the centre of which was a clockwork mouse loaded up with a shot glass of tequila. The mouse was spun around before it set off across the table in a random direction. The mouse stopped when it reached the table's edge and the nearest person had to drink the tequila. This involved squeezing fresh lime juice onto the back of the hand, adding salt, licking it off and then knocking back the tequila. All to the accompaniment of cheering and laughter from everybody else. Until it was their turn. Before long everybody was totally blitzed and in hysterics. Especially Harold. I had to carry him to bed.

Next morning, we recuperated on a paddle-steamer cruise through the 'Thousand Islands', a scenic paradise of some 1,864 islands along the St Lawrence River. A jazz band was playing on the boat, and we were soon clapping along with gusto.

The Kingston concert was in the Grant Hall, a super venue at Queens University. There was an audience of 700 people packed in, and there was a great buzz of anticipation. The choir prided itself on staging professionally, and our marshal meticulously lined us up in the room below the stage. Alternate rows were instructed to simultaneously enter the stage from either side, making for an impressive entrance. The lead man in each row knew his route to the stage and at the signal, the choir members proceeded up twin staircases and onto the stage in perfect synchronism. The applause was thunderous. The marshal stood proudly in front of the choir, observing the staging, which went like clockwork. Then a look of horror crossed his face. The choir was completely arse about face! The baritones were on the right instead of the left. The other three sections were similarly in the wrong place. The choir was a mirror image of itself! The marshal was nothing if not decisive and uttered the command *'swap around boys!'* waving his arms vigorously. We were trained to follow orders and did as we were told. Imagine over a hundred choristers on a tiered stage all clambering over each other to get to their correct positions. Everybody had to move. Some moved quickly, some were more reluctant, others had to be cajoled (there are always one or two). It was mayhem. No-one thought to draw the stage curtains or turn down the lights. The whole sorry manoeuvre was carried out in the full glare of the stage floodlighting in front of a bemused (and much amused) audience. But we did it. When the conductor and accompanists took the stage, the choir was spot on. We opened the concert with *Men of Harlech* and brought the house down. By the time of the final encores, everyone had forgotten the cock-up at the start. Almost.

After Kingston, we were off to Montreal. Here the Welsh community had matched me up with a namesake. Ex-pat Brian Davies and family hosted Harold and I for three days at their delightful house near the St Lawrence river. There was a house party on our first evening and there was much reminiscing about the old country. Next morning, we enjoyed a sight-seeing tour including a visit to the great Oratory at Montreal's highest point. This impressive building's huge dome is second only to St Peter's in Rome. We also saw the Olympic Stadium, but the highlight was undoubtedly the beautiful Notre Dame basilica in historic Old Montreal. I'll never forget the magnificent deep blue ceiling and wonderful stained glass in one of the world's most dramatic religious buildings. Brian then treated us to a speciality Montreal lunch of smoked beef and pickles.

Our evening concert was at the 2,000 seat St James' heritage church, a magnificent venue. The church was packed, with many Welsh exiles in the audience. While we were singing the exiles' song *Unwaith eto 'n Nghymru Annwyl* (Once Again in Dear Wales) I couldn't help noticing a lady in the fourth row, immediately behind the conductor's arm, weeping openly. I started crying myself. I couldn't stop. It was the most emotional concert I've ever experienced. The afterglow was at the Black Watch club where chorister John Williams 300 (ex-Welsh Guards) was in his element. He stood on a table to give a moving monologue about his pride at being a member of the Morriston Orpheus.

Next day our host took us on a car trip to Ottawa, Canada's capital. It was a beautiful day as we admired the National Parliament building (modelled on the Houses of Parliament in Westminster). We also visited the Victoria Library, with its statue of the Old Queen at the centre of the great reading room. In the evening we visited Montreal's red-light district (to further our cultural experiences). Say no more.

Next stop was at Kitchener in Southern Ontario, where we stayed in the Valhalla Hotel. Peter Lowe and I decided to explore the city which included sampling a 'typical' bar. This turned out to be a real dive, with some unsavoury-looking characters in it. We quickly drank our beer and exited, heading for a pub called the 'Duke of Wellington' which was much more friendly.

Our Kitchener concert was in the 'Centre In The Square', a superb new performing arts venue seating over 2,000. Our performance received several encores, and the response was quite humbling. The concerts were getting bigger and more prestigious as the tour progressed.

The following day, there was a choice of excursions: either a visit to a local brewery or a trip to see a Mennonite community. I surprised myself by opting for the Mennonite village where I was fascinated to observe the alternative way of life. People were dressed in old-fashioned clothes and travelled around in horse-drawn carts. They seemed to lead a clean, God-fearing existence, unsullied by modern temptations and were also very friendly and welcoming.

We were based back in Hamilton for the remainder of the tour, and spent a further five nights with our host, Ray Williams. We visited City Hall to meet the Mayor and sang in the Council Chamber. Later, our penultimate concert was held at Hamilton Place, a major concert hall in the heart of downtown. It was uplifting to see the 'Morriston Orpheus Choir' name in lights high up on the giant electronic billboard in the city centre. The concert was spectacular. Alwyn was on great form and the choir excelled as did our two soloists. The music critic of the *Hamilton Spectator*, Hugh Fraser, wrote in his review: 'magnificent is the pale, wan, best I can come up with to describe the performance of the Morriston Orpheus Choir'. We were on a high and looking forward to our finale in Toronto.

On a free day we visited Niagara Falls and marvelled at the spectacle. Some of us decided to get up close and personal with the falls with a trip on the *Maid of the Mist*, a boat that takes you right underneath the falls. This was unforgettable and hilarious with us all kitted out in waterproofs and sou'westers, holding tightly onto the boat's rail while soaking up the mighty mist with the great falls roaring above us. After the falls we were transported to the more tranquil surroundings of Niagara-on-the-Lake, a scenic spot beside Lake Ontario and rated one of Canada's prettiest towns.

Then it was on to Toronto, our final destination, to sing at the city's International Choral Festival . We had time to explore, visiting the CN Tower, one of the world's most famous tall buildings, with its glass floor on the observation deck. The view was spectacular, looking out over the city and Lake Ontario. We were so high up, an aircraft flew past, below us! Just beneath us was the newly opened Skydome, with the world's first fully retractable roof, and home of the Toronto Blue Jays baseball team. Nearby, looking magnificent, was the Roy Thomson Hall, Toronto's iconic circular arts venue and the setting for our final concert. Soon we were rehearsing on its stage and admiring the hall's auditorium and curvilinear glass interior. There was a final photo call in full concert dress and the anticipation was building. We took the stage to a great ovation from the 2,600-capacity audience and opened the concert with Gounod's *Gloria in excelsis deo*. It was electric. The concert seemed to pass by in a flash and before long we were into our finale and encores. I was proud to be Welsh that night. We took Toronto by storm and there followed a glowing review in the *Toronto Star* newspaper. In addition, the concert was recorded by the Canadian Broadcasting Corporation (CBC).

The final day was spent with our friends from the Canadian Orpheus as we sang at a Festival of Praise at Stoney Creek United Church with ex-conductor Lyn Harry.

It was with a sense of achievement that we returned to Wales. We had been described as 'Ambassadors of Song' and 'The Cadillac of Choirs' during our tour and other press headlines included 'Welsh choir gives 100 singing lessons' and 'Welsh leave misty eyes'. We had performed around forty different pieces of music ranging from *American Trilogy* and *Calon Lân* to a medley from *Jesus Christ Superstar* and Alwyn was justifiably proud of our performances. On the flight home he made a point of thanking each one of us individually, a nice personal touch.

Two years later, the Orpheus was invited to make a return visit to North America. This time there were more concerts in the United States and fewer in Canada and our tour soloists were Leah-Marian Jones and Rhian Owen. We were engaged to start the tour in Cincinnati, Ohio, at the Annual Festival and Cymanfa Ganu of the Welsh North American Association. The tour would again end at the Roy Thomson Hall in Toronto.

Initially flying into Toronto, we immediately transferred to London, Ontario, to stay overnight. Next morning saw us cross the Ambassador Bridge over the Detroit River into the USA, continuing south to the fine city of Cincinnati, on the banks of the Ohio River. We checked into the Hyatt Regency for three nights and a message was waiting for me from a family friend, inviting me to a welcome party. Their house was across the river in Kentucky, and I was asked to bring along about eight fellow choristers (no shortage of volunteers!). We arrived at a large house near the riverside, where the great and good of the neighbourhood were waiting to greet us, including numerous 'arty' types. There was a super spread prepared for us, and we circulated and enjoyed a jolly good evening.

Next morning, a few of us were whisked off to a smart Country Club for a spot of golf while many of the choir party went on a paddle steamer cruise on the Ohio River. We were all back in good time to head off to the Music Hall for rehearsal and our evening concert. The Music Hall is a beautiful 3,500-seat concert theatre, built in 1878 and home to the Cincinnati Symphony Orchestra and Cincinnati Opera. Our sell-out concert was part of the North American Welsh Festival and was followed next day by the Cymanfa Ganu hymn-singing festival, held in two sessions, with the choir joined by Welsh exiles and descendants in their thousands, from all over North America. The singing of the Welsh hymns, all in the 'language of heaven', nearly raised the roof of the

Music Hall and there was a great feeling of *hiraeth*.

We had some time to explore downtown Cincinnati and were impressed by the twin buildings that comprise the world headquarters of Procter & Gamble. These two towers have distinctive rounded tops, inevitably referred to locally as the 'Dolly Parton Towers'!

After Cincinnati, we headed north to the township of Howe in Indiana. The minister of the Episcopal Church in Howe originally hailed from Morriston, so we were delighted to perform a concert for his church. We stayed with congregation families and on arrival Bill and I were introduced to our hosts. They lived in a delightful house by a lake and had a boat moored at the bottom of their garden. The boat was a flat-bottomed affair with a frilly canopy, and we did a leisurely lap of the lake, which was relaxing after the frenetic bustle of Cincinnati. This was the Bible Belt, and the family was strictly teetotal, so we had a dry day (and night) and felt very virtuous! Our host was the editor of a newspaper on the other side of the state line in Michigan. The two states had different time zones, so he had two different time schedules, one for work and one for home. It must have been very confusing! After a pleasant family dinner, we went to the Howe Military Academy for our concert at the Bouton Auditorium.

The next day saw us travelling back over the border to Hamilton, Ontario for three nights; it was good to meet up again with old friends from the Canadian Orpheus. This time, Bill and I were hosted by Adrian Williams in the suburb of Burlington. Adrian was the brother of Ray, my host on the previous trip, and made us very welcome. Next morning, we visited the Grand River Indian Reservation, a fascinating experience, before the whole choir went to a lunch party at Joanie Cunningham's fabulous house by the river. Joanie was a key patron of the Canadian choir and a vice president of the Morriston Orpheus. This set us up nicely for our big concert at Hamilton Place theatre in the evening. The 2,200-seat concert hall was again packed, and the choir was on good form, enjoying the splendid acoustics. We had another excellent write-up from Hugh Fraser in the *Hamilton Spectator.*

On the way back to Burlington after the concert, Adrian's car broke down on the Queenie (Queen Elizabeth Highway). It was terrifying. Gigantic trucks were hurtling past, inches from our car, which was stranded on the very narrow hard shoulder with a high wall on the inside. We were eventually rescued, after more than an hour of sheer terror. I'll never forget the Queenie.

Next day, we revisited Niagara Falls. Bill and I decided to take a ride to the top of the Niagara Skylon Tower, 775 feet above the mighty falls and with panoramic views. There's a revolving restaurant and bar at the top so we ordered a cold beer and sat down to admire the unwinding view. We soon became aware of an adjoining buffet bar where a tempting sign said: 'All You Can Eat - $8.00'. Diners were piling their plates high with delicious looking foods and kept coming back for more. They were slowly inching past us, carefully trying to balance large piles of food on their plates. It seemed sheer gluttony but I'm ashamed to say we eventually succumbed. We made about three trips to the buffet, until we were totally, utterly stuffed. We eventually wobbled to the exterior glass elevator feeling slightly sick.

When we arrived back at our accommodation a short time later (still stuffed), our smiling host, Adrian, proudly announced that he had prepared an extra-special meal for us. Home-made faggots, mushy peas and chips! When he saw our looks of horror, he hastily reassured us the chips were healthy, cooked in sunflower oil! I managed to eat about half of my huge plateful, but Bill failed miserably. We were glad later to get some much-needed exercise on the long walk to Burlington Rugby Club. Here we enjoyed some friendly socialising on our last night in Hamilton. And lots of spicy chicken wings!

Next on the itinerary was a concert in Cleveland, Ohio and we went over the border again, following around Lake Erie, heading south-west to Cleveland. We stayed with a lawyer and his family in a big house in Cleveland Heights, an attractive suburb about twenty minutes from downtown, which we explored next morning. We headed for the tallest building, called the Terminal Tower, and took in the view of the city from the observation deck. Our evening concert was in one of Cleveland Heights' fine churches and we were ringing the changes with our repertoire to keep the music fresh. Alwyn again interacted with the audience in his inimitable fashion.

The following day we performed at a Major League Baseball game at Cleveland Municipal Stadium. The Cleveland Indians were playing against the Toronto Blue Jays and the Orpheus sang the United States and Canadian national anthems in the centre of the pitch before the ballgame started. Quite an experience. I watched the game with a regular fan who patiently explained the rules of baseball to me. Sadly, I've forgotten the rules (I've also forgotten who won!).

In the evening our host and family took us out for dinner to the Cleveland Flats, an impressively redeveloped post-industrial area alongside the Cuyahoga River. The renovated Powerhouse there includes numerous vibrant bars and restaurants. Then it was 'off to Philadelphia in the morning' for our next concert.

Or to be accurate, to an overnight stop in Harrisburg, Pennsylvania on our way to Philadelphia. In passing, I recalled the major nuclear accident that occurred at Three Mile Island nuclear power plant, south of Harrisburg, some twelve years earlier.

In Harrisburg we spent the evening unwinding and enjoyed a live band in Rod's Roadhouse before continuing to Philadelphia next day. On arrival, we visited the Liberty Bell pavilion, to see the iconic cracked bell that is the symbol of American independence. We later booked into a Ramada Inn in Essington, near the airport, and gave a concert in the evening in a modern church. In the morning we followed the great Delaware River waterway, with its naval shipyards, along Interstate 95 on our way to New York.

Our next engagement was on Long Island, at the city of Huntington, but first we visited New York City, dropping off in Manhattan near the Empire State Building. Some of us went straight to the top and admired the magnificent view. I had my photograph taken there, with the World Trade Centre Twin Towers in the background. The date was September 11, 1991, which is uncanny looking back. At the time, I made myself a promise to one day go to the top of the Twin Towers but sadly, this was never to be. Exactly ten years later, on September 11, 2001, the Twin Towers were devastated in the terrorist attack. We were destined to revisit New York in the immediate aftermath of the attack.

We had an all-too-brief period to explore downtown Manhattan, but a few of us managed to find an Irish bar on 43rd Street. One of the customers was Welsh: he was a steward on the QE2 liner berthed on the nearby Hudson River. She was due to sail very shortly and he insisted on buying us a round of drinks before departing. We sent him on his way with some Welsh 'hymns and arias'.

Suitably refreshed, we crossed the East River to spend a couple of days at Huntington, Long Island. Four of us were billeted with a delightful lady called Jean-Beth. We enjoyed drinks on her porch while she prepared dinner: her speciality meat loaf was a real treat. After dinner we gathered around a lovely old organ in her parlour, which she played with great gusto while we sang, reading from her songbooks, and adding some tunes of our own.

The next day, some of our party visited Theodore Roosevelt's house on the north shore. The evening concert was at the

University Concert Hall, with an audience including many students. Our programme included a gospel song *Where could I go but to the Lord* in which we all snapped our fingers in time with the music, a difficult exercise of coordination.

The tour continued with a long journey north through New York State to our final destination in Toronto. There was an overnight stop in Syracuse on the way. We checked into the Holiday Inn in Toronto for a couple of nights. Nearby was a well-known restaurant called Ed's Warehouse and that evening we enjoyed a lobster meal to celebrate the approaching end of the tour. Next day, Bill and I took in a baseball game at the magnificent Skydome (since renamed the Rogers Centre). We settled down with around 50,000 other spectators to watch the Blue Jays play the Oakland A's. We were fortunate to witness a 'grand slam' hit by one of the A's batters (in baseball, a grand slam is a home run hit with all three bases loaded, thereby scoring four runs, the most possible in one play).

Our concert at Roy Thomson Hall was a memorable finale as the choir and soloists responded to a tremendous welcome from another capacity audience. It was a poignant ending, however, as our much-loved accompanist, Mair Wyn Jones, was staying on to live in Canada. The Orpheus had once again thrilled the audiences of the United States and Canada and lived up to its reputation as the 'Cadillac of Choirs'.

13 - EXPO SEVILLE

The early nineties saw no let-up, with many concerts and numerous TV and sound recordings. We produced a new album each year and followed our *Hits of Andrew Lloyd Webber* with a range of other albums, winning the 'Choral Record of the Year' award an unprecedented three times. There was also an album called *Christmas from the Land of Song* produced jointly with Treorci and Pontardulais Male Choirs and the Band of the Welsh Guards, which achieved a silver disc. Our repertoire was constantly changing; for example, during 1993, we performed around sixty different pieces, almost all arranged by Alwyn. We also received an invitation to take part in the 1992 international Expo exhibition in Seville.

I remember a trip to Bury St Edmunds, where we sang in St Edmundsbury Cathedral. The town is the home of the Greene King brewery, and our hosts thoughtfully provided a barrel of IPA for the choir, set up in the middle of the changing room. It didn't last long!

Another performance was at Neyland, celebrating the start of the Tall Ships Race from Milford Haven. Sir Geraint Evans was present, and he praised the choir's rendering of *Balm in Gilead*, a lovely, softly sung spiritual that we sustained with careful breathing. At the Brangwyn Hall, we sang with Larry Adler, the legendary harmonica player, who accompanied the choir in *The Rose*.

In March 1992, the choir performed at the National Stadium in Cardiff, for the Wales v Scotland rugby international. We sang the usual 'hymns and arias' and the two national anthems on the pitch. Unfortunately, the Welsh Rugby Union only provided enough match tickets for half the choir, so the other half had to watch on TV in the Cardiff clubhouse. This didn't go down too well, but we held a ballot, and the situation was amicably resolved. Luckily, I got a ticket (and Wales won).

The 'Universal Exposition of Seville' (Expo '92) was a prestigious major event at which the British cultural contribution was masterminded by Major Sir Michael Parker (who also organised our Berlin concerts). The Orpheus party was limited to fifty voices, so Alwyn had the tricky task of selecting the fifty singers. Fortunately for me, I was one of the tenors selected. Most of our party were accommodated near Seville centre but a few of us stayed with the 'crachach' in a smart hotel outside town, including our musical staff and new accompanist, Joy Amman Davies. The 'Hotel Jardin de la Reina' was also the location for our rehearsals with the other performers. There were musicians, dancers, clowns, jugglers, stilt-walkers and pearly kings and queens among many others. Harpists joined the choir in representing Wales.

Expo was held on Cartuja Island alongside the waterway in central Seville and over 100 countries were represented. The designs of the pavilions were amazing, representing a global display of innovative architecture. Our task was to participate in 'British Day' including the official opening of the British Pavilion in the presence of the Prince and Princess of Wales.

We paraded through Expo, singing while marching behind the Band of H.M. Royal Marines, and with the Red Arrows simultaneously flying overhead. We marched past the royal party, saluting with 'eyes left', and afterwards, in the Pavilion, we sang *God Bless the Prince of Wales* to Charles and Diana and the assembled guests. I enjoyed chatting to some of the Red Arrows pilots in the reception afterwards.

After the ceremony, I hitched a ride with our choristers who were staying near the city centre because I wanted to see

116

something of Seville. I was much taken by the great cathedral, but after visiting several establishments with my friends, I found myself alone in the early hours looking for a taxi and trying to remember the name of our hotel!

Next day, we returned to the Pavilion for a full concert performance, sharing the stage with numerous other participants. Some years later, I revisited Seville with Mari, and we took a river cruise past the site of Expo, which has been converted to a technology development area and theme park. It was pleasant to reminisce about Expo '92 and enjoy the many attractions this fine city has to offer.

The week after Seville, we were back at the National Stadium in Cardiff, participating in a spectacular 'World Choir' event. This was reckoned to be the largest male choir ever assembled with around 180 choirs and about 8,000 voices; the event was repeated the following year. Celebrities taking part included Sir Tom Jones and Dame Gwyneth Jones in 1992 and Max Boyce and Dame Shirley Bassey in 1993. A proposal to take the whole show to the USA unfortunately failed due to financial difficulties.

Another event of note took place in November 1992 when the choir sang to a meeting of European Trade Ministers at Brocket Hall, near Welwyn Garden City. The meeting was hosted by President of the Board of Trade, Michael Heseltine (born in Swansea and a keen supporter of the Orpheus). I couldn't attend, but I understand our deputy musical director, Huw Rees, conducted affairs with his customary good humour. The following year we sang at the wedding of Heseltine's daughter at the village church in Marston St Lawrence, near Banbury. Half the cabinet was there, dressed in their morning suits and finery. Our programme included the finale of *Nidaros* and, of course, *Myfanwy*.

The rugby connection continued with a social trip to Scotland for the international. I joined friends from my old choir of Cwmbran together with some from the Orpheus and we stayed in Pitlochry; I took my walking boots, planning on some hill-walking. The local mountain was Ben Vrackie (2,760ft) and its snow-capped summit looked inviting. About a dozen of us decided on the climb and started up the lane towards the village of Moulin. Here there was a nice pub that looked ideal for refreshment on our way back down. We carried on upwards, climbing steeply. I think about five of us made it up through the snow to the summit including Bill, whom we nearly lost at one stage! The weather closed in as we descended and we reached the Moulin pub, ready for a pint, but it was just closing for the afternoon! The landlord refused to let us in, even though we were soaking wet and freezing, We could see locals still drinking in the bar and pleaded with the landlord for a swift half. Eventually, he grudgingly agreed provided we drank up very quickly. We were there for seven hours! Once we started singing, the locals wouldn't let us leave.

This period included concerts at Great Yarmouth, Dudley and Dulverton in Somerset. At Dudley Town Hall I met up with Jeff Bubb and his wife, Jean, who Mari and I first met in the Greek islands. Jeff sang in a local choir and was a Black Country poet and prolific letter writer. Mari corresponded with Jeff for several years. The trip to Somerset allowed Bill and I to do some walking on Exmoor.

Another TV recording was held at Pinewood Studios with Dame Thora Hird for the programme 'Thora on the Straight and Narrow'. Fellow performers included the great American concert organist, Carlo Curley, and The Angel Voices. Dame Thora got on with the choristers like a house on fire - she even came to wave us off when we departed!

The Orpheus also sang at three important occasions I couldn't attend: the Covent Garden Festival; the Wales v New Zealand rugby league international; and the D-Day fiftieth anniversary celebrations at the Royal Albert Hall. I was present, however, when the choir sang to the Prince of Wales at the Brangwyn Hall when he visited Swansea to receive the Freedom of the City.

We also sang at the Commonwealth Universities Congress at Swansea University. There was a free bar afterwards, but it soon closed, so we quickly got a couple in. A delegate from Botswana asked me why I had a pint in each hand. I told him it was customary in Wales. He looked around and saw everyone else was carrying two pints!

Then there was a trip to Hereford to sing at the Cathedral. A few of us stayed overnight in Hereford at a local guest house. After an impeccable concert we sampled the delights of the nearby Wye Valley Brewery before ambling back to our guest house. When I went down for breakfast next morning, I greeted our host with a cheery 'good morning' to be met with a somewhat frosty reception. Apparently one of our number had disturbed him and his wife in the middle of the night. It transpired that Pugh had got up to go to the toilet in the night and had gone out through the front door by mistake. The door slammed behind him, and he was locked out, clad only in his boxers! He hammered on the door to try to rouse someone, but without success. He went around the back and tried again, even throwing stones up at bedroom windows. Still no response. The shivering Pugh was now in trouble. He wandered down the deserted street seeking refuge. In the distance he saw a light. He went for it like a moth to a flame and it turned out to be an all-night petrol station. He entered and asked to use the telephone! The bemused attendant helped him find the number of the guest house and Pugh telephoned, waking up the proprietor and his wife. He was very lucky that they got up from bed and opened the door for him. He was missing at breakfast.

In December 1994, our musical director, Alwyn Humphreys, married our accompanist, Joy Amman Davies. The wedding ceremony took place at Tabernacle Chapel in Morriston where the Orpheus lifted their voices to help celebrate the special occasion.

14 - DOWN UNDER

The Diamond Jubilee of the Morriston Orpheus Choir was celebrated in 1995 and it turned out to be quite a year. There were many special events, but the highlight was the choir's first visit to Australia. There had been a strong demand for the Orpheus to go Down Under for some time, and the Melbourne and Sydney Welsh Choirs were helpful in arranging our tour. Melbourne member, Cyril Jones, was the main promoter and he organised an impressive itinerary of visits and engagements, including a gala concert at the Sydney Opera House.

There was a tour party of around 180, including supporters, and conductor Alwyn Humphreys was supported by soloists Iona Jones (soprano) and Elizabeth Ann Stevens (mezzo), with Clive Williams as organist, and accompanist, Joy Amman Davies. The choir was 112-strong and although the logistics were challenging, everything was well planned. Alwyn prepared a wide-ranging repertoire, strongly Welsh but with an Australian and international flavour. There was a pre-tour concert at the Brangwyn Hall to send us on our way.

A large group of us who were travelling without partners formed an unofficial 'Blobby Club' with garish 'Mr Blobby' ties to be worn at every opportunity (a bit silly but good for a laugh). Mari didn't mind me going on my own: she didn't fancy all the travelling from city to city and living out of a suitcase.

We travelled in style with British Airways and arrived in Melbourne via Singapore and Perth. Our group was split between three Melbourne hotels with some choristers hosted by Melbourne Welsh members. Bill and I stayed at the Palm Lake Hotel near Albert Park (where the Formula One grand prix is held), not far

121

from St Kilda beach.

The first day was spent exploring: we visited the Shrine of Remembrance war memorial and strolled along the vibrant area alongside the Yarra river. For dinner, we joined some of the other 'Blobbies' including the popular Brian Lloyd, a bearded first tenor, and fine soloist, who was fondly known as 'the Pocket Pavarotti'.

Next day we visited the Dandenong mountains and took a ride on the 'Puffing Billy', an historic steam train that runs through the rainforest, with its giant tree ferns and prolific wildlife. Next stop was the Yarra Valley Winery, with obligatory tasting, before a visit to the Healesville Sanctuary, a bushland haven for Australian wildlife. After viewing the koalas and other animals, I decided to have some fun by allocating names of animals to the choristers they most resembled. One particular chorister became the Tasmanian Devil, and I won't mention who was the duck-billed platypus! We finished the day at Bill Bell's Hotel, with its own brewery (far better beer than the usual bland Australian lager). A few bursts of song got rid of any rustiness and lingering jet lag.

Next day was St David's Day, and our first performance was due that evening. But first, Bill and I visited the Rialto Tower, Melbourne's tallest building. At the top we bumped into Clive Williams and Barry Child, two of our choristers who were handling the publicity for the tour (brilliantly). They were being interviewed by the radio station whose studios were in the tower. Afterwards, we went to Young & Jackson's pub near Flinders Street Station to meet Chloe who, as expected, was in the nude (Chloe is the subject of a painting displayed in the pub and is a Melbourne icon).

Our St David's Day Concert was at the Robert Blackwood Concert Hall at Monash University's Academy of Performing Arts. There was a capacity audience of 1,400 and our programme, including the soloists, was entirely composed of Welsh items.

There was much *hiraeth* in the hall that evening. Two days later, we gave a second concert at the same venue with a completely different programme, this time with a more international flavour.

Meanwhile, Bill and I continued to explore Melbourne using the excellent tram system. We visited the Queen Victoria Market (*aka* 'the Vicky Market') to do some shopping. There were exotic fruit and vegetable stalls, and I made the mistake of picking up a prickly pear with my bare hands. Ouch! We made a courtesy call to the Redback Brewery (named after the killer spider) before taking the tram down to St Kilda beach. In the evening, a few of us went to a barbecue at the home of Loretto, the Melbourne choir's accompanist. Loretto was a member at the Melbourne Cricket Ground (MCG), famous for the Olympics, Test cricket and the Aussie Rules Grand Final and next morning, we were given a guided tour of the MCG. We walked out into the middle of the playing area and visited the museum before enjoying lunch in the members' dining room as Loretto's guests. We later walked through the National Tennis Centre, home of the Australian Open championships. We were sad to say goodbye to Melbourne next day when our convoy of coaches set off for Canberra.

It was a long road journey of over 400 miles and our first stop was at Glenrowan where we saw the 'Big Ned' statue of the legendary Ned Kelly: bushranger, outlaw and 'folk hero'. Glenrowan was the scene of Ned Kelly's violent last stand in 1880 before he was captured. He was hanged at the Old Melbourne Gaol and his original suit of armour is preserved at the Victoria State Library (I saw it on a later trip). We stopped for lunch alongside the Murray River, at Albury on the Victoria/New South Wales border. After reaching Canberra and checking in, we headed to a nearby club to chill out.

We explored Australia's capital next morning and, in the afternoon, gave a performance in the Great Hall of Parliament House on Capital Hill. We were invited there by the Australian

Arts Minister and were given a guided tour of the Parliament. There were formal welcomes, and it was an honour to perform at Australia's seat of government, the first Welsh choir to do so. In the evening there was a major concert at the Llewellyn Hall, Canberra's premier concert venue, with another 1,400 present. The hall is named after the Australian National University School of Music's founding director, Ernest Llewellyn CBE (1915-1982).

Next morning there was a trip to the Australian National War Memorial. We later moved on to Wollongong, a seaside city in the Illawarra region of New South Wales. We arrived in high spirits, many of us sporting our Mr Blobby ties.

Bill and I were hosted by June and Bob in their house at Woonona, on the north side of Wollongong. They were connoisseurs of Australian wine and champagne and were keen for us to sample the local cuisine. That evening, we dined on Sydney rock oysters, Balmain bugs (butterfly fan lobsters) and king prawns all washed down with a crisp, dry white. As we drank each other's health, we wondered how the other boys were getting on!

We spent five nights with June and Bob in 'The Gong'. The city is located along a narrow coastal plain between a spectacular rainforest escarpment and the Pacific Ocean. It has a history of heavy industry, especially coalmining and steelmaking, but also has a series of superb beaches making it a diverse and interesting place. On day one, Bill and I visited the top of the escarpment where the Sublime Point Lookout offers great views over the rainforest and the many beaches that span the coastline. We walked very steeply down the escarpment, on a track through the rainforest, marvelling at the wildlife, especially the beautiful birds, and the odd snake (thankfully up in the trees). We reached the Pacific shoreline at Austinmer beach and walked back along the coast to Woonona. It was a stimulating day out, topped off by an evening barbecue for the choir at the Orb Recreation Club at Figtree. I recall that the choir sang for its supper.

Next morning, the choir did a TV recording at the Novotel on Wollongong North Beach, followed by lunch at the Illawarra Steelers Rugby League Club (a few years later the Steelers formed a joint-venture club known as the St George Illawarra Dragons, now one of Australia's top teams). In the evening we performed our main Wollongong concert, at the Church of Christ in the leafy suburb of Figtree. The weather was lovely as we chatted outside beforehand to our enthusiastic audience, many of them Welsh exiles.

The following morning the choir met the Lord Mayor of Wollongong, who officially welcomed us to the city. Lunch was in the nearby RSL Club, which provided excellent dining at reasonable cost. The RSL (Returned and Services League) is a support organisation for men and women who have served in the Defence Force. There are licensed RSL clubs all over Australia and we were fortunate to be welcomed as guests in several during our tour.

Later, June and Bob took us to visit some friends at Kiama, a scenic coastal town south of Wollongong. Their friends had Welsh connections and we spent a pleasant time chatting with them. In the evening, Bill and I took June and Bob out to dinner to their favourite restaurant, repaying them for their kind hospitality. The Panorama House restaurant was superbly situated at the top of the escarpment with breath-taking views of the coast and city at night.

On our final day in Wollongong, some of us visited the giant BHP steelworks at Port Kembla. It was awe-inspiring viewing the great fiery furnaces and interesting to compare the works with our own steelworks at Port Talbot. After lunch we visited the Mount Keira Lookout and later, we gave an informal concert at the Fraternity Club in Fairy Meadow, billed as 'A Night With the Orpheus' and organised by the Australian-Welsh Friendship Club. This was our last engagement in Wollongong.

After fond farewells, we boarded the coaches for the short journey of 60 miles to Sydney. As soon as we had checked into our Sydney hotel, we travelled on for a further 100 miles up the coast to Newcastle. Our driver took us over the Sydney Harbour Bridge to give us our first view of the spectacular harbour and Opera House, one of the most iconic views in the world.

The concert in Newcastle was at the University Great Hall. This port city is the second largest in New South Wales and there were again many people with Welsh connections in our audience. We were getting used to standing ovations at the end of our concerts and our finales were getting longer. Alwyn was really building up the emotion. Bring on the Opera House!

We were very late getting back to our hotel, but happily the bar across the road was still open. We planted our flag there and the bar became our HQ in Sydney.

Our whole group was staying at the Sydney Boulevard Hotel on William Street, near Hyde Park. It was within walking distance of the main sights and also near Kings Cross. There was an RSL Club nearby, handy for lunch on our first day, after which we ascended the Sydney Tower, at that time the highest building in the southern hemisphere. After enjoying the panoramic view, we walked around the Botanical Gardens and down to Sydney Harbour. In the evening there was a welcome dinner with the Sydney Welsh Choir at Eastern Suburbs Rugby League Club, home of the Sydney Roosters.

Next day, a gang of us walked across the Sydney Harbour Bridge. The Bridge Walk over the top wasn't then in operation so Bill and I ascended one of the bridge towers: the view was special. Peter Davies had pre-organised a harbour cruise, including lunch, so we spent the afternoon enjoying the magnificent scene from the boat and taking photographs. The weather was wonderful. The rest of the day was spent exploring Darling Harbour.

The big concert day was next, but the morning was free. Bill and I rode the monorail running above the streets from the central business district to Chinatown and Darling Harbour (since dismantled). We checked out the Pumphouse Tavern (recommended) before having lunch in Chinatown. We sampled genuine Dim Sum among crowds packed into a noisy and boisterous restaurant, surprising ourselves with delicacies ranging from crab claws to chicken's feet. Then it was off to the Opera House.

There were staging rehearsals and photocalls inside and outside the Opera House plus a TV recording. After rehearsals we strolled among the crowds around Circular Quay and passed a well-endowed young lady walking the other way. One of the boys commented to his pals: 'bronau mawr!' which basically means 'big boobs!' in Welsh. To his complete surprise (and embarrassment), the girl stopped and said 'diolch yn fawr' (thanks very much!). Among all those crowds of people from all over the world, she was a Welsh girl living in Sydney! Incredible coincidence. Luckily, she saw the funny side of it, and started chatting to the boys (the guy who made the comment was hiding behind the others).

What can I say about the concert? To say we were keyed up would be an understatement. The Sydney Opera House concert hall had 2,700 people packed in. We'd sung in many great venues around the world, but this was something else. As we were lining up to go on stage, the guy next to me, Tecwyn, a choir veteran, turned to me, shook my hand and said, 'good luck!'. It was the only time this ever happened. I was rarely nervous in the Orpheus, always confident, but that night was different. We came on stage to a tremendous reception. People were cheering and standing. I felt ten feet tall in the front row of the choir. Then Alwyn came on, raised the audience to their feet and everyone sang *Advance Australia Fair*. As they were settling back into their seats, Alwyn turned to

127

the choir and said, 'Give them Hell!'. We launched into *Men of Harlech* (in Welsh) with a passion. It was almost frightening. The place erupted. The scene was set, and the concert went from strength to strength. Our soloists were brilliant. Joy and Clive excelled on the Steinway and Opera House organ. Alwyn was interacting with the audience with his usual great humour as we brought Old South Wales to New South Wales. It was one of those occasions when performers and audience became as one. The song *I Still Call Australia Home* delighted our audience. It was familiar to everyone as it was being broadcast at the time on a TV advert for Qantas Airways. We modified the words to include 'Old Swansea Town'. We sang Welsh hymns and arias including a premiere of *Nessun Dorma* specially arranged by Alwyn for the Opera House. Imagine twenty-five top tenors all singing the high notes of the ending together. The concert's finale went on and on as we received no less than five standing ovations. There were grown men crying that night. As the last *Amens* died away and everyone rose to sing *Hen Wlad Fy Nhadau* we knew this was a night we would always remember.

We got back to HQ and the party started. Everyone was on a massive high. I don't think the pub had ever seen anything like it. In the early hours, the intrepid among us ventured to nearby Kings Cross, renowned for its 'night life' (and every other form of life). Enough said.

Next day we were in recovery mode. It was back on the tourist trail and a trip to the Blue Mountains to see the Three Sisters. This is a famous sandstone rock formation viewed from high up on Echo Point. The scenery was dramatic with steep cliffs and millions of eucalyptus trees. I breathed deeply and my head magically cleared. Then we went for lunch to the pretty village of Leura. In the evening, it was the official Blobby Club Dinner, a properly organised affair, held at the RSL Club in Sydney. All the members of the Blobby Club attended, resplendent in their Mr

Blobby ties and we had a pukka three-course dinner including oysters and Australian port. We had toasts and speeches, including an inspirational one from Chief Blobby (Roy Pugh).

We had one more concert to perform but first I had shopping to do: Aboriginal art, opal earrings, chocolate covered macadamias, fluffy koalas and kangaroos, and a boomerang for my mother-in-law (which didn't go down well). Lunchtime refreshment was found at the Fortune of War, Sydney's oldest pub in The Rocks area near the harbour. The final concert was in the Sutherland Arts Centre, in a suburb some 20 miles south of central Sydney. We were welcomed with great enthusiasm, with banners and Welsh flags festooned all around the concert hall. It was great to finish our musical journey in such a friendly atmosphere.

We had one more free day and many of us went on the Sea Cat across the harbour to Manly. We relaxed on the beach and even had fish & chips! Our final evening meal was somewhat grander, when we dined at the Lord Nelson Brasserie up above The Rocks. The Lord Nelson is my favourite Sydney watering hole, with its own brewery, excellent bar food as well as the top-notch brasserie. I revisited the Lord Nelson numerous times on subsequent choir trips and on a Lions rugby tour.

The choir returned home to some special sixtieth anniversary events including major concerts at the Barbican Hall in London and Birmingham Symphony Hall. We also had concerts in Shrewsbury and Royal Tunbridge Wells. A return visit to Dulverton in Somerset saw Bill and I travel down early to do some walking. We walked right across Dartmoor south to north, about 30 miles. We took two days over it and felt quite proud of ourselves until we talked to a guy in the pub at the end. He told us about a regular challenge in which walkers trek 100 miles over Dartmoor in 24 hours, non-stop!

There were several TV recordings in our anniversary year, both on location and in studios. We also recorded another album with *Nessun Dorma* as the title song. In addition, there was a celebratory dinner at the Brangwyn Hall. All in all, it was a whirlwind year.

The Morriston Orpheus Choir at their home at Calfaria Chapel in the 1980s. The principals at the front are (left to right): Huw Rees (Deputy MD), Mair Wyn Jones (Accompanist), Alwyn Humphreys (Musical Director), Mrs J T Morgan (President), Huw Madoc-Jones (Chairman), Royston Pugh (Secretary) and Alun Tregelles Williams (Organist).

A group arriving at the Nancy International Choral Festival in 1985, and trying to look the part! Sporting headgear are (left to right) John Amour, Peter Davies, Ernie Amour, Roy Pugh, Mair Wyn Jones and Harold Rowe.

At Checkpoint Charlie in Berlin in 1985. This is the Allied side of the Checkpoint.

Chipping away at the Berlin Wall in 1990. The wall had 'fallen' on 9 November 1989.

Orpheus choristers on board 'The Maid of the Mist' underneath Niagara Falls in 1989.

133

At the top of the Empire State Building with the Twin Towers of the World Trade Center in the background. The date: September 11 1991, exactly ten years before the terrorist attack.

With Dame Thora Hird after filming 'Thora on the Straight and Narrow' at Pinewood Studios on 25 July 1993. The group includes Billy Ace, Dudley Williams, Dennis Owen, John Darracott, Les Thomas and Clive G. Williams.

134

Orpheus choristers in good spirits arriving at Wollongong, New South Wales, in 1995. Note the Mr Blobby ties proudly sported by some members (Illawarra Newspapers Holdings Pty Ltd).

The Morriston Orpheus Choir pictured outside the Sydney Opera House before their first performance there in 1995.

An Orpheus group strolling over the Sydney Harbour Bridge, including Eddie Davies, Brian Lloyd, Dave Bowen-Evans, Dudley Williams and Roy Pugh. I think my hat must have blown off!

Some off duty music-making with our friend with the didgeridoo. The would-be musicians are Trev Wills, Eddie Davies, Derek Caldwell, Roy Pugh and Harold Rowe.

136

Our official guide showing our group around the famous Melbourne Cricket Ground.

The back of the bus: a happy group of Orpheus choristers on the way to Poland in 1996.

137

Performing at the Bydgoszcz Academy of Music at the International Choral Festival in Poland 1996. The concert was recorded by Polish Radio.

Morriston Orpheus Choir on stage at Carnegie Hall, New York, on 21 October 2001, in the aftermath of the devastating terrorist attack.

The fabulous Carnegie Hall in New York (Wikimedia Commons Cheburashka).

15 - BYDGOSZCZ POLAND

It was January 1996 and snowing hard. We were in Blaenavon, at the head of the Eastern Valley, just a couple of miles from Garndiffaith, where I grew up. The Orpheus was singing at Blaenavon Workmen's Hall and our buses had somehow managed to get there through the snow. I knew our singing would be appreciated because they know their music in Blaenavon, with its fine male choir and town band. I was delighted to bump into my ex-Cwmbran conductor, Gareth Whitcombe, who was at the concert. Blaenavon was our first concert of the year; by contrast, the following week, the Orpheus was at the Grosvenor House in London.

Another busy year lay ahead, and I'll mention some of the highlights. We had an overnight trip to Bridport in Dorset and then the unique experience of singing in an underpass. Morriston had acquired a new bypass road which travelled through a huge underpass, and for its official opening, the Orpheus sang on a specially erected stage in the underpass. The authorities wanted to name the underpass after the Orpheus but apparently there was some objection. Shame. We had to be content with the headline 'Orpheus in the Underpass' (apologies to Offenbach).

In May 1996, the choir took part in an International Choral Festival in Poland. The Festival was centred on Bydgoszcz, a university city in the north of Poland, with events also held in surrounding towns and cities. Most of us made the long journey to Poland by coach while the musical staff and some choristers flew to Warsaw then travelled by train to Bydgoszcz. We set off from the Red Lion in Morriston just before midnight in high spirits, and caught an early ferry across the Channel, crossing northern Europe to reach our overnight stop in Hanover. There was a recommended brewpub in Hanover city centre, so Bill and I made a beeline, with half the choir following, and enjoyed a cracking evening to break our journey.

We bypassed Berlin before crossing the Polish border to reach Poznan, where we turned north to head to Bydgoszcz, arriving at our hostel accommodation by late evening. The hostel was a dump, way out in the sticks, with no facilities other than dormitories and shared showers. It was also cold and some of the beds were damp. After urgent discussions with the warden using sign language and broken English, the beds were eventually sorted out. Arrangements were made to ship in crates of local beer. He also offered some 'other services', which we politely declined.

Next morning, we trooped into a large room for breakfast. You could either have borscht or borscht (beetroot soup). Wow. At least it was a nice purple colour. Then we met our guides/interpreters and went for a short tour. Our guides were students of English from the university and would remain with us throughout the festival.

First stop was the city of Torun, on the wide Vistula river. The medieval old town is a World Heritage Site, and we explored the Gothic architecture, mercifully undamaged by the war. Then it was on to nearby Bydgoszcz where we took part in a parade through the city to celebrate the opening of the Choral Festival. We joined the other choirs from various countries, walking through the streets and waving to the crowds. Afterwards, we had time to explore the city. Because the exchange rate was very generous and things were cheap, we had lots of zlotys and groszys (1 zloty = 100 groszys). The boys called them all 'grottys' (I called them smarties). We went into a bar/restaurant for a meal. The menu was chalked up on a blackboard and was completely unintelligible. No-one in the bar could speak English so I selected the item that had the most 'z's in it. It turned out to be tripe floating in a kind of broth. We also made our first acquaintance with Zubrowka (buffalo grass vodka). We met Zubrowka a few more times before we left Bydgoszcz (but never, ever, since).

The buses collected us and took us back to our hostel. We were fully organised now, with a makeshift bar in a spare room, and choristers taking it in turns to serve. The money collected paid the man who supplied the beer, with some tips going to the students. A happy arrangement. The musical staff were safely tucked away in a city-centre hotel.

Next day we headed northwards to the city of Gdańsk, Poland's main seaport and historical capital of Pomerania (Gdańsk was also the home city of Lech Wałęsa and the *Solidarity* movement that helped end Communist rule across Eastern Europe). I had been looking forward to visiting Gdańsk and a tune had been in my head. The choir sometimes sang *Let's Face the Music and Dance*, and I'd changed this to *Let's Face the Music and Gdańsk!* Silly.

We presented our music in St Mary's in Gdańsk, the largest brick-built church in the world. The sheer size of the basilica was enough to take your breath away. It can reputedly hold 25,000 people (useful during the 1981-83 period of martial law, when many members of *Solidarity* took refuge there). We gave our performance of mainly sacred music, and the experience was awe-inspiring. The sound was magnified and echoed in the high vaults. It must have been difficult for Alwyn conducting, waiting for all those echoes to return! This was the first time a Polish audience had heard the Orpheus. After the concert we were able to spend time visiting the old port and getting a feel for Gdańsk.

Next day's concert was in the town of Żnin to the south of Bydgoszcz. The town was deserted as we went to a hall to change, and I feared the worst for the concert attendance. But when we went to our concert venue at the central church the whole town was packed inside. People were standing, crammed in all the spaces, even sitting on the floor. The church was another huge brick building and beautiful inside. I was informed that most churches in

Poland, even the ancient ones, are brick-built because of the shortage of native stone.

The local choir sang first, beautifully, *a cappella*. I thought we would do well to match them. But we had a great reception. The people particularly loved *Va, penserio (Chorus of the Hebrew Slaves)* from *Nabucco*. Clearly it was a chorus that meant a lot to them. Performing for those people was uplifting. The local choir took us to a sports club afterwards and provided food and drink but had none for themselves: we were the guests. It was emotional linking arms and embracing our Polish counterparts when we departed.

In the evening some of us escaped the hostel and went by taxi to the best hotel in Bydgoszcz for dinner. We invited our student guides (they had never been inside a hotel!). The prices were very cheap by our standards, but way beyond their means. It was a pleasure to wine and dine them: it was only smarties after all!

A few of us decided on a repeat performance for breakfast next morning. We were heartily sick of beetroot soup! This time we went to the Holiday Inn (which catered mainly for foreign businesspeople). For about a fiver, we had a breakfast to die for. Cold meats and cheeses, fruits and cereals and a hot grill with a chef cooking whatever we wanted. All washed down with Bloody Marys! There was even champagne. It made me feel a bit ashamed.

Afterwards I went shopping. One of the festival people whisked me off to a gallery where one of her friends was exhibiting paintings (they could clearly see I had currency to spend). I ended up buying a modern, colourful watercolour of Bydgoszcz for Mari.

In the afternoon, the choir did a recording session and gave our main concert in Bydgoszcz, at the Academy of Music. I remember our programme included *Nos A Bore* by the Welsh composer, William Mathias. It was nice to sing at the heart of the festival after our outlying adventures. Afterwards, some of us started singing in a bar, but it became obvious the locals didn't like it. They thought we were showing off, spending freely, and singing loudly. Then John Davies (he was a Samaritan) offered to buy them all a drink, which they grudgingly accepted. Things improved and we quietened things down out of respect. Diplomatic relations thawed, and Bill drank too much Zubrowka. He later threw up on the stairs back at the hostel. Dudley said it was the only time he'd seen someone smiling and spewing at the same time! Bill said the vodka had been too cold.

Our final Sunday at the Bydgoszcz International Choral Festival was busy. We started by singing at a Catholic Mass at a church in Świecie, a town north of Bydgoszcz. We must have sung non-stop for well over an hour, with no applause allowed. The acoustics were good, and, by the end of it, the congregation had heard a fair selection from our repertoire, most of it sacred. They listened very attentively and thanked us warmly afterwards.

We returned to Bydgoszcz for the final concert of the festival, which featured all the participating choirs. This was held at the 'new' opera house. This was so new that it was only half-built! Backstage was like an obstacle course with scaffolding planks everywhere and wiring hanging down. There were even holes you could fall through! Each choir was given a slot and we were conducted by our deputy MD, Huw Rees. We sang a short programme of Welsh music to demonstrate our culture, as did the choirs from the other countries. Then we clambered out of there.

The final night was party time in our bar at the hostel. There were about twenty of us having a brilliant singsong, mainly '60s hits, until late. Two of the girl students were with us and were really enjoying the singing. Then a choir official, usually the life and soul of the party, came in and objected to the noise. I couldn't believe it; it was our last night. I told him he wouldn't be very popular if he stopped the party. This seemed to touch a nerve, and he launched into a tirade of insults. I was conscious there were two young girls present and didn't retaliate. Maybe I should have. Anyway, it was the end of the party. Next morning, I reluctantly shook his offered hand. Luckily the incident came at the end of what was an enjoyable and interesting experience. Later, the choir raised funds to make it possible for three of the students to visit Wales. It was the least we could do after all the help they had given us.

We headed west early next morning hoping for another pleasant night in Hanover. But our bus broke down on the autobahn. By the time we reached our hotel it was too late to go downtown so we stayed in the hotel bar. They were serving a special Bock beer in attractive tankards, and I asked if I could purchase one as a keepsake. When I went to collect it at the end of the night, the whole stock had vanished! Next morning at breakfast a splendid buffet was laid out. After the usual eating fest, all remaining food on the buffet was hoovered up and taken onto the buses (for lunch). But the plates and cutlery were hoovered up as well! The indignant hotel staff had to enter the buses to recover their missing cutlery and crockery. But they didn't get the tankards.

We returned to our normal concert programme. We sang at the Tiverton Spring Festival and at an interesting concert in Monmouth, at the Wyastone Concert Hall. This is the recording studio of the Nimbus Foundation and sits in a glorious setting in the Wye Valley. The concert was for the Royal Monmouthshire Royal Engineers, the only regiment with two 'Royals' in its title. Their Honorary Colonel, the Duke of Gloucester, was present at the concert, which became a regular booking. Shortly afterwards, we did some BBC TV recordings at Tabernacle in Morriston and at Oystermouth Castle with our old friend, Sir Harry Secombe. We also recorded our own weekly TV series with S4C, with various guest artistes.

Then there was a charity concert in the beautiful Derby Cathedral. This was to be my final concert singing in the first tenors. I'd been struggling with the high notes for some time and consulted the choir doctor, Mr Julian Bihari who examined my vocal cords but found nothing fundamentally wrong. I discussed the problem with our musical director who gave me a voice test and as a result I became a baritone.

Our repertoire was constantly changing, so I could learn the new work as we went along. I had to re-learn the 'standards' in our repertoire and my fellow baritones were very helpful. My first concert in the baritones was at Birmingham Symphony Hall on 21 September 1996. This is where I happily remained, enjoying my singing. I can still sing tenor on a good day, but the baritone range now suits my voice much better.

Another concert was at the Grimsby Auditorium. On the way back, Bill and I headed to Chepstow to walk Offa's Dyke from Chepstow to Knighton, which took us five days. I was working in Cardiff at the time, and putting in long hours, so it was good to put on my rucksack and boots and get away from it all.

Towards year end, we visited Cornwall, as guests of Penryn Male Choir. We sang at Truro Concert Hall and the Penryn choir also contributed an entertaining section. The Orpheus stayed overnight at a large seafront hotel in Falmouth where we had a lively afterglow. I took my son Phil on the trip, hoping he would be encouraged to join the choir. He enjoyed the experience, particularly when we called at the Seven Stars, an old Falmouth pub whose landlord was a vicar! On the day of our return, the 'Songs of Praise' programme we'd recorded with Sir Harry was broadcast.

16 - THE DEEP SOUTH

Another year, another tour, this time to the deep south of the USA. But first there was a visit to Scotland where an Edinburgh promoter had booked the choir for a concert at the Festival Theatre to coincide with the Scotland v Wales rugby weekend.

After a long coach journey, we arrived at our hostel accommodation in Linlithgow on Friday afternoon. Bill and I were allocated the world's smallest room. It was a cupboard with bunk beds in it. You had to open the door wide to get into your bunk then reach out to close the door after you were tucked in. All our gear was squeezed under the bottom bunk. I was in the top bunk, with my nose almost touching the ceiling.

That evening, we were proud to be singing at Edinburgh's number one venue. In the dressing rooms we changed into our concert dress, preening ourselves in front of mirrors surrounded by light bulbs. On cue, we smartly made our stage entrance, ensuring we didn't blink in the glare of the stage lights. We gave total attention to the conductor, launching into our opening item and ending with our usual flourish. Then we realised. There was nobody there! Zero audience, apart from a few sundry individuals in the front row who clapped apologetically. Our esteemed promoter had seriously miscalculated: nobody wanted to go to a concert on a rugby weekend in Edinburgh. I take my hat off to Alwyn, he directed the entire show as if there were 2,000 people in the audience. The promoter was impressed … once he overcame his deep sickness.

Our afterglow was at the Prison Officers' Club (no kidding). There were far more punters there than in the theatre. We gave another mini concert with a bagpipe band. Then we headed back to Linlithgow and crawled into our cupboard. Exhausted.

Next day was match day. Arrangements had been made for the choir to be welcomed to the Caledonian Brewery to view the match on a big screen. We arrived, were given free tasters of beer (and a Scotch pie) and everyone settled down. Those of us with match tickets proceeded to Murrayfield where Wales defeated Scotland 34-19. Hooray! We returned to the brewery to celebrate, then caught the train back to Linlithgow. A jolly evening was spent at a pub called the Four Marys (the Marys in question were the four ladies-in-waiting of Mary, Queen of Scots, who was born across the road in Linlithgow Palace: perhaps it should have been Five Marys?). Afterwards, we slept in our cupboard as well as if it were the Ritz. We travelled home to Wales happy.

There were a couple of TV recordings and local concerts to follow, then in April (1997), we were off to the southern states of the USA with a concert 'en route' in Toronto, at the Roy Thomson Hall, our third appearance there in eight years.

On our first day in Toronto a small group of us explored the shoreline of Lake Ontario and the downtown end of Yonge Street. This is reputed to be the world's longest street, at an incredible 56 kilometres (35 miles). We walked about one mile of it before heading for the Greek quarter of Danforth. After lunch in a taverna we descended on a recommended bar called Allen's. There were lots of craft beers and the place was full of atmosphere. It was run by a friendly New Yorker and he and his friends were impressed that we were singing at the Roy Thomson Hall. They immediately resolved to come to the concert. Furthermore, they decided they would 'capture' a group of us after the concert and bring us back to the bar for a party!

The concert was as good as the previous two, and straight after the show about six of us were whisked off in taxis to Allen's bar. There was bubbly to greet us, together with a buffet supper and the bar was packed with well-wishers. We sang, of course, and everybody had a rare old time. We eventually had to say regretful farewells. We were up early next morning for our flight to Atlanta, Georgia, via Chicago.

Atlanta was very different, an attractive city that played a prominent part in the 1960s Civil Rights movement (the Martin Luther King Junior National Historical Park is situated there). We checked into our downtown hotel before going out for a stroll. There weren't many people about apart from a few vagrants who approached us for cash. We kept a wide berth and stayed in groups, although they seemed mostly harmless. We soon found some decent bars and restaurants. We were based in Atlanta for six nights.

Next day we crossed the state line into Tennessee for a concert in Chattanooga. We viewed the famous 'choo choo' locomotive before heading to our concert at Collegedale Seventh Day Adventist College where we performed to an audience of around 1,000, mainly students and staff. They were incredibly friendly and appreciative.

The following day some of us visited the Georgia State Capitol which houses a brilliant museum featuring the natural and cultural history of Georgia. Then we walked to the Olympic stadium. The Olympic Games was held in Atlanta the previous year, but the stadium had already been reconstructed as a baseball park, home of the Atlanta Braves. Our evening concert was at Peachtree Presbyterian Church, described as a 'megachurch'. There was a substantial Welsh presence in the audience. I recall that one of the boys had a 'funny turn' on stage and Alwyn halted the concert. Luckily, he had only fainted.

Next day we were on the road again, but not until after lunch at a pub called the Prince of Wales! There were two other similar pubs in Atlanta, and they had a double-decker London bus running a shuttle service between the three pubs. You could buy a pint in one pub, take it on the bus, enjoy the sights of Atlanta, then get off at the next pub and so on. Great idea!

After lunch we were off to Gainesville, Georgia, situated in the foothills of the Blue Ridge Mountains. We sang at the Mountains Center Theatre and afterwards the *Gainesville Times* music critic wrote 'the choir sang with a buoyancy and control reminiscent of Robert Shaw's professional choirs of the 1950s'. Praise indeed.

Bill and I continued exploring Atlanta next morning, passing by the CNN studios and the Philips Arena, home of the Atlanta Hawks basketball team. We headed for the Georgia Dome, the mega-stadium home of the Atlanta Falcons football team. It took us about half an hour to walk around the perimeter. Afterwards, we walked back through the Centennial Olympic Park, built as a showcase for the Games. The park was targeted in a terrorist bombing during the Games: the explosion sadly claimed the lives of two people, injuring over 100 others. Security guards cleared many people from the area before the device went off, avoiding many more casualties. The security guard who initially discovered the device and raised the alarm was hailed as a hero, but later the FBI suspected him of being implicated. He was soon exonerated, but it was seven years before the true culprit was arrested and subsequently convicted.

Later in the morning we were off to another state, to Greenville, South Carolina, where we were entertained to lunch at a smart golf and country club. Our concert venue was the Bob Jones University, a well-known learning establishment noted for its conservative policies. The concert was in the university's auditorium, so large it was called an 'amphitorium'. We had a staging rehearsal then some spare time before line-up. Bill and I decided to look for a cold beer. We left campus and started walking along the highway. There was no sign of anything, but we kept going. The road was a long straight boulevard leading towards downtown. Eventually, we saw a faint neon glow in the very far distance. It was past the time to go back, but we weren't going to give up. The sign gradually materialised. It said 'Budweiser'! Our pace quickened, and it turned out to be a wonderful little roadside bar (actually it was a dump, but Budweiser had never tasted so good). We ran all the way back. The boys were changed and ready to go on stage. Some had gone the other direction and found a bar just around the corner! Typical. We did a quick 'Superman' change and joined the line-up just in time … in a lather.

The amphitorium was packed with 3,000 students. We sang a mainly religious programme, but with some secular numbers. The pastor who introduced the concert specified 'no applause' for the religious items. Because much of our programme was in Welsh, the audience didn't know whether to clap or not! In the interval we met some of the students. They were all immaculately dressed, with the boys in smart suits and the girls in long dresses, carrying flowers. They were unfailingly polite and friendly. The press review later described Alwyn as 'probably the most charming man on the planet'.

On our final day in Atlanta, we attended a farewell reception at Peachtree hosted by the Welsh Society. Our chairman, Hugh O'Neill (a non-Welsh speaker) delivered a lengthy speech in Welsh, without notes, which was much appreciated.

In the evening it was the Blobby Club Dinner, at Azio's Italian restaurant in downtown. We invited Jill Padfield and Joanne Thomas, our two brilliant soloists. Afterwards we went up the glass elevator in the Westin Hotel tower for drinks. This is one of the tallest buildings in Atlanta with 73 storeys and the views from the revolving bar at the top were stunning. It was a brilliant way to end our stay in Atlanta, with a jazz pianist playing and singing *Georgia on my Mind*. It was 'just an old sweet song' made famous by the late, great Ray Charles. Georgia has certainly remained on my mind.

We flew on to Miami. When we exited the airport, the heat hit us like a blast. It was a relief to board our air-conditioned coaches for our trip north on Interstate 95 to Orlando for a four-day break. Our hotel was on International Drive with all amenities close by. I soon found a restaurant specialising in Cajun food and a pub, improbably called the 'Cricketers Arms', which became our HQ.

I'd previously visited Orlando with Mari, so had been to most of the theme parks. On our first day we went to the Florida Mall for some retail agony. The following day we visited Epcot and Church Street Station (for the Country & Western). Then Peter Thomas and I ventured on a trip to Busch Gardens in Tampa Bay. This is an African-themed park famous for its extreme state-of-the-art roller coasters. There were three in operation: the Scorpion, Montu and Kumba, and we determined to ride all three. We started with the Scorpion. It was horrendous. The G-forces were greater than anything I'd ever experienced. I was in danger of having an abdominal dysfunction. And this was the mildest of the three, the Mickey Mouse one! After staggering off the Scorpion, I point blank refused to contemplate Montu and Kumba. Peter agreed. I was distinctly below par at the 'farewell to Orlando' party at our hotel that evening.

Next day we travelled back south to West Palm Beach for three nights and to perform the final concert of the tour. This was at the Kravis Center Amphitheatre, an open-air venue with a capacity of about 1,400. It was nice to perform outdoors in the balmy weather. Next morning, Bill and I walked over the bridge to Palm Beach itself for Sunday brunch. In the evening a group of us walked to an 'Ale House' that served about twenty different beers, but they all tasted the same. Cold and gassy. The number of beers was matched by the number of TV sets featuring every ball game taking place. We enjoyed a convivial last evening in America before our flight home from Miami, via Chicago. It had been interesting to experience a different part of America.

After a few more UK concerts, the Orpheus visited Machynlleth in mid Wales to celebrate the 60th anniversary of the choir's first success at the National Eisteddfod. The choir won the Chief Male Choir prize at the Machynlleth Eisteddfod in 1937, when the audience of 10,000 in the pavilion acclaimed the Orpheus as the undisputed winner among eight choirs competing. Our visit was the choir's first return to Machynlleth since then, and it was organised by our chairman, Group Captain Huw Madoc-Jones (popularly known as 'Huw Magic', or sometimes 'Biggles').

A few of us travelled up a day early to climb Cadair Idris. We ascended the Pony Path to the summit and scrambled back down the scree on the Fox's Path. It was exhilarating. We sang at the Bro Ddyfi Leisure Centre in the evening and stayed over in the Wynnstay Arms. The choir revisited Machynlleth several times over the following years and I returned myself when walking the route for my 'Walk Through Time' book series in 2009.

A tragic event took place on 31 August 1997 with the untimely death of Diana, Princess of Wales, in Paris. A couple of days afterwards, the BBC asked the Orpheus to take part in a special memorial 'Songs of Praise' televised live at Liverpool's Catholic Cathedral. The other performers included Michael Ball and it was a very moving occasion held in the cathedral crypt. As we were singing the Welsh hymn *Gwahoddiad*, I couldn't help remembering singing to Diana at Expo in Seville a few years earlier.

Later in the year I was out of action for a while and missed concerts at Birmingham, Ipswich, Leominster and Brighton. I attended a concert at Walsall Town Hall, however, before the usual Christmas concerts ended 1997, another memorable year.

Christmas Eve, 1997 saw my last day working full-time for SWALEC. My company had recently been taken over, and I took the opportunity to negotiate a favourable early retirement. At a

153

relatively young age, my full-time professional career was ending, but I had all sorts of future plans. The choir would remain important, although I didn't realise that writing would eventually take over my life.

I drove home from St Mellons to Mumbles having said farewell to my colleagues, to be greeted with the news that my brother-in-law, Steve, was in dire straits in hospital in London. I turned the car around and headed to London with Mari and her mum and we spent Christmas at the Royal Free Hospital. Steve pulled through, but I was soon to have my own health issues.

17 - LAND OF THE LONG WHITE CLOUD

My first year after 'retirement' started well enough, with the usual concerts and a new CD recording called '*A Tribute to Elvis Presley*'. Unfortunately, I soon began to experience chest pains. After a concert at St Chad's Church in Shrewsbury, we were hurrying to the Boat Club for our afterglow, when my chest pains became worse. Six days later I had a heart attack.

Hospital, followed by recuperation, put my choir activities on hold. I missed a trip to Ireland where the choir sang at Ennis Cathedral in County Clare. But I attended the MOCSA concert, sitting in the audience, and particularly enjoyed the choir's performance of *The Glory of Israel* from *Nabucco*. My singing return was at Afan Lido in Port Talbot followed by a Cymanfa Ganu at Tabernacle and an inspiring concert in Brecon Cathedral. I missed a trip to the Savoy Hotel in London and the recording in London of another new album called '*Sounds of Cardiff Arms Park*' featuring rugby favourites such as *Calon Lan, Delilah, Swing Low, Sweet Chariot* and *Flower of Scotland.*

Then came a TV recording at the almost-completed Millennium Stadium in Cardiff. The choir donned hard hats and sang from the stands in what was still a building site, becoming the first choir to sing in the new stadium. As 1998 ended, all the talk was of a forthcoming tour to New Zealand and Australia, due in February 1999. This would be the choir's first time in New Zealand, but in my heart of hearts (literally) I knew that the trip was too soon for me.

January 1999 saw us performing at the official opening of the new five-star St David's Hotel in Cardiff Bay. We sang on the circular balconies of the hotel's high atrium and the hotel's owner,

Sir Rocco Forte, was delighted. He even conducted the choir in a spirited rendering of *Cwm Rhondda*! The champagne was flowing freely afterwards.

I sang at the choir's pre-tour concert at Siloh Chapel in Landore with mixed feelings. We performed the tour repertoire including *Pokarekare Ana*, a traditional New Zealand love song in the Maori language that became a big hit on the tour. I had a lump in my throat when I wrote a letter to the choir wishing them a successful tour.

The Orpheus blazed a triumphant trail through New Zealand, singing in all the major concert halls in the main cities to packed audiences. They even sang at Eden Park rugby ground in Auckland and at the New Zealand Parliament in Wellington. The tour was covered on NZ television and the choir's recording of *'Sounds from Cardiff Arms Park'* reached number four in the NZ classical charts (surpassed only by Bryn Terfel, Cecilia Bartoli and Andrea Bocelli).

The choir party also enjoyed the spectacular scenery of New Zealand before flying on to Australia to revisit Wollongong and again perform at the Sydney Opera House. The tour's promoter was very happy. New Zealand press reports included: 'their diction lifts the words off the page, giving the impression they sing in capital letters' and praised the 'stunning unaccompanied sustained pianissimos'. The *Otago Daily Times* hailed 'The Rolls Royce of male choirs'. What a tour to miss!

The next highlight was the official opening of the National Assembly for Wales in Cardiff Bay on 26 May 1999. The Orpheus took part in the 'Voices of a Nation' spectacular in the presence of HM The Queen and Prime Minister, Tony Blair. The event was televised live by the BBC and the Orpheus was introduced as 'one of the greatest choirs in the world'. We performed with The Alarm rock group singing *A New South Wales* and with all the top Welsh stars including Tom Jones, Charlotte Church, Max Boyce and the irrepressible Dame Shirley Bassey, magnificent in a flowing dress made from the Welsh flag. Shirley was a real star, engaging in banter with the Orpheus boys and posing for pictures. Quite an occasion.

The Rugby World Cup was soon on everyone's mind. Wales was proudly hosting the event and the new Millennium Stadium was ready. The Orpheus was booked for numerous rugby engagements, the most prestigious of which was probably the 25th anniversary reunion of the 1974 British Lions rugby team at Cardiff International Arena. All the great players were there including most of the 1971 and 1974 Lions and it was a thrill when they joined us on stage to sing *Flower of Scotland*, conducted by Scottish winger, Billy Steele (they'd sung this on their invincible tour of South Africa).

There were concerts at Exeter Cathedral and Sherborne Abbey before the World Cup was upon us. The Orpheus was booked for an event at the Park Hotel in Cardiff on the day of the Final and the hosts were my old company, now called Hyder. The centre of Cardiff was ablaze with colour, with rugby followers from all over the world mingling and enjoying the atmosphere that only Cardiff can provide. Phil and I had tickets for the Final and watched Australia defeat France to win the World Cup for a second time. Afterwards, I set off to the Park Hotel in high spirits, reaching there before the choir and spending a pleasant hour chatting to a loquacious Irishman in the bar. By the time the choir arrived I was well up for it!

We entertained the Hyder people and their corporate guests, and I was personally made very welcome by my ex-colleagues. My PR friend, who organised the event, ensured the free bar for the choir remained open after the main performance, and we joined other revellers in the hotel bar. They were from many different countries, and we had a great sing, with Alwyn standing on a table and conducting. It was a memorable international occasion.

The year ended with great news: our promoter in New Zealand wanted the Orpheus to return! The new tour was planned for August 2000, with the promoter meeting most of the costs. This would virtually be a professional tour and we would present a 'complete show' with Alwyn as compere and conductor and with our own lighting and sound technicians. I would get to visit the Land of the Long White Cloud after all.

The year 2000 started with a return to the Millennium Stadium for a BBC recording, then another visit to the Stadium to sing at the Welsh Cup Final (Llanelli 22 Swansea 12). It was almost becoming a second home. In between, there were a couple of concerts that I missed for family reasons. One was at Gloucester Cathedral (Alwyn's 500th Orpheus concert) and the second was an important function at the Natural History Museum in London. For this, the choir arrived early enough for some of the boys to escape for a pre-performance pint. They had to explore South Kensington before finding a suitable watering hole and inevitably, they were late getting back for staging. The musical director was not amused. Their excuse was that they got lost trying to find their way back to the museum. This was a ridiculous story, and they were hauled before the committee and handed a severe reprimand. They became known as 'The London Eight' and entered choir folklore. It's a good job I wasn't there, or it would have been 'The London Nine'!

Things soon settled down and at our Millennium Annual Concert at Tabernacle we gave our first performance of *Ave Signor*, the great prologue chorus from *Mefistofele* by Boito. We also performed another concert at the beautiful Derby Cathedral.

On 11 August 2000, our advance party flew from Heathrow to Los Angeles, for an overnight stop en route to New Zealand. After the 11-hour flight we checked into our LA hotel, then had almost a full day relaxing before our ongoing flight to Auckland. Some visited Universal Studios, but Bill and I went ten-pin bowling. Our onward flight from LAX lasted 12 hours, then we transferred to our Auckland hotel before exploring the city.

First port of call was the Sky Tower, soaring high above the Sky Hotel and Casino, with great views of the city and harbour. Lunch was at the 'Shakespeare Tavern' where there was a photograph on the wall of the Barbarians v All Blacks rugby game held at Cardiff Arms Park in 1973, famous for the Gareth Edwards try (voted the greatest try ever). I proudly boasted to the barman that I had been present at the game. He calmly replied, 'I played in it!' He was Ron Urlich, the All Blacks hooker, and was the proprietor of the Shakespeare Tavern. He later kindly presented some mementos to choir members.

Two days acclimatising in Auckland allowed me to visit the harbourside and take a boat across to Devonport, for a walk up Mount Victoria. I also went to Eden Park rugby ground and watched the Blues training. The main choir party soon arrived, and we relocated to Hamilton for three nights. Our first two concerts were at the Gateway Centre in Hamilton and Alwyn was on great form, entertaining the audience and bringing out the best from the choir. It was a real 'show' including tour soloists, Camilla Rhian Roberts and Siân Wigley Williams with accompanists, Joy Amman Davies and Lois Davies, and organist, Tudur Pennar Jones.

While in Hamilton, many of us went to Waikato rugby stadium to see Waikato play Northland in a Ranfurly Shield game. Waikato won 52 points to 14 to retain the huge shield and the home crowd enthusiastically rang their cowbells throughout (Waikato is an agricultural area). The choir was presented with a Waikato cowbell afterwards!

Our third concert was back in Auckland, at the Aotea Centre, the city's main concert hall. The hall was packed with 2,200 enthusiastic people who enjoyed our programme, including *Hine e hine*, a beautiful Maori lullaby.

159

We moved on to Napier next day, stopping at scenic Lake Taupo on the way. It was fascinating travelling through this volcanic region to reach Napier, situated at Hawkes Bay on the eastern coast of the North Island. Napier is a lovely city, rebuilt in art deco style after the 1931 earthquake. Our hotel was on the waterfront promenade and next day, we toured Napier's art deco buildings, also visiting a tannery producing sheepskin products and the Mission Estate Winery. Our evening concert was at the Municipal Theatre, another fine art deco building, and it was a lovely warm atmosphere at one of the nicest concerts of the tour. Napier was memorable in many ways.

Next, we headed south-west to Palmerston North in the Manawatu-Wanganui region of the North Island. Some of us visited the New Zealand Rugby Museum, one of the best rugby collections in the world (Kiwi Graham Henry was coach of Wales at the time and a vice-president of our choir). The curators were delighted to meet a group of rugby-loving Welshmen.

The evening concert was at the Regent Theatre on Broadway, described as NZ's leading provincial theatre. Another sell-out crowd cheered the choir on and particularly enjoyed some of our rugby-related items. The Celtic Inn next to the theatre was a popular venue for after-concert rugby chat.

After our one-night stay, we took the scenic coast road down to Wellington, New Zealand's capital. Our hotel in Oriental Bay overlooked the magnificent Wellington harbour and was near the Te Papa Tongarewa Museum, the national museum and art gallery of New Zealand, where I spent a rewarding afternoon. The museum's name means 'the place of treasures of this land' and it brilliantly showcases the country's culture and diversity.

Soon, it was time to move off to Wellington Town Hall for rehearsal and the evening's concert. Another lovely building and another great concert: our finales were getting longer as the tour progressed. Afterwards, many of us made for the Welsh Dragon Bar, the only uniquely Welsh pub in New Zealand where a warm welcome awaited! Next day was free after three concerts on consecutive nights and we were buoyed to read the *Dominion Post* review: 'the men of Morriston Orpheus Choir have the voices of angels and their music is a gift of gods'.

We toured Wellington, visiting the Parliament Building, popularly known as the Beehive (where the Orpheus sang previously). We also visited the Botanic Gardens and Mount Victoria Lookout for the fantastic views. From here, I could see the distinctive 'cake tin' shape of the Westpac Rugby Stadium, which I wanted to visit. I phoned the stadium and was told I would be very welcome (I'm sure being in a visiting Welsh choir helped). I was met at the stadium by a PR person who gave me a guided tour. They even gave me some souvenirs to take home. On my walk back I called in a little bar and realised I was the only non-Maori in there!

Next morning saw us leave Wellington airport on our flight to Dunedin, in the south of the South Island, for a one-night stand at Dunedin Town Hall. There was no time to explore Dunedin. At the theatre, Elfed discovered he'd left his black shoes at the hotel. He ended up singing the whole concert in black-stockinged feet, much to the amusement of the rest of the choir. It was another concert at a top venue with a pleasant afterglow at our hotel with some of the punters. We were off to Christchurch in the morning.

Our professional tour manager, Bert Queenin (a Kiwi, and brilliant organiser), had arranged a treat for the journey to Christchurch. He'd chartered a private train to take the choir party on the scenic route up the east coast. We arrived expectantly at the station and boarded the special train, looking forward to the four-hour trip. Then we discovered there was no beer on the train. So, we disembarked in protest! There must have been an urgent call to Speight's Brewery because before long, crates of ale were being loaded up. We happily re-boarded and set off on our merry way, admiring the views of the snow-capped Southern Alps off to our left and the Pacific Ocean to our right. We didn't over-indulge, as we had a concert in Christchurch in the evening.

Christchurch Town Hall is, to my mind, the finest concert hall in New Zealand; it's just a beautiful place to perform in. The audience was over 2,000 and the atmosphere was tremendous. Alwyn was at his consummate best and the choir responded in great style, with our accompanists, organist and soloists all combining to create a memorable experience. Afterwards, the promoter was cracking open the champagne in the musical director's dressing room and I was taking my turn at the choir merchandise stall, signing autographs and shaking hands with the crowds.

The party in our hotel afterwards was subdued, however, because one of our choristers had suffered a heart attack earlier in the evening and was taken to hospital where he was to remain for a couple of weeks. Touring is not always a bed of roses.

Next day I walked around the Botanic Gardens, then did some shopping at Christchurch Arts Centre. The obligatory tram trip was followed by dinner with Welsh exile, Donald Preece, an uncle of a friend back home. The following day, Donald took us on a trip to the port of Lyttleton, from where Captain Scott's ship, the *Terra Nova*, departed in 1910 for the heroic, but ill-fated expedition to the South Pole. Donald also took us to the Jade Rugby Stadium, and we visited the Canterbury Museum where there's a brilliant Polar Exploration exhibition. I was delighted to obtain some images of Scott's party at the South Pole for use in a book I was writing at the time (among Scott's companions was Petty Officer Edgar Evans from Rhossili in Gower, who tragically lost his life with the rest of Scott's party on their return journey from the Pole in 1912).

In the late afternoon it was time to head back down the coast for a concert in Timaru. By this time, I had developed a heavy cold and should have skipped the concert, but at the last minute I grabbed my gear and climbed aboard the coach.

Timaru is a port city, about 100 miles down the coast from Christchurch, and the concert was at the Theatre Royal. I sang on stage for the first half but was really struggling. I stayed backstage for the second half feeling sorry for myself and was glad to get back to the hotel in Christchurch and get my head down.

Our Christchurch concert had been professionally filmed and next morning, before departure for Australia, the choir were given a showing of the video at an airport hotel. It was good to see our concert recorded for posterity and it was another commercial opportunity.

After our flight from Christchurch to Brisbane we transferred to the Twin Towns Resort at the southern end of the Gold Coast. The twin towns of Coolangatta and Tweed Heads are right on the border between Queensland and New South Wales. We were amazed when we saw our luxury accommodation in Coolangatta (fondly known as 'Cooly'). Our apartments were by the beach and Bill, Peter and I had a high-level two-bedroomed apartment with two bathrooms, lounge and kitchen and a fabulous balcony overlooking the ocean. It was great to settle in for seven nights of comfort after all the travelling in New Zealand. Breakfast was provided in the adjoining hotel and the weather was gorgeous.

I was still suffering but luckily, the next day was free. There was an early morning photo-call (that I missed) and when I surfaced, I went for a gentle stroll along the coast and had dinner at Fisherman's Cove. Most of the boys spent the day on the beach where there was another (unofficial) group photo taken. About fifty of the choir lined up in formation in the sunshine, and in their bathers. But right in the centre of the front row, one of the boys was doing a moonie!

There were now five concerts on consecutive nights, but

163

daytimes were free. I hopped on a bus to Surfers Paradise. There, I wandered along the golden beach and took a trip on the amphibious Aquabus. The evening concert was at the Twin Towns Services Club where the audience filled the auditorium. There was a party atmosphere all evening which carried on afterwards with music and dancing at the casino until very late. Next day I was still in recovery mode when I took the stage for our second concert at the Services Club. Good job the other 90-odd in the choir were on fine form! The following day's concert was at the Empire Theatre in Toowoomba, an attractive city situated on the crest of the Great Dividing Range, around 700 metres (2,300 ft) above sea level.

Next day we travelled to Brisbane for the first of two big concerts at the Brisbane Concert Hall in the Queensland Performing Arts Centre (QPAC) on the South Bank of the Brisbane River. We had a tremendous welcome from the audience of nearly 2,000, including many of Welsh extraction. It was the first time for the Orpheus to sing in Brisbane and we returned the following day for a repeat performance, and an equally enthusiastic reception. It was an emotional finale for our tour.

After the second show we returned to the Twin Towns Resort for our end of tour party. The tour promoter was generous in his praise (and his hospitality). There was a warm glow of satisfaction amongst Alwyn and the choir and the incredibly hard-working musical staff and soloists. We left Australia with the Orpheus reputation further enhanced.

We departed the following afternoon for Singapore and a one-night stopover. The heat and humidity hit us when we left Changi Airport in the evening to transfer to the Peninsula Excelsior Hotel. Some of the boys headed to Raffles Hotel for a 'Singapore Sling' and others found a bar with karaoke and quickly became the stars of the show (this lot were very late coming back to the hotel that night). Bill and I contented ourselves with a few Tiger beers in the hotel bar.

An early start next morning saw us reach our group check-in at Singapore Airport to discover three of our number were missing; it transpired that they were still asleep in their hotel rooms! (they were part of the karaoke party). They were hastily roused and bundled into a taxi and made it to the airport in the nick of time. We now had 'The Singapore Three' to add to 'The London Eight' (the three individuals were, of course, members of both groups). They were given a final warning by the committee but survived to sing another day.

I arrived home almost four weeks to the day after leaving, having travelled right around the world. I managed to pass my bug on to Mari when I got home, which she didn't thank me for, although I brought some nice gifts for everyone. Soon afterwards we were devastated when Mari's mum passed away. The choir would take a back seat for more important matters.

In October 2000 the choir made another CD recording, at the Angel Studios in Islington, with Gordon Lorenz as the producer. In between recording the tracks, the larger-than-life Gordon entertained us with his very funny jokes. At around that time, I took over as the choir recruitment officer (the post fortunately didn't require me to be on the committee). Happily, one of my first new recruits was my son Phil, who joined the Orpheus on 8 October 2000, a proud moment for me. He joined the top tenors and when I asked Alwyn how his voice test had gone, he replied 'he's almost as good as you used to be!'

The following week there was a trip to Tonbridge in Kent where we sang in the hall of Tonbridge School, followed by a trip to Berkhamsted. A couple of appearances at St David's Hall in Cardiff and our usual Christmas concerts brought a memorable millennium year to a close.

18 - NEW YORK, NEW YORK

We were in the middle of Ireland. The date didn't seem significant: it was September 11th, 2001. Mari and I were travelling from Connemara to Dublin, having spent a delightful holiday touring the west coast. We were looking forward to a couple of days in Dublin and were listening to the music and banter on Radio Éireann as we drove along. Suddenly, there was an interruption to the programme. The announcer reported that a plane had flown into one of the Twin Towers in Manhattan. I turned up the volume as the second plane hit. Then a third plane crashed into the Pentagon. America was clearly under attack; it seemed as if war had broken out. My immediate thoughts turned to my choir friends Bill Kenny and Terry Jones who were in New York finalising arrangements for the choir's visit in a few weeks' time (Bill was choir chairman and Terry was the choir tour manager). They were in New York meeting our American promoter to discuss our tour, including our concert at Carnegie Hall.

We checked into our Dublin hotel and watched the horror on television. In Temple Bar, the normally boisterous restaurants and bars were very subdued. Everyone was watching TV screens, some were crying, saying it was World War Three. Mari wanted to go home immediately so we curtailed our holiday. We arrived home to the news that Bill and Terry were safe but stranded. They had witnessed the whole tragic event from their high-rise Manhattan hotel, but eventually managed to reach Long Island. They stayed there until they could get a flight home, two weeks later. Meanwhile the prevailing view in the choir was 'the tour must go ahead'.

The year had started on a sad note with the passing of Glynne Jones, the much-admired conductor of Pendyrus Male Choir. Some of us from the Orpheus attended the funeral in Merthyr along with Alwyn, our conductor. Also in January 2001, I helped to organise a concert at St Mary's Church in Swansea to raise funds for the Cardiac Rehabilitation Centre at Singleton Hospital. This was my son Phil's first concert with the Orpheus, and we raised over £4,400 for the Centre.

In the months before our New York visit we sang in Chepstow, Ross-on-Wye and Stoke-on-Trent. At the Annual Concert at Tabernacle, Phil and I sang side by side, with me on the inner end of the baritones and Phil next to me in the first tenors. There followed another CD recording entitled '*The Impossible Dream*' and concerts at Ipswich Corn Exchange and the Newbury Spring Festival where we shared the stage with Dame Gwyneth Jones. Her voice was spellbinding, as always. Our Welsh concerts included Llandaff Cathedral in the south and the Criccieth Festival in the north. There followed concerts at Malvern, St Albans Cathedral and Ludlow.

The 18th of August was a happy day for our family as my daughter, Lucy, was married to Mike at St Peter's Church in Newton. The Orpheus sang at the wedding, and I'll never forget the thrill as Lucy and I arrived outside the church to hear the choir singing before the ceremony, then my pride as we walked down the aisle together.

In September, I tried recruiting students from Swansea University for the choir. I booked a stall at the Freshers' Fair and set up a TV playing videos of the choir. There was plenty of interest and after two days, I had a list of eighteen names. Of these, around half actually joined the choir. It was difficult holding on to these guys as they settled into university life, but a few stayed for extended periods. One of them, Dan Emberson, who'd previously sung in Lichfield Cathedral Choir, stayed with the Orpheus for several years, and went on some of our overseas tours. Around this time the choir acquired Welsh tartan waistcoats and green bow ties to add a bit of pzazz!

In the following weeks, there was much discussion about our imminent visit to New York. We would be taking part in the 'UK in New York' festival, a major series of events to promote the UK in the city. After the terrorist attack it was decided to change the festival name to 'UK *With* New York' with everything going ahead as planned, as far as possible. There were understandable concerns about the safety of flying and one of our soloists and a few choristers dropped out, including Phil, soon to be engaged to Gail. However, a virtually full choir of 100 choristers made the trip, with a full musical team. We were determined to show our solidarity.

In the late evening of 17 October, we arrived at the Millennium Hotel, UN Plaza, a skyscraper hotel on East 44th Street, close to the UN building. We crowded the elevators to reach our rooms where the views were spectacular, but there was a slight problem. They were all double beds. Now, we're all good friends in the choir, but draw the line at cwtching up in bed together! My bottom-bass pal Peter Holborow was sharing a double bed with the tenor soloist! I was sharing a room with Bill, who had the difficult task of sorting everything out with Terry and the hotel reception. I found the situation hilarious but eventually, we were reallocated twin rooms, with some lucky choristers relocated to a swish hotel in Times Square.

We soon headed out and found an Irish bar on Second Avenue. We were given the welcome news that all local bars were open until 4am. On a more sombre note, the bar we chose had pictures and tributes on the walls to brave firefighters who had died in the Twin Towers. The bar was used by the local fire ladder (crew) and they had lost some of their own people. The disaster was still very raw, and we tried our best to empathise (I'm writing this with great sympathy to all those who lost their lives on September 11, and their loved ones, including the heroic firefighters, NYPD police officers and other emergency workers).

Next day, we had an engagement at Huntington Town Hall on Long Island where the choir was officially welcomed, and we sang on the lawn in front of the town hall. In the afternoon there was a 'Wales With New York' event at Grand Central Station. We sang in the vast and magnificent Vanderbilt Hall to thousands of people in the terminal. The Vanderbilt Hall is noted for its history, architecture and grandeur and has a 48-foot-high ceiling with five golden chandeliers. The acoustics were superb. There was much evidence at the station of the Twin Towers disaster, with photographs displayed of the people still missing and very many messages and flowers.

Next daytime was free, so I hopped on a bus along 42nd Street to Pier 83 on the Hudson River. I joined some Orpheus boys on a boat trip around Manhattan island, taking in the Statue of Liberty, Brooklyn Bridge etc. There was a hushed silence as we sailed past Lower Manhattan and the site of the Twin Towers attack. I got chatting to a New Yorker and it was uplifting to listen to his perspective. He said that New York would carry on as normal, defiant and unbowed. My new friend later directed me to the Landmark Tavern, one of New York's oldest pubs, opened in 1868.

Our evening concert was a formal affair at the Huntington Townhouse and the patrons had pre-concert cocktails and a buffet supper included in their tickets. Before the show, the choir waited patiently backstage, as instructed, but there were a few incursions into the cocktail party (me included). We mingled happily, enjoying drinks and listening to our deputy accompanist, Lois Davies, playing the harp. After the show, everybody joined together for the supper. It was a very pleasant evening apart from the traffic snarl-up on our way back to Manhattan through the Queens Midtown Tunnel. It was after midnight when we arrived back, but fortunately our adopted little bar was open until 4am.

The following morning, I went on a solo exploration, walking up Fifth Avenue and visiting St Patrick's Cathedral. I had a good walk around Central Park, before catching a bus to Greenwich Village to meet choir friends at the White Horse Tavern, where Dylan Thomas spent his last evening before his untimely death in 1953. We admired the mural of Dylan in the bar, and I quietly sang *Eli Jenkins' Prayer* from 'Under Milk Wood' as a personal tribute. After a convivial lunch in the tavern, one of the locals urged us to visit an old speakeasy nearby. He led us to Chumley's, a historic pub and former speakeasy tucked away in the West Village. We reflected on the days of prohibition-era raids, when the bartender would magically get word whenever the police were coming. There was a trapdoor into a cellar where people used to hide and a back door for a quick escape! Chumley's has recently reopened as an upmarket restaurant, but I'm glad I saw it in its original form.

Afterwards, some of us caught a bus down to the devastated World Trade Center at Ground Zero to pay our respects. There were many people there, I'm sure for many different reasons. I was staggered by the sheer scale of the devastation as I looked through the barriers and saw the skeletal lattice steelwork above the immense mound of rubble, an enduring image seen on millions of television screens around the world. The smoke and dust were still in the air. We just observed, taking in the scene quietly, lost in our own thoughts, before walking slowly away down Wall Street.

Next day was the big one: Carnegie Hall. In the morning Bill and I strolled north along Second Avenue as far as 61st Street, where we took an overhead tram ride to Roosevelt Island in the East River. Walking back along Park Avenue, we went into St Bartholomew's Church where we spontaneously joined a service for a brief period of prayer and reflection. Next was the Waldorf Astoria Hotel where we viewed Cole Porter's piano on the Cocktail Terrace. Porter was a resident at the hotel for thirty years and composed many of his famous songs there. We walked back along Madison

Avenue to get ready for the big show.

The coaches took us to Carnegie Hall, where there was tight security, and we were given our backstage passes. We took the stage for rehearsal to be greeted by Alwyn wearing a Carnegie Hall T-shirt which stated, '*If You Haven't Played It, You Haven't Made It!*'. The place had an aura about it and there was a feeling of anticipation and pride at being there. There was an audience of well over a thousand people which was fantastic considering recent events. As well as the great and good of New York, there were many Welsh exiles there and we received a great reception. To open the concert, Alwyn had specially arranged a 'Tribute to the USA': a medley of three anthems, *America the Beautiful*, *God Bless America* and *The Star-Spangled Banner*. This rousing opening set the scene and by the time we sang an emotionally charged *New York, New York*, they were dancing in the aisles. The concert went by in a blur. There was a distinctly Welsh flavour in our programme, particularly in the finale. We also sang the Caccini *Ave Maria* and *Senzenina*, a Zulu chant. I also remember the performance of *Stars* from *Les Misérables* by one of our young baritones, Simon Gray, with the choir accompanying him. Simon was unfazed and took his solo performance at Carnegie Hall in his stride. What a thrill it must have been for him. Our two professional soloists Iona Jones (soprano) and Huw Rhys Evans (tenor) were also brilliant as were our accompanists Joy and Lois (who again played the harp) and organist Rob Nicholls. We finally left the stage after standing ovations and many, many tears. It was a very special night that none of us will ever forget. The Welsh American newspaper *Ninnau* later reported: 'The concert was the perfect antidote for New Yorkers who had been so recently stunned by the unbelievable happenings of September 11th. The concert culminated with an extremely charged audience standing, stomping and demanding encore after encore'.

There was a humdinger of a party back at the Millennium Hotel. It seemed half the audience had followed us there. The nearby liquor store did a roaring trade in six-packs which were brazenly hauled back to the (expensive) hotel bar. When the party eventually started to ebb, a crowd of us went to Muldoon's bar, where the real party started. I have hazy recollections of Eddie Davies standing behind the bar performing his party piece and, to quote Max Boyce, 'we sang Cwm Rhondda and Delilah' (I hope they didn't both sound the same!).4am came and went. It was a memorable night in so many ways. Next morning was spent gift shopping on Fifth Avenue before a return to Muldoon's and fond farewells. It was an emotional departure.

Four days later we were singing in Shrewsbury, then after a couple of local concerts it was the Queen's Hall in Derby, followed by the usual Christmas engagements. To cap off 2001 on a very happy note, Phil and Gail became engaged on Boxing Day.

19 - THE QUEEN'S GOLDEN JUBILEE

The Queen's Jubilee year of 2002 started with a rare visit to the Rhondda Valley. The Pendyrus Male Choir asked the Orpheus to help their Trust Fund in memory of their late conductor, Glynne Jones, and we offered them a concert. It was a bit like going into the lion's den when we arrived at Ystrad Rhondda Leisure Centre, with many Pendyrus choristers and followers in the audience, but we were determined to put on a good performance. Alwyn had composed a special arrangement of the Welsh hymn *Nazareth* in memory of Glynne, and we gave its first performance during the concert. Alwyn's conducting of this beautiful hymn delivered pathos and power and we received an emotional response. Afterwards we enjoyed a convivial afterglow with our Pendyrus friends.

There were other Welsh concerts to follow, including one of our regular visits to Ammanford and an engagement in Fishguard. There was also a visit to Northampton that I couldn't attend. This was a very sad occasion because one of our baritones collapsed during the rehearsal and tragically passed away. Cyril Lewis was a choir stalwart, always cheerful despite his incapacity, and would be greatly missed.

There were visits to Cannock, Cardiff City Hall and Monmouth, then on 3rd June we were off to London to take part in the Queen's Golden Jubilee Festival. The Orpheus was honoured to be invited, and to work again with our old friend and choir vice president, Major Sir Michael Parker, legendary organiser of so many major events (including our Berlin and Seville adventures). Michael worked by three basic principles:

1. If it is easy to do it's not worth doing.

2. If you know it is going to work you are probably doing something wrong.

3. Unless everybody enjoys it, don't bother.

The logistics of his events were always mind-blowing, with thousands of performers and often with huge pyrotechnics, lasers and cannons. He was always cheerfully optimistic and completely unflappable. He was a pleasure to work with and everything (nearly) always turned out right in the end.

For the Jubilee Festival, the choir was sent a 50-page book with the scores of all the musical arrangements, just two weeks before the event! This was the music to accompany the Queen's Procession from Buckingham Palace to St Paul's Cathedral and was entitled 'Progress for The Queen'. We would be joined by a symphony orchestra, massed bands, a large mixed choir, a gospel choir and another Welsh male choir. The Orpheus would also perform solo sections for the vast crowds outside the Palace with our deputy musical director, Huw Rees, conducting. The narrative of our two-day sojourn in London goes something like this:

Monday, 3rd June: Rehearsal and Queen's Concert with Fireworks

Arrived in London at lunchtime, checked into the Thistle Victoria Hotel with Mari. We walked up to our staging position on the South Stage facing the Queen Victoria Memorial and Buckingham Palace. We were positioned next to the Gospel Choir and Caldicot Male Choir, with massed bands in front of us. Another large mixed choir was on the North Stage together with the symphony orchestra. Sir David Willcocks was the main conductor, with TV and audio monitors positioned to allow the shadow conductors to keep the beat.

Mari and some other choir wives were on the Green Park

(north) side of the palace to watch our rehearsal and were in good position to view the Queen's Concert, with its galaxy of stars, in the evening, relayed from the Palace Gardens onto big screens and followed by the much-anticipated fireworks display. The crowds were so vast that I asked Mari to stay exactly where she was so I could join her straight after our rehearsal. Most of the choir stayed on the stage for a grandstand view of the concert and fireworks but I battled through the crowd to join Mari. The crowd was about a million strong and after about half an hour of pushing and shoving and being diverted several times by the police, I reached Mari's spot, but no Mari! The other wives were there and told me Mari had headed back to the hotel! Why? I fought my way back through the crowd, and eventually made it back to the hotel. But still no sign of Mari. I was getting worried now. Luckily, Eddie was there and had a mobile phone (one of the few). He contacted his partner at Green Park who confirmed that Mari was okay, having returned there after failing to get through the crowd. There was no way I could get back again, so I went with a few of the Orpheus boys to the Stage Door pub and watched the show on TV. When Mari returned to the hotel much later, having enjoyed the spectacular show live, a few words were exchanged!

Tuesday, 4th June: The Queen's Procession and Festival Pageant

Up at the crack of dawn. On stage by 07.30 for the main event. It took a couple of hours to get all the choirs and musicians in place, with numerous sound and visual checks. The proceedings were being televised and broadcast around the world. Eventually, on schedule, The Queen and Prince Philip exited the palace in the Golden State Coach to the cheers of the massed crowds and our great musical ensemble greeted her with *Zadok the Priest*, followed by *Here's a Health Unto Her Majesty* and *Men of Harlech, Londonderry Air* and *Scotland the Brave*. As The Queen progressed down The Mall and on to St Paul's Cathedral there were further choirs and bands leading and performing and we continued singing, with everything synchronised. There were popular songs, songs from the shows, folk songs and even Cockney favourites. Incredible! Everything was transmitted to the crowds along the Mall and in the Royal Parks on twenty-two huge screens. The crowds joined in, including Mari and my daughter, Lucy, who had travelled up from Oxford. They were in a great position in front of our choir stage.

Later, we sang several spots on our own, with Huw conducting brilliantly. The crowd was vast, over a million. It was our biggest ever live audience. We had a great reception, with a lively spiritual called *I'm Gonna Walk* a particular crowd favourite. The other choirs took their turn and periodically, the massed choirs, bands and orchestra performed together.

The Queen and royal party returned to take up their viewing position in the royal box in front of the Queen Victoria Memorial, just in front of our stage. The pageant and parade that followed was fantastic, with Notting Hill performers in their amazing carnival costumes, steel bands and many colourful theatre floats. All the UK's main organisations were represented and there was even a parade of vehicles from the 1950s onwards, including classic cars, buses, ambulances, fire engines and police cars. Then came a vibrant parade of performers from the Commonwealth countries. It was a spectacle of colour and noise lasting for hours, and we had a grandstand view. Our choirs and musicians joined in on cue, singing *Rejoice, Rejoice*, an anthem specially written for the Jubilee. Eventually, the Royal Family returned to the palace and appeared on the balcony to more cheers, waving to the crowd and witnessing the fly past. The RAF's finest screamed overhead in formation, including Typhoons and Tornados then finally, right over our heads, Concorde accompanied by the Red Arrows with their red, white and blue vapour trails. Wow! What a finish to a memorable show. Another triumph for Major Sir Michael Parker!

We continued the party back at the hotel with Lucy and her friend Bethan joining us. What a day! Next day, the Orpheus group visited Windsor Castle to complete our royal experience. Later, we each received a certificate to mark our participation in the 'Golden Jubilee Festival Celebrations'.

Ten days later we were back in London performing at the Chelsea Festival. That summer, we also sang at three Welsh cathedrals: Bangor, St David's and Llandaff. We also gave a concert at Worcester Cathedral, another magnificent building that was a joy to perform in.

Swansea University's next Freshers' Fair yielded another crop of potential recruits. Later, we sang at Margam Orangery to celebrate the retirement of George Edwards, Editor of the *South Wales Evening Post* and an old friend.

Then there was an unusual event at a Cardiff hotel: a convention of undertakers! Although they were all dressed in sombre black, the event was more like a Halloween party. It was great fun mixing with these people in the bar after our spot, particularly with one female undertaker who looked just like Morticia from the Addams Family!

20 – WHISTLE STOP TO OZ AND NZ

Early the following year we embarked on a whirlwind tour down under. Our promoter made us work especially hard this time, with lots of flights and one-night stands covering all the major cities.

Our pre-tour concert was at Tabernacle in Morriston, and my old friend Des Downes and his wife Anne came down for the show (Des was now a member of the Ardwyn Choir in Cardiff, a high-class outfit). The following week, we returned to the Victoria Hall in Stoke-on-Trent for another concert promoted by Alan Beckett, one of our vice-presidents. Our concert included the appearance of a young violinist called Nicola Benedetti and we could see a star being born.

On 25 February 2003, we boarded a Cathay Pacific overnight flight to Hong Kong for a one-night stopover. Having checked into the Majestic Hotel in Kowloon, a group of us set off down Nathan Road towards Victoria Harbour. We didn't get far before calling into a bar to celebrate the start of the tour. A few bottles of Tsingtao beer later, we carried on and it was dark when we reached the harbour and gazed at the magnificent view across the bay to the skyline of Hong Kong Island's waterfront. We jumped on the Star Ferry which took us over to 'Central' on the island, the commercial hub of Hong Kong. On disembarking, we grabbed some delicious street food and enjoyed a wander.

Next day we had an organised tour before our onward flight to Brisbane. On Hong Kong Island we ascended The Peak by the famous tram, one of the world's oldest and steepest funicular railways. On reaching the Sky Terrace, we took in the panorama from the highest 360° viewing point in Hong Kong. Next stop was Repulse Bay, a beautiful crescent-shaped beach. Then it was

Stanley Market, a mix of eateries and little shops selling souvenirs. I noticed some 'ivory' Buddha figures that looked interesting. On closer inspection, I found that many of them were extremely vulgar, particularly if you looked underneath! I chose one as a joke for Mari and it still sits grinning at us from our conservatory windowsill. Our next delight was a sampan cruise in Aberdeen fishing village, a floating community of junks. We floated serenely around waving to the boat people and wondering at the incongruity of the modern skyscrapers alongside the harbour.

Back in Kowloon, serendipity found us at a bar with the unlikely name of 'Ned Kelly's Last Stand' (reputed to be the oldest pub in Hong Kong). We noted that live jazz would be playing there when we were due to return to Hong Kong and made a date with the Aussie proprietor. Then Bill and I decided to have a 'proper' Chinese dinner at a typical restaurant with a fish tank with numerous species swimming around happily, unaware of their impending fate.

Our overnight flight to Brisbane landed in time for lunch. Clive Arnold and I decided to visit the Gabba cricket ground in the afternoon, where Queensland were playing Victoria in a 'Sheffield Shield' game. They let us in free, so we were able to relax watching the cricket for a couple of hours. After dinner, it was early to bed; tomorrow was St David's Day, and our work would begin in earnest when we would give two concerts in one day at Brisbane's main concert hall.

There was time in the morning for Bill and I to take a 'City Cat' catamaran ride along the Brisbane River. Then it was off to the Queensland Performing Arts Centre (QPAC) for a staging rehearsal followed by our matinée concert. Our tour soloists this time were Iona Jones (soprano) and Dewi Wyn Williams (tenor) with guest accompanist Jan Ball supporting Joy Amman Davies, and organist Robert Nicholls.

As it was St David's Day, our programme had a strong Welsh flavour, including *Aberystwyth* and *Y Nefoedd*. Between shows we enjoyed a stroll along Southbank as far as the iconic Goodwill Bridge. The evening concert was a repeat performance, with a second sell-out audience. As ever, we had a stall in the foyer, selling a range of choir merchandise (including a CD produced especially for the tour). The stall was manned by supporters and by choristers signing autographs after the show. There were many Welsh exiles gathered there, keen to reminisce about home and congratulate the choir. The Welsh must be the most homesick people in the world - the *hiraeth* was very evident in Brisbane. The afterglow on our hotel patio went on late into the night despite a very early start next morning for our onward journey to New Zealand. We would return to Australia later in the tour.

Up at the crack of dawn and bleary-eyed, we left Brisbane for our flight to Auckland. We arrived at our hotel in Logan Park and after a quick meal transferred straight to Auckland Town Hall for our evening concert. We received our customary great reception in Auckland and would return in a week's time for a second concert (added to the tour due to demand). Afterwards it was straight back to the hotel; there was another early flight next morning. It had been a hectic start to the tour with three long flights, three countries and three concerts in two days. The choir performed well despite tiredness and jet lag but an extra day's rest in Brisbane would have been better.

We flew to Wellington and arrived at the Portland Hotel around lunchtime; Mansel Richards and I went for a stroll, and after dinner at the Emporium, it was off to the Michael Fowler Centre, Wellington's main concert hall. The auditorium was modern and impressive, and the concert was very enjoyable (although I thought Wellington Town Hall had more character).

Next day's concert was in Palmerston North, in range of coach travel so, thankfully, no airports and no flights. The journey north to Palmerston North took about an hour and a half and on arrival we were treated to a roast beef dinner. We then checked in at the Regent Theatre for our concert, after which it was straight back to our Wellington hotel. It was my daughter's birthday and I phoned Lucy to wish her a happy birthday. It was midnight in Wellington and midday at home.

Another day, another flight, another hotel, another concert. We flew from Wellington to Christchurch and checked into a hotel near the airport. There was a short time to relax, some of the boys having a dip in the pool, before it was off to Christchurch Town Hall. I'd managed to get my friend, Donald, a couple of complimentary tickets. The atmosphere was superb, as always, and it was reckoned to be 'one of the great concerts'. After the show there was great demand for CDs and autographs and Alwyn and the music staff were almost besieged.

We had a few hours free in Christchurch in the morning so a few of us enjoyed a walk by the river and around the beautiful gardens in this 'most English of New Zealand cities'. After lunch, we flew south to Dunedin and transferred to the Pacific Park Hotel before being quickly moved on to the theatre.

I wanted to visit Carisbrook rugby ground, also known as the 'House of Pain'. There was very little time, so I hailed a taxi. The driver was delighted to take a Welsh rugby fan to 'The Brook' and soon escorted me onto the hallowed turf itself. I mentioned the infamous 1959 British Lions test match against the All Blacks, when the Lions scored four tries only for Don Clarke to kick six penalties to win the match 18-17. The referee was a Kiwi and every time he awarded a penalty to the All Blacks, he said 'a penalty to us!' The taxi driver had been at the game as a young boy, standing on the 'Scotch Bank' up behind the posts, from where a good view could be obtained free of charge (many of Dunedin's inhabitants are of Scottish descent, and the idea of watching the game without paying was very appealing, hence the

181

bank's nickname!). I managed to get back in time for the concert in the Regent Theatre. Tomorrow we would be flying back to Auckland and after six concerts on the bounce we were looking forward to a rare night off.

An early flight from Dunedin to Auckland saw us back at our hotel by lunchtime. We were able to chill out and do some laundry - all those white shirts needed to be worn again!

Our concert dress for the tour was a black dinner suit with white shirt and black bow tie, with the addition of a daffodil in our lapels (our blazer uniform was for less formal occasions). In the evening we visited some of our previous haunts, including a walk around Auckland harbour, spectacular at night.

Next morning, we visited the Americas Cup Centre to admire the magnificent racing yachts. The great sailing event had taken place the previous week and New Zealand had unfortunately lost the Cup they won so famously. I noticed there was a guy on the harbourside sketching caricatures of people and he seemed to have plenty of customers. I soon realised that it was Emlyn Williams, one of our first tenors (and a talented artist) who was taking the opportunity to earn a few dollars during his free time!

Dudley and I decided to do the 'bridge walk' over Auckland Harbour Bridge, but by the time we were getting kitted up we realised we wouldn't be able to complete the climb before our concert, so we had to abort.

At the concert, our second at Auckland Town Hall, a week after the first, Alwyn was in fine form, entertaining the audience with his Welsh humour as well as conducting brilliantly. We sang a version of the Max Boyce song *Hymns and Arias* with some altered words that amused the rugby-loving crowd. The ovations the choir received were, if anything, greater than the week before. It was a fitting end to the New Zealand leg of our tour. In our week in NZ, we had given six concerts in the main cities of both North and South Islands, and it was now time to return to Oz; Sydney was the next port of call.

We were visiting Sydney for one night only! After our early flight we transferred to the beach resort of Coogee where we were accommodated in beachside apartments; but we wouldn't have time to enjoy the delights of Coogee and Bondi Beach. Five more choristers had flown out to join us and our staging strength was now increased from eighty-five to ninety.

I wanted a couple of our younger recruits to see something of Sydney, and I wanted some publicity pictures, so we hopped into a taxi to take us early to Sydney Town Hall, our evening concert venue. We stowed our concert gear then headed down to the harbour where I took photographs of Dan and Andrew with the Harbour Bridge and Opera House as a backdrop: ideal for our website. We made it back to the Town Hall just in time for staging.

Sydney Town Hall was an impressive venue with a magnificent organ which Rob Nicholls made full use of. It was good to perform at Sydney's other major venue after our appearances at the Opera House. After the show, it was straight back to the Coogee apartments where I hung up my suit and crawled into bed. We were flying to Melbourne early in the morning.

We arrived at our hotel in downtown Melbourne to find that our rooms weren't ready. This was annoying, particularly as we were working to such a tight schedule. It had been the Australian Grand Prix the day before and all the hotels had been booked out with Formula One people. They'd been slow to get out, hence the delay.

Perhaps I should say something here about the logistics of a major tour. The concert schedule is agreed with the promoter months in advance and a detailed tour itinerary is produced for every chorister. This includes flight details and timings, concert venues, hotel arrangements and coach travel details. The choir and travelling supporters are sometimes split among several flights and there are normally three or four coaches for transfers to hotels and concerts. Everyone is allocated a designated coach number for the whole tour and the luggage and suit bags are labelled with names and coach numbers. When the bags are recovered from airport carousels, they are collected from us and taken to the appropriate buses. After transfer, the hotel staff unload the bags and deliver them to the correct rooms. This avoids choristers having to handle their luggage and normally works very efficiently.

Eventually, we could freshen up before transferring to the Hamer Concert Hall at the Melbourne Arts Centre. This is a lovely circular building near the riverside and is Australia's largest performing arts venue; this was the Orpheus's first visit there. Afterwards, we walked through the vibrant riverside area to the casino, enjoyed a nightcap, and said hello and goodbye to Melbourne.

Very early next day we flew to Adelaide, where we would be staying for three nights. What luxury! We could unpack our suitcases properly. We arrived at the Holiday Inn mid-morning, and after a short walk established HQ at a nearby pub called The Brecknock. After lunch we took a circular bus ride around Adelaide. This was our first visit to this attractive city, and we admired the fine buildings. Our evening concert was at the Thebarton Theatre. The 'Thebby' is one of the most well-loved venues in Australia and the Adelaide audience gave the Orpheus a warm welcome. A favourite concert item was the aptly named *What Would I Do Without My Music*.

Unknown to us at this stage, our promoter had arranged an additional concert for the following day, at Tanunda, in the Barossa Valley. This was not in our agreement, so we refused to do it. There was an urgent meeting after breakfast, where the promoter advised that the concert was a sell-out and offered to pay every chorister generous expenses. We didn't want to let the fans down, so we agreed to go, knowing we had most of the day to explore Adelaide beforehand.

Clive and I took a bus to Adelaide Oval cricket stadium to tour the ground and admire the statue of Sir Donald Bradman. Then it was a lunchtime drink at the Strathmore Hotel, a popular downtown venue, with some of the other boys. Peter Thomas turned up wearing a singlet, shorts and flip-flops (his normal off-duty attire). They refused to serve him because he was improperly dressed, much to our hilarity. He was advised to go to the backpackers' hostel around the back, but was refused there as well, the cue for even more laughter! Afterwards I visited a Don Bradman exhibition at the State Library of South Australia. One display related to The Don's final innings at The Oval in London in 1948 when he needed to score just four runs to average exactly 100 in Test matches. He was out for a duck and ended with a career average of 99.94. There was an apt quotation that said: 'however great, no player is greater than the game itself'.

After an early dinner, we enjoyed a scenic drive through the Barossa Valley to the delightful town of Tanunda (home of Jacob's Creek Wines). The concert venue was the Brenton Langbein Theatre, and many people had travelled long distances to be there. I had a pleasant surprise after the show when I met John Bowkett from Cwmbran, brother of Graham, my friend from Cwmbran Male Choir days. John was a professional singer, now living in Australia, and it was great to meet someone from the Eastern Valley in the Barossa Valley! Reports from the show afterwards were stunning with many people saying 'it was the best show they had ever seen'. On our return to Adelaide there was a great party at The Brecknock; it was good to let our hair down knowing that tomorrow was a free day.

After a late breakfast, many of us took the vintage tram down to Glenelg (note the palindrome) to chill out on the beach. In the evening, four of us went to a smart restaurant called Le Blanc for a nice dinner, washed down with Clare Valley Riesling.

Our last internal flight was from Adelaide to Perth for our final two concerts. Our party was split between three flights, and we arrived in Perth to be told that one of our choir wives had been taken ill on the third plane. She was taken off the plane in Adelaide and rushed to hospital. She was very ill indeed and was hospitalised for a considerable time.

We transferred to our hotel in downtown Perth for four nights (including a couple of extra nights to wind down). After check-in we ventured over to Northbridge (a vibrant hub) and discovered the Brass Monkey, a brilliant bar which became our Perth HQ. Later the coaches took us across the Swan River to the Burswood Concert Hall, a 2,300-seater at a huge entertainment complex including a Crown hotel and casino. This was our venue for two concerts on consecutive nights. There were many Welsh exiles at both concerts and the first one was very emotional, particularly as it was our first visit to Perth. After the show we hopped back over to Northbridge to be greeted by mayhem. It was Friday night, and the place was absolutely bouncing. So, we joined in the fun.

Next morning, Clive and I visited the WACA cricket stadium where there was a club match going on between Subiaco and Claremont. Later, we caught the train down to the port city of Fremantle and met some of the lads for lunch at the Sail and Anchor. As we were munching away, Bill suddenly pointed out of the window. There was a girl walking past wearing nothing but green paint! Wow! Thus began our love affair with Fremantle. We reluctantly dragged ourselves away and took a boat up the Swan River back to Perth. This must be one of the most scenic boat trips in the world with countless yachts sailing by as the Swan River widens out to greet the impressive skyline of Perth.

The final Perth concert was even more emotional than the one the night before. The finale and encores went on and on. We sang the lovely Henry Mancini number *How Soon* and Alwyn left the stage halfway through, leaving the choir singing unconducted, eventually reaching a final decrescendo, almost to a whisper. You could hear a pin drop for a long few seconds before the audience burst into applause. When the choir was finally allowed to leave the stage, we all came off at the front, straight into the audience, walking down the aisles, giving high fives and throwing our daffodils into the crowd. It was fantastic. And it was party time. We celebrated back at the hotel and at a pub called The Melbourne just around the corner. It was difficult to tell which was the best party, so I ended up going back and forth between the two. What a night!

Next day we couldn't resist another trip to Fremantle. This time we reversed the process and sailed the other way down the Swan River. Fremantle has a brilliant indoor market, with an emphasis on indigenous products. The market also has a great bar with live music, and we enjoyed a good session there. Then it was down to Fremantle's fishing boat harbour for the best 'fish 'n chips' ever, sitting at the water's edge. The evening was spent at HQ, the Brass Monkey.

One more day in Perth and time for some last-minute shopping. Duty done, I set off on my own for a long walk. This took in Kings Park and Botanical Gardens, one of the world's largest and most beautiful inner-city parks, with stunning views overlooking Perth and the Swan River. I spent hours walking there before dropping down to the riverside to follow the scenic route back to the city. I naturally called into the Old Swan Brewery on the way. In the evening there was a final tour dinner. We reflected on a barnstorming tour, the Australian sections of which had seen us visit the country's five main cities, giving eight concerts. Our final drinks were at the Moon and Sixpence pub where many of the choir had gathered to say goodbye to Australia.

Despite our early morning departure, it was after 10.00pm local time when we arrived at our hotel in Hong Kong. We quickly headed off to 'Ned Kelly's Last Stand', as planned, where the live jazz was in full swing. We had a late supper and some decent beer while enjoying the music well into the early hours. There was now no rush and no hassle. Our departure next day was mid-morning so there was time to wander the teeming streets of Kowloon before leaving for the airport.

We arrived back in Morriston tired but happy. We had travelled a total of 28,000 miles to the other side of the world and back, with thirteen different aircraft flights and fourteen sell-out concerts in the major venues of Australia and New Zealand. We deserved to be happy. Then the taxi driver taking Bill and I home to Mumbles told us that the Iraq War had started. I spent the next week glued to the television.

21 - A TRIP TO TAIWAN

After our tour Down Under, the rest of 2003 stretched ahead, and the choir continued to move forward. We developed a state-of-the-art website that won a prestigious award (and a £2,000 prize) and the following year, the choir opened its own shop in the High Street Arcade in Swansea.

The choir's first post-tour concert was at Chichester Cathedral, one that I missed because of the birth of our first grandchild. Megan was born in Oxford on 10 April and the family was thrilled.

Two weeks later, we were singing in Luton, at the Stopsley Auditorium, an excellent venue. Our hosts provided a nice buffet afterwards which was quickly demolished. We stayed overnight at a town-centre hotel and were soon enjoying our afterglow in the hotel lounge. One group in the far corner (who'd probably missed out on the buffet) decided to order a tray of sandwiches for their table. This was a mistake. A trolley arrived laden with sandwiches, but as it was wheeled across the lounge, hands reached out from other tables to grab a sandwich as it passed. By the time it reached the group in the corner, the trolley was empty.

I should mention here that refreshments were frequently provided at concert venues. These ranged from tea and biscuits to generous buffets and even three-course meals. Sometimes, we even had beer provided! After the show, there was always a rush from the dressing rooms to reach the food and beer. It was every man for himself. Speed getting changed was vital as was your position in the changing room (preferably near the door). If you planned carefully and changed quickly, then sprinted to the buffet still in a state of partial undress, you would still find half the choir there before you, some of them already going up for seconds. If you hesitated while deciding whether to go for the beer or the food, you were sunk. Even the most generous of buffets would be demolished in seconds, leaving only crumbs and the odd lettuce leaf for late comers. But the very first choristers arriving at the buffet were always the same ones. They were unbeatable.

Next up was Lincoln Cathedral and Bill and I decided to make a weekend of it. On the way we called at the Three Kings in Hanley Castle, one of our all-time favourite pubs. In the evening we explored the ancient city of Lincoln and next morning visited the cathedral and saw the famous Imp. This is a little stone 'grotesque' high up on the cathedral wall, said to be an evil creature sent by Satan but turned into stone by an Angel. I wondered who it reminded me of? We also visited Lincoln Castle to view the Magna Carta, one of only four original copies of this history-changing charter of liberties, dating from 1215. The concert in the evening was great, with around 1,000 people packed into the cathedral.

Then we sang at Hereford Shire Hall. I chatted to a member of a local choir afterwards and he said our performance was 'what we all aspire to', which was pleasing to hear. After another concert in Monmouth, it was our annual concert, moved from Tabernacle to the Brangwyn Hall so that a full orchestra could be accommodated. Our programme included *Finlandia* by Sibelius with the full orchestral score. A week later we were in Corby for a concert at the Willows Arts Centre with the well-known Travelsphere Band.

The following week I attended the annual concert of Cwmbran Male Choir at the Congress Theatre (I was invited every year as a Life Member). I was joined in the audience by my old friends Des and Barry, and we were invited to join the choir on stage at the end to sing *Gwahoddiad*, a particular pleasure.

I missed our next concert in Cardigan but then came another big event at the Brangwyn Hall where we shared the stage with two

190

previous MOCSA winners who had both achieved international fame. Bryn Terfel and Rebecca Evans joined the choir to thrill a capacity audience. The two stars were as down to earth as ever, both very good friends of the Orpheus. A week later it was the actual MOCSA concert at the same venue with a new generation of talented young Welsh singers.

Another week and we were at the De Montfort Hall in Leicester. My sister, Peggy, came down for the show. An after-concert dinner had been arranged for the choir at a village pub in Cropston some five miles due north of Leicester centre. So, what did our coaches do? They headed due south. When we reached Blaby, some six miles south of the city, our transport masterminds realised we were going the wrong way (a fairly regular occurrence). We eventually arrived at the pub at about 11.00pm to tuck into our roast beef dinner! Happily, the bar stayed open.

At that time my daughter, Lucy, was a Macmillan Nurse living in Oxford, and son-in-law Mike was a surgeon there. I decided to organise a concert at Oxford Town Hall to raise funds for Macmillan Cancer Support. Coincidentally, there was an invitation from Oxford Welsh Male Choir for the Orpheus to come to Oxford to help celebrate their 75th anniversary. It was agreed to combine these two events and happily, the Oxford Welsh undertook most of the work. I was delighted when both choirs performed on stage at this lovely venue. We managed to raise over £3,000 for Macmillan.

Our next CD recording was entitled *Mansions of the Lord*, including the title song from the film 'We Were Soldiers'. The CD also included *Unfold ye Portals* from Gounod's *Redemption* and the Karl Jenkins *Adiemus*.

Our last trip of the year was to Malvern College and the usual Christmas concerts followed. A small group also joined me at the Newton Inn (my local) for some festive singing. We revived the

Mumbles Horse's Head tradition using the skull of a horse dating from the 19th century. This was decorated with ribbons and its owner, Len Bowden, hid under a sheet, holding the skull on the end of a pole while snapping its jaws! This variation of the 'Mari Lwyd' tradition has been carried on in Mumbles over many years. We learned the traditional *Horse's Head Song* specially for the occasion.

We performed a total of 34 concerts in 2003, with eleven in Wales, nine in England, eight in Australia and six in New Zealand. The year ahead would be just as exciting, with two overseas tours. But 2004 would also be the last year for our musical director, Alwyn Humphreys, to conduct the Orpheus: he would be leaving the choir after twenty-five years of distinguished service. His announcement to leave was unexpected and came as a shock and surprise to us all. But at least there would be plenty of time to appoint a successor. Alwyn would be a very hard act to follow.

Our first concert of 2004 was at Midsomer Norton. I remember little about this, as during the following week, my mother sadly passed away. At the funeral service, a recording of the Orpheus singing *The Old Rugged Cross* was played which helped the family to come to terms with the loss.

Our next concert was at the Brangwyn Hall, again with Rebecca Evans, followed by a BBC recording at the Pontardawe Theatre. A concert at Newport Leisure Centre was followed by a tribute at St Thomas Church in Swansea to our old friend, Sir Harry Secombe.

Shortly after this, Mari and I flew to the USA to visit Lucy, Mike and baby Megan. Mike had been appointed to the Mayo Clinic in Minnesota on a year-long contract. We flew to Chicago, where we spent a few days, before driving west through Wisconsin, then following the Mississippi north. We spent happy family times with Lucy and celebrated Meg's first birthday in Minneapolis. Lucy was a bit homesick, but a large Welsh flag pinned to her lounge wall helped a lot! Our USA visit meant that I missed the choir's participation in a memorial event for the great Welsh footballer, John Charles, and a prestigious performance at The Snape Maltings at Aldeburgh in Suffolk.

Lucy and family later flew back home for the wedding of my son Phil and Gail at St John's Church, Gowerton and the Orpheus honoured us by singing at the wedding service. Our annual concert at the Brangwyn Hall was Alwyn's last and was a memorable occasion, with the National Orchestra of Wales joining the choir.

The process of appointing a new musical director was now underway. The choir committee decided to advertise the post and four people were eventually selected for interview and audition. Our accompanist, Joy, didn't apply for the job but was happy to continue as our accompanist. The committee interviewed each of the candidates, who also conducted the choir in some set pieces chosen by Alwyn. The choristers then voted for their favoured candidate, and it turned out that one candidate received more votes than the other three added together. Alwyn provided help and support throughout but declined to state his personal choice, leaving it for the choir to decide. The committee subsequently confirmed the choir's choice and there was a further choir vote to ratify it. The successful candidate would be announced publicly after our imminent trip to Taiwan.

The choir had received an invitation from Taiwan's Institute for Information Industry to visit the country for their 25th anniversary celebrations. This was a prestige corporate event, culminating in a major concert at the National Concert Hall in Taipei. On 20 July 2004, we took off early from Bristol for Amsterdam on the first stage of our journey. There were a few hours to kill at Schiphol before our ongoing flight to Bangkok, so I browsed for a bit before venturing into one of the bars. There, seated around a table, was a group of Orpheus choristers playing crib. Pints in front of them, crib board in the centre, they could have just as easily been in the

Landore Social Club!

After an overnight flight to Bangkok, we took our final flight to Taipei where we transferred to the smart Holiday Inn Asiaworld (now called the Sunworld Dynasty) for a four-night stay. There was an 'interesting' dinner to greet us, with all manner of dishes labelled in Chinese with vague English translations. One of the boys thought he was eating 'elephant', but it turned out to be 'eggplant'! Afterwards, we explored but only got as far as the Shannon Bar, a pseudo-Irish pub with an Australian landlord. This naturally became HQ because (a) it was near the hotel (b) it was the only bar around and (c) it was brilliant. We soon became very comfortable indeed.

Next morning, we had an official visit to the new '101 Tower', at that time the tallest building in the world. I was gutted that we couldn't go to the top: the 101st floor wasn't yet accessible for visitors. We enjoyed a reception at a lower level, where our hosts welcomed us to Taipei. In the afternoon there was a televised press conference at which a small group of choristers was required to sing. Alwyn chose a group for this and the rest of us were free for the remainder of the day.

Back at the hotel I asked the concierge if it was possible to arrange a guided tour around Taipei. Within the hour a coach and guide were outside the hotel ready to roll. Our guide was called 'Danny' and spoke very good English, soon enjoying the banter with the boys who started calling him 'Danny Boy' (with musical accompaniment). We were first taken to the National Chiang Kai-shek Memorial Hall, built to commemorate the memory of the leader and former President of the Republic of China (as distinct from the *People's* Republic Of China). The ROC continues to exist on the island of Taiwan (once called Formosa) since it lost control of mainland China in 1949. The CKS Memorial Hall is situated in Taiwan Democracy Memorial Park, a lovely central park also containing the National Theatre and the National Concert Hall (where we would be performing). Leaving this impressive setting,

194

we travelled to the National Revolutionary Martyrs' Shrine, dedicated to the war dead of the Republic of China. There we witnessed the changing of the honour guard, a ceremony carried out with extraordinary precision. Next call was the National Palace Museum which houses a magnificent collection of ancient and beautiful artefacts from throughout the dynasties of Chinese history. Finally, we were taken to a Taoist Temple, an oasis of calm and spirituality in the busy city. I'm sure we had a more interesting afternoon than the ones who sang at the Press Conference!

Next morning, we went for a walk past the Taipei Stadium as far as the Keelung River. The traffic was very busy, not with cars but with thousands of motor scooters that moved in a great swarm! Later, we moved on to the National Concert Hall for a photocall and staging rehearsal. This beautiful Chinese palace-style structure seats over 2,000 people and was sold out for our concert. The Orpheus sang a couple of traditional songs from Taiwan in the Mandarin language. These were translated as *The moon represents my heart*, and *Ode to Formosa*. These were wildly applauded by our audience who also enthusiastically responded to our Welsh and international repertoire, including *Rachie* and *You'll Never Walk Alone*. Our fine soloist, Samantha Cole, was also very well received. Our hosts laid on a splendid reception afterwards where each chorister was presented with an engraved solid glass paperweight as a memento. This sits on my desk as I write.

At the Shannon Bar later it was party time. There was a live band, and everybody was dancing. We were the only Westerners there but joined in with gusto. At the party's height, our Aussie barman persuaded us to get up on stage to sing. We sang, in Mandarin, the *Ode to Formosa*. The emotional effect was stunning. Everybody in the bar was in tears. They were mainly young people who were clearly deeply moved by this bunch of Welsh guys singing about their homeland. We were feted afterwards, and the experience was just as memorable as the concert. Another precious night in the catalogue of Orpheus memories.

Next day we were taken to the north-east coast of the island. First stop was the Juming Sculpture Museum at Chin-shan, a fascinating outdoor sculpture park showcasing the work of the contemporary Taiwanese artist, Ju Ming. Then we were taken to the scenic cape of Yehlui to be entertained to lunch at a special seafood restaurant. We sat at circular tables with large revolving serving trays. Various dishes started to appear - firstly, rice and noodles and vegetables and salads and bottles of water. Then large bottles of beer and fish of every description: large fish that we could carve, lobsters and crabs and shellfish. As we were tucking into this feast, there suddenly emerged, from the depths of the salad, the largest centipede you've ever seen. It was at least four inches long, more of an animal than an insect! It scuttled quickly across the table straight towards Peter Holborow who was sat next to me. The centipede shot off the edge of the table and landed on Peter's leg (he was wearing shorts). We all jumped up, Peter kicked it off his leg and the centipede escaped to somewhere else (to the next table, we hoped!). We all laughed nervously and got on with the serious business of eating the seafood. But the salad remained untouched.

In the evening we were guests at a function hosted by the Welsh Society of Taipei. This was held around a hotel's rooftop swimming pool, and we gave a concert at the poolside, under the stars, with all the proceeds going to the Disaster Relief Fund for the devastating typhoon that struck Taiwan two weeks earlier. Afterwards, the party degenerated nicely, and it became inevitable that someone would end up, fully clothed, in the pool. We were all in concert dress and our accompanist, Joy, was in a splendid flowing gown. She and our soloist, Samantha, were paddling at the poolside and it was such a lovely evening, and the water looked so inviting, that Joy dived in, in her posh frock! A great cheer went up and then Dan Emberson, one of our younger members, jumped in as well. Everybody else quickly edged away from the poolside. Joy and Dan were soaking wet on the coach going back to the hotel, but Joy said afterwards that it was the best and most memorable swim she'd ever experienced! Later, we headed back to the Shannon Bar for fond farewells.

On our last day we were taken to a Ceramics Museum in Yingge before being entertained to dinner at a hotel in Taoyuan City. A few of us went for a walk, but the place was teeming and there was a danger of getting hopelessly lost so we doubled back and boarded the coaches for the short journey to Taoyuan International Airport. At Bangkok there was a last opportunity for airport shopping (T-shirts and toy elephants) before our overnight flight to Amsterdam. We had most of the day to wait at Schiphol before our connecting flight to Bristol so a group of us hired a minibus to take us on a guided tour of Amsterdam, a good way to end our tour.

Four days later we were performing at Oystermouth. At this event it was announced that Siân Pearce was to be the new musical director of the Morriston Orpheus, the choir's first lady conductor. At the afterglow at Mumbles Rugby Club, all the talk was of our new conductor and the different style she would undoubtedly bring. At the audition she had put the choir through a range of vocal exercises in addition to conducting the set pieces. She had left a very favourable impression and was clearly a skilled singing teacher. As recruitment officer, I thought a new approach might help us to attract more younger members. Having said this, the following day was my 60th birthday! Lucy and Megan flew home from the USA for the party and Bill brought his guitar along. As my family and friends sang together in our garden, the future looked bright.

The choir's view of events outside Buckingham Palace prior to our participation in the Queen's Golden Jubilee Celebrations in 2002.

My friend Bill Kenny and I enjoying a City Cat ride on the Brisbane River in 2003, before our concert at the Queensland Performing Arts Centre. The Story Bridge is in the background.

Enthusiastic supporters on our tour Down Under in 2003.

The Orpheus honoured our family by singing at Phil and Gail's wedding in May 2004.

199

The Orpheus on stage at the Taipei National Concert Hall with conductor Alwyn Humphreys, accompanist Joy Amman Davies, organist Rob Nicholls, and soloist Samantha Cole.

The Morriston Orpheus at the choir's spiritual home, Tabernacle Chapel in Morriston, in 2006.

200

The Opening of the new Audi Showroom in Cardiff in 2006 with the Orpheus conducted by Siân Pearce (courtesy Cardiff Audi).

The Orpheus on stage at the Sydney Opera House in 2007, with conductor Siân Pearce and accompanist Sally Tarlton.

Siân Pearce and the newly-formed Morriston Phoenix Choir (Pat Ward)

Members of the Phoenix Choir with Siân Pearce and choir president Bonnie Tyler, pictured at the Mumbles (Pat Ward).

The Phoenix Choir 'on the rocks' at Limeslade Bay'. This photoshoot had painful consequences for Simon Davies! (Pat Ward).

Mumbles A Cappella, conducted by Phil Orrin, in performance at the magnificent St Bavo's Cathedral in Ghent, Belgium, in 2022 (Sam Bevan).

Members of Mumbles A Cappella tour party visiting the very moving Yser Tower World War One Museum during their Belgian tour (Sam Bevan).

Mumbles A Cappella à Paris - on tour in 2023 (Sam Bevan).

The Mumbles A Cappella choir performing a recital at the Église de la Madeleine in Paris. Singing here was a great experience (Sam Bevan).

The magnificent neoclassical Église de la Madeleine in Paris.

Église Saint-Sulpice is the third largest church in Paris and has a great acoustic.

22 - ARABIAN NIGHTS

It was the summer of 2004, and the new conductor of the Orpheus had been appointed, although Siân would not be officially taking over until the end of the year. There were several major events planned for Alwyn and the choir before his farewell, including a tour to the Middle East.

Firstly, there was another concert at the Victoria Hall in Stoke-on-Trent, this time with a professional orchestra, and it was good to see Siân in the audience. Back at our hotel, Bill played his guitar and Siân clearly enjoyed the afterglow. The following week was Alwyn's final MOCSA Concert at the Brangwyn Hall where our distinguished panel of adjudicators comprised Stuart Burrows, Patricia O'Neill and Huw Tregelles Williams. The winner was soprano Nicola Hughes of Neath. Three days later we were off to the United Arab Emirates and the Sultanate of Oman.

Mari came with me on the trip, and we joined other choir members for a couple of nights in Dubai at the start of the tour. We stayed at the Mövenpick Hotel, and after checking in took a taxi to the Old Quarter. It was very hot as we strolled to the Dubai Creek and browsed around several souks.

There was an English-style pub/bar in our hotel and even a happy hour (popular with some friendly Russian ladies). In the evening we had dinner at the Dubai Yacht Club followed by nightcaps at Vu's Bar on the 50th floor of the Emirates Towers Hotel.

Next day was the 'Dubai city tour', including visits to Jumeira beach and the Burj Al Arab Hotel (the one shaped like a sail). There was also a little 'abra' boat trip across the Creek to see the spice souk and the famous gold souk. Later we enjoyed a dhow cruise with dinner, sailing out into the Persian Gulf. All touristy stuff but enjoyable in good company. Overall, I found the old part of Dubai interesting but most of the city was a bit modern and glitzy for me.

Next day we travelled along the desert road to Abu Dhabi to meet the rest of the choir at the Millennium Hotel. A crowd of us hired some taxis for a tour around the harbour and along the Corniche to the Breakwater Marina. In a café there, a few of us smoked hookah pipes.

Next morning, we were taken on a proper guided tour of Abu Dhabi. The trip included a visit to the carpet souk, where the merchants were highly skilled in the art of selling. Mari and I were taken with one particular carpet which we could picture in our lounge at home. I started to barter with the man, with some of the choir urging me on, and after much haggling, a price was finally agreed. But the man wouldn't take a credit card. He wanted cash in dirhams, but I didn't have enough, so he agreed to deliver the carpet to our hotel if I could get the cash in the meantime.

Later that afternoon two determined-looking Arabs in dishdashas knocked on my hotel room door. They had the carpet, folded and packed, but I still didn't have the dirhams. Next thing I knew, I was being whisked away in their unmarked van to a distant cash machine. It was like being abducted. I withdrew the cash, which they carefully counted before taking me back to the hotel where Mari was relieved to see me!

The evening concert was at The Cultural Foundation, under the patronage of H.H. Sheikh Abdulla Bin Zayed Al Nahyan, Minister of Information and Culture. Our soloist was Rebecca von Lipinski (soprano). The audience seemed to be a mix of Emiratis and ex-pats and there were several VIPs sitting at the front, dressed in immaculate white dishdashas. Our programme started with *It's a Grand Night for Singing* and it was interesting to perform in a completely different culture. I'm not sure what they made of our Welsh items. Our after-concert drinks were in the 'Cellar Bar' of a nearby hotel.

It was a very early departure, at 5.00am next morning, for our flight to Muscat in Oman. At Abu Dhabi airport, I shrink-wrapped my bulky carpet for further protection: it became the 'choir carpet' as it was carefully escorted onto planes and buses. (When we eventually got it home and laid it down, the creases magically disappeared, and it looks beautiful).

We arrived at Muscat Airport and proceeded to Customs, where there was an unaccountable delay. Firstly, Steve Pearson, who oversaw choir merchandise, was detained whilst attempting to import the choir CDs and videos. There was apparently a suspicion that these may contain salacious material! They had to be viewed by customs officials before they could be released. Steve was allowed through, minus the recordings, which were impounded. We didn't retrieve them for another couple of days.

There was another reason for our delay: chorister Robbie Harrison left his walking stick leaning against the wall in the customs area and wandered off to the toilet. The eagle-eyed security officers thought it looked very suspicious: maybe it was a 'stick bomb'! The walking stick was carefully taken away for examination and was taken apart to see if it contained drugs or explosives. When it was realised that it was just a walking stick, the broken remains were returned to Robbie. He unfortunately had to buy a new one!

We finally arrived at our hotel mid-morning, still laughing about what had happened at the airport. The five-star Al Bustan Palace was the most magnificent hotel I'd ever seen. I remarked to our tour leader that this must be one of the best hotels in the Middle East. He replied that it was one of the best hotels in the world! The great high atrium with its central fountain and beautiful scents greeted us. It was the very best of Islamic art and style and we were welcomed by the hotel staff, immaculately dressed in Omani costume. They led us into a beautiful room, with another fountain, for coffee and pastries. We had been advised in advance to observe a modest dress code and to behave with great decorum. So, what happened? Immediately after we were served coffee, one of the choristers spilt the hot coffee onto himself and whipped his shirt off to avoid being scalded. He stood there with his grey hairy chest (not a pretty sight). Then Dennis Owen slipped on the spilt coffee and fell in the fountain! There he was, lying in the water with his coffee cup and cakes floating around with the rose petals. We watched open-mouthed and couldn't decide whether to laugh or cry. The hotel hostesses were brilliant. The shirtless chorister was quickly covered with a large towel and Dennis was fished out of the fountain. They were both ushered away while the rest of us carried on with our coffee, embarrassed at the impression we had made. We'd only been in the Al Bustan Palace for about ten minutes!

Our rooms were fantastic with views of the Gulf of Oman and the spectacular mountains. There were brightly coloured birds flying around - it was paradise. When we gathered for lunch at the restaurant on the private beach, another little saga was related (again featuring Dennis). Terry Bennett and Dennis had discovered their room had a large double bed (two singles joined together). It required a member of staff to separate the beds. While they were waiting, they lay alongside each other, having a rest. When the man eventually appeared, Dennis said to him, "it's too late, I'm pregnant!" (not sure the man got the joke). Next minute, there was a tremendous crashing sound from their bathroom. They had hung their dress suits on a rail above the bath and filled the bath with hot water so that the rising steam would ease out the creases. The rail had collapsed, and the two suits were floating in the bath water. Another job for the hotel laundry!

The Al Bustan Palace has a helipad on the roof with the penthouse reserved for the private use of the Sultan of Oman. The hotel also has its own superb purpose-built theatre known as The Oman Auditorium and this was the venue for our evening concert. We were told that there would be members of the Omani Royal Family present as well as high-ranking officials and members of the international community. I like to think we gave a performance fit for royalty, in keeping with the splendid surroundings. Afterwards, we were treated to a pukka reception, rubbing shoulders with the 'crachach'. We remained in our dress suits for this occasion. The man whose shirt had been covered in coffee told Mari his laundered shirt had never been so white!

Oman is a nation of diverse terrain, including desert, rocky mountains, lush riverbed oases and a long, beautiful coastline. It is everything you think of when you conjure up an image of Arabia and Arabian Nights. It is also a devout Muslim country: our local guide explained to me the Five Pillars of Islam which helped me to better understand the Muslim faith.

On our tour the next day we visited the busy fish market at the waterfront Muttrah quarter of Muscat. It was a different world, with the clamour of the merchants bartering noisily and a huge variety of fish. There were also live chickens that were slaughtered to order. Our next visit was to the great Sultan Qaboos Grand Mosque. The vast floor of the mosque was covered in a beautiful carpet, all in one piece. I was told it was the largest single carpet in the world.

Then we went inland, to the historic Nakhal Fort, one of many such fortifications in Oman. It dates from pre-Islamic times but has been rebuilt numerous times. It stands on a hilltop, keeping guard over the ancient village of Nakhal and the area oasis. It is surrounded by orchards of palm trees and offers great views of the craggy mountains from its battlements. The fort also hosts a weekly goat market.

We moved on to the nearby springs and a forest of date palms near the old village. We ventured close to the village and saw scenes that seemed almost biblical. The women were washing clothes in the stream and the young men were slaughtering a goat. The goat was hung from the branch of a tree and killed halal-style, then skinned. The skin was cast aside for the flies and the carcase was quickly butchered. It was a glimpse of a completely different, yet harmonious lifestyle. The scenes left a lasting impression.

Lunch was taken at a beach resort where they were offering camel rides, and several Orpheus boys and girls couldn't resist. Another hilarious interlude! Then it was back to Muttrah and its labyrinthine souk. This was an authentic and typical Arabian souk, and I was very taken with the decency and fairness of the traders.

As we were leaving the souk, there was an Arab standing at the entrance selling things. He was dressed in a long white dishdasha and Arab headgear and there was a crowd gathered around him. I discovered that he was offering Welsh cakes and dirty postcards! Then I realised it was Danville Griffiths, one of our baritones, dressed up. He looked exactly like one of the locals.

The evening was spent relaxing at our wonderful hotel. After dinner, Bill decided to show off his climbing skills and started to scale the steep cliff at the back of the beach. He did well, with the rest of us watching with bated breath. Much later, we were perched at the beach bar, gazing out towards the ocean at night when we realised Bill had disappeared. We eventually found him stretched out on a bench near the swimming pool, fast asleep. The end of another Orpheus day.

On our last day at the Al Bustan Palace there was swimming in the pool and in the Gulf of Oman followed by a long and leisurely lunch. A group of us were given a guided tour of the hotel. We saw the magnificent ballroom and the private suites at the top end of the hotel. These had unimaginable luxury with silk furnishings and gold-plated taps. We weren't allowed to see the Sultan's quarters, which were apparently even more luxurious. We were reluctant to drag ourselves away from our Arabian paradise when we left for Muscat airport for the short flight to Abu Dhabi followed by an overnight flight to Gatwick and home. We carried our magic carpet all the way.

23 - BOHEMIAN RHAPSODY

The week after we returned from the Middle East, we were singing at Ammanford, a friendly place but not quite the same as Muscat. The following day was Siân's first rehearsal with the choir and she would be alternating with Alwyn for a short handover period. After a series of vocal exercises, we started on *Bohemian Rhapsody*, the 'Queen' classic. This almost became a signature tune for the period ahead and I was delighted.

Alwyn led us on a trip to Cornwall where we sang in Truro as guests of the City of Truro Male Voice Choir. We had a great welcome from our fellow Celts and enjoyed singing Ivor Novello's *Rose of England* which Alwyn conducted with a Welsh flag! One of our hosts commented that the Orpheus made a greater sound than all the choirs in Cornwall put together! (a bit of an exaggeration). There followed two university concerts, at the Great Halls of Aberystwyth and Exeter.

On 8 December a group of us sang festive songs at Swansea's High Street Station which was Siân's first opportunity to conduct the choir outside rehearsal. Alwyn conducted the Christmas concerts at St David's Hall and St Mary's Church in Swansea to end our 2004 programme.

In the new year, Alwyn's final concert was a magnificent farewell event at Tabernacle in Morriston where our guests were Fflur Wyn and Bryn Terfel. The soloists interacted superbly with the Orpheus and Bryn joined us in a performance of *Brenin y Sêr*. Alwyn was in inspired form and the 110 choristers on stage responded with a memorable performance that ended with *The Dawn* from *Nidaros*.

This was the end of an era. Alwyn was leaving the choir after over twenty-five years. I was privileged to be a choir member for most of that period and, like everyone, was very sorry to see him leave. It was an emotional evening at which the Orpheus honoured Alwyn with the title 'Conductor Emeritus' to go with his previous well-merited MBE.

We were soon getting used to Siân conducting our twice-weekly rehearsals with vocal exercises at the start of each practice. She would also spring surprises like moving us around and mixing up the parts. If she was trying to get us out of our comfort zone, she succeeded. She revived numerous pieces from our extensive repertoire, whilst retaining some of the 'standard' items. The only completely new number at this stage was *Bohemian Rhapsody*.

Siân conducted her first full concert at St David's Cathedral in West Wales. The concert was a resounding success with great ovations, particularly for the powerful piece *If You Only Have Love*. There was a buzz among the choir at the Rugby Club afterwards.

The following month, the Orpheus celebrated its 70th anniversary with a dinner at the Tower Hotel. The guest of honour was Gerald Davies, the rugby great and big fan of the Orpheus. Another important event to celebrate the anniversary was a major Morriston Orpheus exhibition at Swansea Museum that was open to the public throughout the spring. This impressive display of memorabilia illustrated the choir's worldwide appeal over seven decades.

At Siân's first annual concert at Tabernacle I was presented with a long service award, having completed 21 years with the Orpheus. Earlier in the day, Phil and I saw Wales win the Grand Slam in Cardiff, so there was much to celebrate that evening!

Our next performance was at Swansea University, followed by a 'Meet the Orpheus' recruitment evening in Mumbles where Siân put the audience through their paces as well as conducting the choir. Afterwards, she held auditions for those wishing to join the choir and five were successful, including two new members from Brecon who had travelled down for the event.

Siân was supportive of my recruitment efforts, and we held a meeting with some of our younger members to listen to their ideas. Later in the year we became involved in a schools project with a progressive teacher from Caerphilly who incorporated recordings of the Orpheus into his on-line music modules. We also held another 'Meet the Orpheus' recruitment evening, at Penlan Social Club, linked to a charity fund-raiser for the Wales Air Ambulance.

In the spring and summer, there were several cathedral concerts starting with Winchester Cathedral. This one seemed a bit below par, but the following week, the concert at Lincoln Cathedral was much better and Siân and the choir excelled themselves. I missed the concert in Norwich but then there was another excellent concert at Hereford Cathedral followed by a return to St David's. During this period, our family was delighted to welcome Carys, our second granddaughter, into the world.

The MOCSA concert in September was the perfect opportunity for our first live performance of *Bohemian Rhapsody* which was very well received. This was followed by a concert at Llandovery College before an appearance at the Millennium Stadium in Cardiff. This was a large corporate affair for European businesspeople held on the covered pitch with the roof closed, and the choir sang on a raised stage in the centre.

I was very much behind Siân, as were most choristers at this stage, although there were a few grumbles. She had a hard act to follow but was an accomplished singing teacher and was conducting well in my opinion. A possible disadvantage was her inability to speak Welsh. The Welsh language repertoire was an important part of the choir's DNA, and a fair number of the choristers were Welsh speaking. She had also banned drinking before concerts, which may have upset a few!

Our next concert helped to keep the faith. This was a return to Luton, to the Stopsley Auditorium, where the audience gave us a great reception. Our two new members from Brecon, Alastair Jones and Derek Hill, had settled in well and would become good friends in the time ahead. They were delighted to be part of the Orpheus, and they thought Siân was terrific. We had a brilliant afterglow at the Stopsley Workingmen's Club where a crowd of us took to the stage to give a spontaneous mini concert.

Our next engagement was at the Millennium Centre in Cardiff Bay, our first appearance at the prestigious new venue. Our performance included *Bohemian Rhapsody* with a full rock band: the guitar riffs were tremendous, and the packed house loved it. A few days later we were back at Leicester's De Montfort Hall. We stayed at the Holiday Inn and enjoyed a late curry in Leicester's Indian quarter! I missed another visit to Exeter but attended the Leukaemia Christmas Concert at St David's Hall in Cardiff. Our Christmas Concert at St Mary's in Swansea was a bit different, as Siân asked various choir members to contribute individual items, readings and poems. Thus ended 2005, a year of major change. There were good reasons for optimism and there was a trip to Ireland to look forward to in the new year.

For me, the new year started with the delivery of my first book to the publisher and I was making plans to invite the Orpheus to sing at the forthcoming book launch. In January, the choir had a couple of local concerts then we were off to County Clare in Ireland for a return visit to the town of Ennis. Mari and I were in Egypt the week before, so Ireland was a complete contrast!

I was delighted to have Phil for company, and we decided to fly from Bristol to Shannon rather than face crossing the Irish Sea by ferry. On arrival, we transferred to the historic Old Ground Hotel

219

in Ennis, opposite the cathedral that was our concert venue. Everybody was in high spirits and the hotel was very welcoming. There was a private party going on in one of the lounges and we were invited to sing to the guests. I ended up conducting the choir and our songs went down very well. Siân said later that she could hear the singing from her hotel room!

Next day, we visited an unusual pub called 'The Usual Place'. It was the day of the England versus Wales rugby international and after lunch we watched this with gritted teeth as Wales lost 47-13! The defeat didn't affect our singing in the evening, however, when around 1,300 people packed into the Cathedral of St Peter and Paul to hear 'the Welsh choir'. The acoustics were great and Siân led us in a spirited performance. The whole town seemed to be at the concert and at the afterglow in the Banquet Suite of the Old Ground Hotel. This went on until the early hours and I remember us singing *The Fields of Athenry* with Bill playing his guitar.

On Sunday morning we attended Mass in the cathedral and gave another performance that included the Gounod *Gloria*. The rest of the day was free, so a crowd of us hired a bus to take us on a trip to the coast where we visited some of the places that had impressed Mari and I on an earlier trip. First was the spectacular Cliffs of Moher, rising to 700 feet above the Atlantic Ocean, a sight that almost took your breath away. Our driver then took us into The Burren, a unique and vast landscape of limestone. Our main destination was Doolin village, renowned for traditional Irish music. Our plan was to visit Gus O'Connor's Pub, famous for its music sessions. When Mari and I visited, Gus put us up in his bungalow. In return I had to sing for my supper in the pub! It was great to take a group from the Orpheus to O'Connor's Pub to listen to the session music and to offer some of our own Welsh singing. The singing continued when we eventually got back to the Old Ground Hotel.

Next morning, there was time for a walk around Ennis before a last visit to 'The Usual Place'. After lunch we departed for Shannon Airport in buoyant mood. It had been a very successful trip to Ireland.

It was still early February and there was a busy year ahead. Among these was the opening of the new Audi showroom in Cardiff, an interesting experience for the 'Rolls Royce' of choirs! There was another concert at Brecon Cathedral and a recording in Morriston before a concert in Wolverhampton.

My first book entitled *Mumbles and Gower Pubs* was published in May. I held the book launch, appropriately, at the Dylan Thomas Centre in Swansea and the Orpheus came to entertain the guests and help me launch the book in style. Afterwards, the choir and guests enjoyed a couple of barrels of beer kindly donated by Rory Gowland of the Swansea Brewing Company. It was great to have all my family there to share in the occasion.

Also in May, we made a return visit to Marston St Lawrence in Northamptonshire, where we previously sang at the wedding of Michael Heseltine's daughter. The concert was again in the village church and Lord Heseltine eloquently thanked the choir on the audience's behalf.

The next engagement was an interesting one at the 'Big Anthem Fawr' Festival in Pontypridd. The event celebrated both the 150th anniversary of the Welsh National Anthem (written in Pontypridd in 1856) and the 250th anniversary of 'Yr Hen Bont', Pontypridd's famous old bridge over the River Taff. The festival was held in a huge marquee in Ynysangharad Park with several thousand present. We shared the stage with Max Boyce, Aled Jones and our old friend Mike Peters of The Alarm. In June we appeared in Burry Port followed by our annual concert and another visit to Derby Cathedral.

It was a busy July with five engagements in the Swansea and Gower area followed by a concert at St Peter's Church in Cardiff

221

to dedicate the new organ in memory of Sir Julian Hodge, the choir's late patron. Then it was the White Lady Festival at Oystermouth Castle, an outdoor event featuring various well-known Welsh groups and named after the ghost of a young lady reputed to haunt the castle!

The choir visited Devizes in August and there was the MOCSA concert in September, with four finalists chosen from over thirty young Welsh singers who applied. This was the 30th annual 'Young Welsh Singer Competition' organised by the Orpheus subscribers and *The Times* newspaper reported it as 'one of the UK's five top cultural events'. We included *An African Trilogy* as part of our programme, and I hoped this successful concert would ease any unrest regarding our new musical director.

There was then a concert at Shirehampton in Bristol followed by some local events and another return to Exeter. The choir was about to record a new album (Siân's first) and the recording company filmed the choir at its next concert, at the Princess Royal Theatre in Port Talbot, as part of the publicity. There were over 100 on stage (always a good turn-out when there's filming!). Next was a return to Machynlleth where I stayed overnight so that I could do some recce work for my next book project, a planned walk through Wales.

In December, the recording sessions for the choir's new CD, entitled *One Thrilling Combination*, were held at Trinity Chapel in Sketty and the BBC Studios in Swansea. The disc included *Back to The Sixties* (a medley of popular '60s numbers) and, of course, *Bohemian Rhapsody*. The Christmas concerts ended a busy 2006, during which we had undertaken thirty-five engagements. Mari and I had a wonderful Christmas present when our third granddaughter, Bethan, was born on 21 December.

The new year of 2007 started with plans being made for a further major tour Down Under. I was surprised when a group of extra singers turned up at rehearsal one night hoping to be 'recruited' for the tour. These were members of other choirs who had been 'invited' along (in the event, only four of these joined the choir). Shortly afterwards, I decided that I would be giving up the recruitment role after almost seven years in the job.

The forthcoming month-long tour to Dubai, Australia and New Zealand was an important one and we managed to put together a decent-sized choir for the trip, despite some choristers opting out. Before the tour, our concerts included the Celtic Manor, Chichester Cathedral and the Riverfront Theatre in Newport. There was also a supposedly 'low-key' concert at the Cwmfelin Club in Swansea at which there was an unfortunate disagreement between our musical director and a choir official. This was to become a very divisive issue in the choir, with people taking sides and opinions becoming polarised. On a more positive note, the choir voted (narrowly) to add white tuxedos and black shirts to our concert dress.

Another development at this time was our MD's decision to enter the Orpheus into the televised 'Britain's Got Talent' show (a decision not supported by everyone). We turned up at the Millennium Centre in Cardiff Bay to compete against the other acts in the Welsh regional round. We were met backstage by the very chatty Ant and Dec before taking the stage in front of the three judges, Piers Morgan, Amanda Holden and Simon Cowell, and an audience of 2,000 people. Siân decided we would sing *Senzenina*, an unaccompanied Zulu chant featuring soloists from our second tenors. This atmospheric but unusual piece seemed to confuse our judges a little. Amanda Holden said she found it very moving but voted NO! Piers Morgan was impressed and voted YES, so it was down to Simon Cowell. He entered a conversation with Siân on stage which resulted in the choir singing an impromptu, unaccompanied version of *You Raise Me Up*. This did the trick and Simon voted YES to send us through to the next round, to be held in London. Unfortunately, the date of this clashed with our overseas tour, so we had to withdraw. At least we could say that our brief sortie into the competition had been a qualified success!

24 – DISCORD DOWN UNDER

By the time the choir took off for Dubai on 6 April 2007, opinion in the choir was becoming more divided, although I'm sure most of the choristers just wanted to get on with the singing. I was on the side of the musical director, as were most of the committee, who were trying to deal with this difficult issue. This resulted in an atmosphere in the background during the tour, but we were all determined to pull together to give our usual professional performances. The musical staff and choristers worked very hard to achieve this in what turned out to be a largely successful and enjoyable tour. Our musical team for the tour included MD Siân, accompanist Joy, deputy accompanists Jo Scullin and Sally Tarlton and organist Jan Ball. Our soloists were Jo Appleby (soprano), Andrew Rees (tenor) and the young Welsh violinist, Sali-Wyn Ryan. I'll describe the tour in the positive way that it unfolded and return to the 'discord' later.

We stayed at the Novotel in Dubai's World Trade Centre for a couple of nights and went on the obligatory city tour. This included Sheikh Mohammed's Palace and the Racecourse where I was surprised to discover that robots were used as jockeys in some of the camel races! The first concert of the tour was at the Dubai Country Club, hosted by the Dubai Welsh Society. This was a very pleasant, outdoor affair with a nice social event afterwards.

My roommate on this tour was Paul Stableforth, a retired orthopaedic surgeon, and we were determined to make the most of our trip. Next day we visited the Sheikh Saeed Al Maktoum House, the historic former residence of the Ruler of Dubai. I was interested to see the wind towers that provide a cooling interior environment during the hot summer months. We found a place discreetly labelled 'The Pub' alongside the Creek for lunch before transferring in the late afternoon to Dubai Airport for our overnight flight to Perth.

In Perth, we transferred to the Holiday Inn and soon made a beeline for our old HQ, the Brass Monkey in Northbridge. On this tour, there was plenty of free time and the next day, Paul and I enjoyed a long walk to Kings Park, and paid our respects at the memorial to the victims of the Bali bombing. The afternoon was spent on a tram ride around Perth followed by a choir rehearsal at the hotel.

Next morning, after breakfast, there was another rehearsal at our hotel which turned out to be a rather tense affair! Afterwards, we took the boat to Fremantle and visited the Whaling Tunnel and Fishing Harbour, followed by a CAT ride around Fremantle town.

The early part of the next day was free, so I visited the Perth Mint, an historic building that opened in 1899 in response to the discovery of rich gold deposits in Coolgardie and Kalgoorlie. I saw some huge gold nuggets that had been mined in the area and witnessed a gold melting and pouring demonstration. I was also able to handle a large gold bar worth many thousands of dollars - quite an experience. I bought some solid silver Australian dollars for my grandchildren. Later, I visited the Subiaco Oval, a major Aussie Rules football stadium.

The concert in the evening was at the Burswood Centre, a venue we'd performed at before. We were surprised that the concert was not a sell-out, as all our previous concerts in Australia had been. Perhaps the Orpheus was becoming a bit over-exposed, having visited Down Under five times in twelve years. Another factor was the price of the tickets: eighty dollars was pricey by any measure. Nevertheless, there was an audience of around 1,200 in the Burswood Centre to appreciate our performance, which went very well. Our conductor could be pleased with everyone's efforts, including that of our soloists and young violinist.

Next day we flew from Perth to Melbourne without accompanist Joy who sadly had to return home due to a family bereavement. She would return later in the tour, but in the meantime, Jo, Sally and Jan performed brilliantly. In Melbourne, we stayed at the Novotel in the heart of the city and next morning I visited the Ian Potter Museum of Art. This fine museum showcases a rich collection of Australian art, and I enjoyed browsing for an hour or two before our afternoon concert, which was a return visit to the Hamer Concert Hall. The concert was terrific right from the start and set the tone for a great show. Unfortunately, one of our choristers was taken ill and my doctor companion, Paul, attended him and got him rushed off to hospital. The chorister remained in hospital following emergency surgery and took no further part in the tour. Happily, he made a full recovery.

In the evening, we went to Young & Jacksons pub (to say hello to Chloe) then visited the casino. Tomorrow we would be heading for New Zealand. The first week of the tour had seen three concerts, in Dubai, Perth and Melbourne, and there had been lots of free time (in comparison to previous tours).

We flew from Melbourne to Christchurch and installed ourselves in the Millennium Hotel in Cathedral Square (a devastating earthquake was to strike Canterbury and Christchurch three years later, resulting in the deaths of 185 people and badly damaging the lovely cathedral).

We had dinner followed by drinks at a pub called The Bard on Avon, a reminder of Christchurch's very English character. Next morning, I visited Canterbury Museum, to say thanks in person to the curator who sent me material on Captain Scott's polar expedition for my book. Later, it was off to Christchurch Town Hall for our concert. The audience gave us their usual very warm Christchurch welcome.

Next day some of our party went whale-watching at Kaikoura while the rest of us went to Hanmer Springs. We called at the Mud House Winery for lunch, then a very small group of us decided to go jet boating at Thrillseekers Canyon. It was frightening! We rocketed along the river canyon at breakneck speed, bouncing off rocks and scraping the bottom. After a while, it became exhilarating but when I eventually got off, my legs were like jelly and my heart was racing. Afterwards, I bought a DVD of our boat ride (I've never played it!). It was a relief to move on to the thermal sulphur springs where I immersed myself in the very hot spring water and gradually felt some normality oozing into my trembling body. It was an experience I'll never forget.

My mate Paul had gone out on a boat whale-watching all day. Unfortunately, they didn't see a single whale! I consoled him by arranging our evening dinner in a smart restaurant. The green-lip mussels were delicious.

Our next port of call was Nelson in the north of the South Island, and we travelled by coach on a scenic route through the National Park. This was a beautiful journey through hills and valleys with the low white clouds clinging to the peaks, illustrating why New Zealand is called 'the Land of the Long White Cloud'. This memorable trip took us into the famous Marlborough wine region and the lovely coastal town of Nelson. Our party was split into two for accommodation and Paul and I were allocated to a hotel at Tahunanui Beach, a superb location. For dinner, we enjoyed some seafood followed by crème brûlée made with Manuka honey. Then there were drinks (and songs) with the rest of the gang at the Smugglers Bar. This was the place to be!

Next morning, we walked along the coast into Nelson and enjoyed lunch at an atmospheric bay-side restaurant called The Boat Shed (scallops and sauvignon blanc). Later, I walked up onto the bluff to look at the fabulous views over Tasman Bay. Our evening concert was at the Trafalgar Centre, with a somewhat changed concert programme. We wore black shirts without jackets, in good All Black tradition. Afterwards, it was back to the Smugglers Bar, where our hosts kindly provided free hot platters of food.

In the morning, there was a massive change of plan. We were due to take the ferry across the Cook Strait from Picton to Wellington. But our promoter now wanted the choir to head back to Christchurch to take part in a TV broadcast to boost publicity for the tour. We would sing at a Super 14 Rugby match between the Crusaders and the Hurricanes at Jade Park Stadium, then fly to Wellington after the match. We dropped off our supporters at the Picton ferry terminal, then the choir proceeded back south to Christchurch, following the east coast road through Blenheim and stopping in Kaikoura for lunch. Looking out to sea from the beach at Kaikoura, we spotted a whale! You can imagine the mickey-taking of those who'd spent an abortive day at sea on their so-called whale-watching trip!

We rocked up in Christchurch and were given a slap-up dinner before heading to the rugby stadium. There to welcome us was none other than Graham Henry, our vice-president. It was good to shake hands and have a brief chat. We sang at the pitch-side before the evening game, televised by Sky, then settled in to watch the match. The stars were all playing, including Dan Carter and Richie McCaw and the Crusaders won 23-13. Our music staff and officers were entertained in a hospitality suite where they met several All Black greats. After the match, we were whisked off to the airport, where two private executive jets were waiting to take us to Wellington. It was great to have the VIP treatment and we arrived at our Wellington hotel around midnight. Happily, the bar was still open.

I love Wellington. It's a fine city in a beautiful setting. Paul and I took the cable car up to Kelburn for lunch before our concert at the Michael Fowler Centre. It was great to see Joy, who had rejoined us following her flying trip home. Our afterglow at the Welsh Dragon pub was another pilgrimage to this little bit of Wales on the other side of the world.

The show then moved on by coach to Palmerston North where we checked in at the Novotel. Then it was off to the Regent Theatre, another excellent venue visited several times previously. We marked the concert at nine out of ten. At the Celtic Inn next door after the show, we got into some rugby discussions with the locals. One of our Kiwi friends was full of praise for Andy Haden for diving out of the lineout in the infamous match against Wales in 1978! His cheating resulted in a penalty for New Zealand that allowed them to win the match in the dying seconds, denying Wales a famous and deserved victory. He insisted that it was 'not against the laws of the game'. How one-eyed can you get?

Our coaches continued northwards, heading for Auckland, stopping for lunch at Taumarunui in the King Country. Our base for two nights was the Mercure Hotel, superbly located near Auckland Harbour. After dinner we visited the Sky Tower, to marvel at the view of Auckland by night.

The following day we had a concert double-header at Auckland Town Hall. The matinee concert was followed by a light meal before the evening performance which I thought was one of the best concerts of the tour. There were repeated standing ovations and I felt proud coming off stage. I was disappointed to hear some choristers criticising Siân's conducting, particularly after such an outstanding concert. After the show, there was a drinks party in the hotel bar, but Siân didn't join us; she was keeping to herself and probably didn't want to socialise, such was the pressure she felt under from some quarters. I was sad about this, especially as the tour was progressing so well musically. In my view, Siân was doing a great job, and this was certainly the view of our promoters and audiences.

230

In the morning, we transferred to Auckland Airport for our flight to Brisbane. We stayed at the Holiday Inn and in the evening in the hotel bar, I made a point of quietly chatting to some choristers to encourage support for Siân. I was surprised to find that some weren't as supportive as I expected. There would clearly be a reckoning when we returned home. In the meantime, it was on with the show!

Next day was another double-header, at the QPAC Concert Hall on the South Bank. A walk along the Brisbane river in the morning was followed by the afternoon matinee; the evening concert was another nine out of ten. Performances were continuing at a high standard, and everyone was looking forward to Sydney and the Opera House.

Our flight to Sydney went smoothly and we were soon installed in the Holiday Inn, Darling Harbour. We walked down to Circular Quay to view the Harbour Bridge and the Opera House and were very fortunate to view a fantastic fireworks display over the Harbour Bridge. It was like New Year's Eve! We spent the evening at The Rocks, visiting the 'Fortune of War' and the 'Lord Nelson' (my favourite Sydney pub).

The following day was free, so I did my own thing. I spent some time in the State Library of New South Wales (I love libraries) before walking through the Botanic Gardens to Circular Quay. I wanted to have lunch at Doyle's famous seafood restaurant, so I caught a ferry to Watson's Bay and had my wish, enjoying my lunch overlooking the idyllic bay. I then went on a walking trail to The Gap and the South Head, right at the mouth of Sydney Harbour where the scenery was spectacular. I followed the trail back along the coast as far as Rose Bay before catching a ferry back to Circular Quay. I really enjoyed being on my own for the day.

Next day was our final double-header at the Sydney Opera House. When the choir assembled for a staging rehearsal, Siân told us that her dressing room had a beautiful Steinway piano and a panoramic view of Sydney Harbour Bridge. She was like a kid in a sweet shop! After the usual sound checks we were ready for the matinee concert. Although the concert hall wasn't completely full, the atmosphere was great. It was clearly an international audience and we entertained them with a varied programme. In the break between shows, our promoter addressed the choir and thanked us for a highly successful tour. He was particularly fulsome in his praise of *Bohemian Rhapsody* and the modern repertoire. The final concert in the evening was quite emotional and Siân conducted brilliantly. In my view she passed the ultimate test. We scored the concert at nine and a half out of ten. The last week of tour had seen the high standard maintained, with repeated standing ovations at every concert. Siân could be proud of the choir and her own courageous performances. I found it unbelievable there was still opposition to her.

The party at the hotel afterwards was something else. Disagreements that had been hidden in the background were coming out and when Bert Queenin, our Kiwi promoter and road manager, made a speech and proposed a toast to our 'magnificent musical director' (his words) there were cheers, but also jeers. The situation was lightened by a virtuoso performance from bottom bass Elwyn Summers, one of the characters of the choir. There was also sadness as one of the choristers received news that a close relative had passed away back in Wales. A large group of us were now looking forward to a three-day break in Singapore. Siân was heading straight home but wished us well for our stopover.

We flew from Sydney to Melbourne, then Singapore before transferring to our hotel on Clarke Quay, alongside the Singapore River. Next day we walked along the river to Raffles Landing and the futuristic concert hall (where we were originally scheduled to

232

perform). Afterwards there was a city tour. This included visits to Little India and a Hindu Temple, then Chinatown and a Buddhist Temple. Mount Faber was also visited, with its panoramic views and finally the tropical Botanic Gardens. The tour gave us an insight into this fascinating multicultural island city-state.

We were fortunate to have a brewpub near our hotel, called the Pump House, which became HQ for a couple of days. After dinner on the Boat Quay, we finished the evening with songs and drinks with the gang.

The following morning, we went to the Changi Museum and Chapel which provided an emotional exploration of Singapore's wartime history during the Japanese occupation. There was a soundtrack playing which included a Welsh male choir singing *Hen Wlad Fy Nhadau*. This sounded very much like the Orpheus, which was quite a coincidence. After lunch we visited the incredible Bugis Street Market, one of the biggest, cheapest and best places to go shopping in Singapore, before taking in a Singapore River cruise.

In the evening we went to Raffles Hotel to try a Singapore Sling. We started with a beer in the downstairs bar and watched a young barman mixing drinks in a kind of stainless-steel machine. We found out he was mixing the pink Singapore Sling cocktail and decanting it into containers to be sent upstairs. This 'mass production' was apparently necessary to cope with demand! But when we went upstairs to the cocktail bar, the legendary drink was served in the traditional way and was most enjoyable. There were free peanuts, and the bar was ankle-deep in peanut shells, another hotel tradition. Having ticked off Raffles, we had chilli crab on the quay, another Singapore 'must'. A huge crab was served in a thick, very spicy sauce. All you needed was a tool kit and a bib. Very messy but delicious.

On our last day, a few of us decided to go on a trip across the causeway to Johor Bahru in Malaysia. After passing through Customs, we were treated to a demonstration of Batik painting then listened to some relaxing bamboo music. We visited the Sultan Abu Bakar Mosque (reminding us we were now in a mainly Muslim country) before visiting a traditional kampong village. Here we were entertained with dancing and were bitten by mosquitoes.

Back in Singapore, we decided to make the most of the afternoon before our evening flight. We caught the monorail over to Sentosa Island (a delightful spot). Our main intention was to catch the Skyway cable car back across to Mount Faber and we had just about enough time to do this before our airport departure. There we were, Paul and I, in a cable car high above Singapore Harbour, nervously taking in the view, when suddenly and inexplicably, the cable car stopped! We were mid-span at the Skyway's highest point, hundreds of feet up, gently swaying in the breeze. We looked at each other, trying not to panic, persuading ourselves that we would start to move again in a minute. But we didn't. The time started ticking away, thoughts of emergency rescues and missed flights began to plague us. Then after what seemed an eternity, just as I was about to press the red emergency button, we creaked into movement. Slowly, with our fingers crossed, we continued to Mount Faber. We managed to get back to the hotel in time to hurriedly pack and even had time for a quick, much-needed drink at the Pump House before our transfer to Changi Airport and our overnight flight to Dubai, and then on to home.

It had been a long, successful and enjoyable tour despite the off-stage tensions, but we all knew there would be trouble ahead. What follows is the story of the unfortunate split that ultimately occurred. This is told from my own perspective, although I acknowledge that there are two sides to every story.

After our return from Down Under, the atmosphere in the choir was very unsettling. Two weeks afterwards, we sang at Trowbridge United Church in Wiltshire. The church has a stated aim of being 'where people of all ages, backgrounds and opinions can work together in a safe, respectful and friendly atmosphere'. This must have temporarily worked for our divided choir, because the concert was excellent. The following week, we performed on the opening day of the Hay Festival, singing in a large pavilion to an appreciative festival audience. Siân compered in her own style and was well-received (particularly by the Festival Director).

The following day, the choir was filming at Bracelet Bay for a video to accompany our new CD recording. We were filmed on the beach, with the sea and lighthouse in the background, singing *You Raise Me Up*, resplendent in our white tuxedos, with Siân conducting off camera. The video was to prove extremely popular (it's still available on YouTube). As we were leaving the beach, I was told that Siân had sent a resignation letter to the committee. I was upset and phoned Siân next day asking her to reconsider. On top of this, our long-serving and popular accompanist, Joy, announced she would be leaving the choir after the forthcoming annual concert. There was clearly a crisis in the choir, but I hoped we could rescue the situation.

A week later there was turmoil at rehearsal. Most of the committee were supporting Siân but they seemed unable to resolve the divisive issues. It looked as if our MD would be leaving, but I hoped she would hang in there until we could try to turn things around.

The annual concert was in two days' time and the committee decided to call an Extraordinary General Meeting for the following rehearsal. This would involve a vote on a motion to back the committee's decision to support the musical director. This would effectively be a vote for or against Siân. But first, the important annual concert had to take place. It was to be our accompanist

Joy's final concert and would potentially be Siân's last concert with the Orpheus if the vote turned out against her.

In the event, the concert was a great success. There were over a hundred choristers on stage and the response from the packed Brangwyn Hall audience was terrific. There was an ovation for accompanist Joy, and they were stamping their feet and applauding the choir's performance. The programme included a selection of arrangements by our previous maestro, who was also present at the concert. The *Matt Monro Medley* went down a storm and there were some newer pieces introduced by Siân such as *You Raise Me Up* and *African Trilogy*. Coming off stage following the standing ovations was a proud moment. How anyone could be saying that Siân was 'rubbish' after that show defeated me completely. With her brave effort, Siân had shown she was still in there fighting. I felt that we still had an uphill task, but we were getting our act together before the EGM.

And so, to the Extraordinary General Meeting. Both sides had prepared their cases and several speakers addressed the choir, presenting both sides of the argument. Several committee members spoke in support of Siân, and the choir official and his key supporters spoke against. I made a prepared speech, in support of Siân and the committee.

There were several 'points of order', clearly designed to muddy the waters, and the meeting became almost farcical at times, but eventually a vote was taken. Unbelievably, the result was tied with exactly half the choir voting for the motion and half against. After this, Siân finally decided she couldn't carry on, with half the choir against her. I also decided I would immediately resign from the choir and informed people that evening. I later sent the following email to the secretary of the Orpheus to make my resignation official:

'Due to recent events, it is with very great regret that I tender my resignation from the Morriston Orpheus Choir. I will arrange to return choir property in due course. I have been proud to be a member of the choir for over 23 years, and this is a very sad day for me. I wish the Orpheus well for the future'.

In the final analysis, the issue was a matter of principle, and I've endeavoured to reflect this in my account.

25 - PHOENIX RISING

Two days after the Extraordinary General Meeting, Mari and I flew to the Algarve for a much-needed holiday. I couldn't escape the repercussions even in Portugal! We stayed at our usual apartment, and I called at the local shop for bread and milk etc, and a British newspaper. I could only get the *Daily Mail* (not my favourite) and I was sitting on our patio in the sun, idly leafing through the pages, when I came across a photograph of Siân and a substantial article about her departure from the Orpheus. The inference was that she had been forced out of the male-voice choir because she was a woman. This became a recurring theme in the media, although it was largely a red herring.

By the time we returned home, things were going a bit crazy. There was talk of Siân forming a new choir and there was a lot of national media interest. In the *Western Mail* on the Monday there was a full-page article, mainly sympathetic to Siân (as was most of the media coverage). I phoned Siân and offered to help setting up her new choir. She asked me to talk to the media who were clamouring to speak to someone, but I wasn't happy to do this. I didn't want to deride the Orpheus on television; it had been part of my life for too long. I had already said my piece in the privacy of the EGM and part of me still hoped there would be a future reconciliation. In the event, Terry, one of Siân's supporters from the committee was interviewed on television. He compared the imminent split with the way the Orpheus was formed in 1935 when the choir broke away from the Morriston United Choir. It seemed that history was repeating itself.

I agonised about joining the breakaway choir and had mixed emotions. I wanted to support Siân, but I didn't want to harm the

Orpheus. I was having sleepless nights but, in the end, I decided to go ahead with the new choir. Around thirty other choristers felt the same way as me, including five past-chairmen of the Orpheus and most of the committee. I helped to organise the new choir and a few days later we held a photoshoot at Bracelet Bay for the Press. We all wore black outfits and very much looked the part. The picture appeared in the following day's *South Wales Evening Post* whose front page two days earlier had held a massive headline which read 'Disharmony' with a picture of the Orpheus with a tear right down the middle. It was sad it had come to this.

Following the photoshoot, we met to discuss the formation of the new choir. Rules were made and officers appointed and there was a lot of positivity and determination. During the meeting, two more 'disgusted' choristers arrived straight from the Orpheus rehearsal. We decided that our name would be 'Morriston Phoenix Choir'. We felt that we should retain 'Morriston' in our title and 'Phoenix' represented a rising from the ashes of the bitter dispute that had torn us apart. The date of formation was 27 June 2007 and on 1 July, the Morriston Phoenix Choir held its first rehearsal at the historic Mynyddbach Chapel, the oldest independent chapel in Swansea.

There was a great deal of outside support for Siân and the Phoenix Choir after all the media coverage, and offers of help came flooding in. Right from the start we were fortunate to have the services of two skilled accompanists in Robert Marshall and Richard John. We soon established ourselves as a viable choir and it was an exciting new beginning. Clearly, a lot of hard work lay ahead but the mood at our first rehearsal was overwhelmingly positive. Twenty-nine of us had made the break and twenty-eight attended the first rehearsal, including my friend Bill and my son, Phil. The Orpheus would miss the ones that left, because they were all committed choristers, but with around ninety singers remaining they could carry on without us. I was gratified about this despite the bitterness.

At our second rehearsal, BBC Radio Four turned up to record the Phoenix singing and to carry out interviews. Being recorded for radio when the choir was just a few days old must have been some sort of a record! Apparently, they also recorded the Orpheus on the same evening. The Orpheus had by now appointed long-serving accompanist, Joy Amman Davies, as their new musical director.

Two weeks later, I returned all my Orpheus property and it felt like a final act of separation. The following week, Bill and I met socially with my old friends Des and Barry in Cardiff Bay and over several beers I related the whole story. Des admitted it was the first time he'd ever listened for so long without saying a word! I wish I'd recorded the conversation: it would probably have been a more accurate account than my memory now allows me.

The following day, the Phoenix gave its first live performance at a wedding reception at the Brangwyn Hall. There were over a hundred guests present, and we received a great response, which was very encouraging. Our repertoire didn't contain anything specifically arranged for the Orpheus: we performed only published music and songs introduced by Siân. This gave us a varied programme that included fresh, modern pieces and Welsh classics. Our early repertoire included *You Raise Me Up*, *Back to the Sixties*, *African Trilogy* and, of course, *Rhythm of Life* and *Bohemian Rhapsody,* as well as another Queen hit *Don't Stop Me Now* (arranged for the Phoenix by Mark Burstow, conductor of Bournemouth Male Voice Choir). Our Welsh favourites included *Men of Harlech* and popular hymn tunes, including Siân's own arrangement of *Calon Lân*. The song *Don't Stop Me Now* became something of a Phoenix signature tune.

The Phoenix set-up was deliberately different from the Orpheus. We had a 'board' instead of a 'committee' and some of the choir's officers were wives and partners, making it more inclusive. Our MD was on the board: after her Orpheus experience, Siân wanted to be part of the decision-making process. All this didn't stop disagreements, of course! We rehearsed on the same nights as before but now had an interval for tea and coffee. Instead of a chairman, we had a spokesperson, and Bill was the first to occupy this position. We set about raising funds and soon put ourselves on a sound financial footing. We approved a Constitution within the first month and Phil soon had an attractive website up and running, featuring our new logo. We received loads of supportive messages online. One of our number returned to the Orpheus but we were soon over thirty voices, aiming for forty.

One month after our formation there was a very sad occasion that brought the Phoenix and Orpheus back together for the first and only time. This was the funeral of Dennis Owen, a much-loved Orpheus chorister. At a moving ceremony in Margam crematorium we joined together to sing *Gwahoddiad* and *You Raise Me Up*, with Joy conducting. Afterwards, I shook hands with several Orpheus choristers; we were still friends despite what had happened.

Two weeks later the Phoenix was singing at the Swansea Bay Beer Festival at the Brangwyn Hall. There was a special ale brewed for the occasion called 'Phoenix Rising', brewed 'in celebration of the formation of Wales's newest Male Voice Choir'. We sang a selection of sixties hits and 'Queen' numbers from the Brangwyn Hall stage to a rousing reception from festival goers.

A week later we were invited to sing at the 30th birthday party of Sonny Parker, the Welsh rugby international, at the Oceana Club in Cardiff. The whole Welsh rugby team was there after playing France in the afternoon. Our performance was a surprise birthday present for Sonny, and it was a great to mingle with the Welsh team and to enjoy a good singsong with them after our performance; the team also joined us on stage for photographs. The only pity was they'd lost to France!

Our list of forthcoming engagements was beginning to look

241

impressive; we even had grand plans for an overseas tour! There was a double-header on consecutive days at the National Botanic Garden of Wales where we had our first official choir photo taken in the splendid surroundings. Then we recorded some items on a CD and posted them on our website for the world to hear. When Mari and I went to South Africa on holiday shortly afterwards, I proudly played the Phoenix recording in our hotel foyer for the pleasure of the other guests. Other early engagements were the Monkey Bar in Swansea (a great music venue), Langland Bay Golf Club and the Marriott Hotel. All these gigs were fee-paying, helping to swell choir funds. We also took part in a show at the Grand Theatre with the Habibi Dancers, in front of around 700 people. It was the first time I'd ever shared the stage with belly dancers! We were being praised for the energy and movement we were putting into our performances.

We were also committed to helping local communities in Swansea. There was an event at the Leadfield in Clase, near Morriston, an area of open grassland. The location enjoys great views but on the actual day in November, the weather was miserable, and we ended up performing in the rain to the proverbial three men and a dog with the local kids riding round and round the choir on their bikes! It was a far cry from the Sydney Opera House! The following week, singing at a wedding at Llanrhidian was a doddle by comparison.

The choir membership soon reached forty and we were kitted out with new, modern black suits with snazzy ties. In early December, BBC Wales asked the Phoenix to take part in the 'X Ray' television programme. Lucy Owen and the crew came along to our rehearsal to record the choir and interviewed several choristers about issues of concern to viewers. All good publicity. By this time, we had relocated our rehearsal venue to St Teilo's Church in Clase.

Leading up to Christmas, we performed at Bonymaen and took part in the Festival of Carols at Tabernacle in Morriston. There

242

were also some social events, including a Christmas lunch at the Dolphin Hotel and a Christmas party at rehearsal. Despite the challenges, we were an ambitious and happy bunch. Our final event of the year was a Christmas concert at Clyne Golf Club. What a 2007 it had been!

Another social event kicked off 2008 when a coach load of Phoenix members and partners went on a trip to Torquay. Two days after our return we performed in the splendid surroundings of Cardiff City Hall. There was more good news when, thanks to our accompanist Rob's approach, Bonnie Tyler agreed to become the President of the Phoenix. We were delighted to have a big star on board, and we went down to Mumbles for a photoshoot with Bonnie.

Up to this time, I had been helping with recruitment, but I now took over from Terry as choir events manager. Among our next series of events was a concert in Rhiwbina, Cardiff, in aid of Leukaemia Research. We presented a full concert programme, including the Robbie Williams song, *Angels*.

The Phoenix soon moved its rehearsal room again, to a more suitable and welcoming venue at Penlan Methodist Church, which became the choir's permanent home. Regular engagements continued, and we held a open rehearsal in Mumbles. On a family note, we celebrated the birth of Seren, Phil and Gail's first child and my fourth granddaughter.

Although the Phoenix was progressing well, there was plenty of plain speaking about the way ahead. Siân was determined to have her say about things and we did our best to accommodate her wishes. I could understand her concerns after what had happened at the Orpheus.

The next couple of months were hectic. The choir sang the

National Anthem on the pitch at Cardiff Arms Park for the Welsh
Varsity Match between Swansea and Cardiff before a crowd of
around 7,500, the choir's biggest audience to date. There was a
photoshoot at Limeslade Bay that had very painful consequences.
We were posing on the rocks when one of the older choristers
slipped and started to fall. Simon Davies dived to save him and
went flying through the air himself, landing on rocks below and
badly injuring himself. He was off work for several months as a
result of his heroic act. We later held a sponsored walk and raised
substantial funds by walking the ten miles from Morriston to
Mumbles Pier. Then there was the first Phoenix AGM and a
meeting with a concert agent who was keen to promote the
Phoenix in venues across England. Things were moving ahead.

Later in May, the Phoenix was invited to sing at a joint concert
in Bournemouth with the Bournemouth Male Voice Choir. Mari
and I drove down and joined everybody at our Bournemouth hotel
for a two-night stay. The concert at St Stephen's Church was a
complete sell-out and I was a bit apprehensive before the show as
the larger Bournemouth choir were a slick outfit. In the event, Siân
inspired us to give our very best performance. We had a great
ovation from the packed church, repeated when the two choirs
joined together at the end. We were on a high when we returned to
the hotel for the best afterglow ever. Siân and Bill were playing
their guitars and we sang well into the early hours. Mark Burstow
and some of the Bournemouth boys joined us and my friends Geoff
and Dubby from Lee-on-the-Solent were also there. We were still
buzzing the following day.

Shortly afterwards, I received a call asking for the choir to sing
at a big funeral in Burton-on-Trent. The choir would be
accommodated overnight in a plush hotel and sing in a large
marquee at the post-funeral gathering. I was unable to attend but
made the necessary arrangements for the choir. Next, we recorded
some songs on a CD as requested by Classic FM and I was starting
to become concerned about our ability to fulfil the ambitious
programme facing us!

The Choir's first anniversary was fast approaching, and it was decided to hold our first Annual Concert to mark the occasion. We arranged this at the Grand Theatre in Swansea for 12 July 2008 and Siân booked the well-known entertainer Mike Doyle for the show, billed as the 'Morriston Phoenix Choir Founders' Concert'. We also invited the Counterpoint School of Performing Arts to perform contemporary dance and to join the choir for several items. This innovative approach was typical of Siân, and it was a new experience to sing with the young dancers moving around us. It added colour and graceful movement to the traditional line-up of men in black suits and we were encouraged to add some movement ourselves! Our President, Bonnie Tyler, wrote an inspirational foreword to the programme and the icing on the cake was the appearance of Philip Madoc, the famous Welsh actor, who acted as compere for the evening. An audience of around 800 packed into the theatre and the whole evening was a resounding success. Much of the work for the event was done by our two Brecon members, Derek and Alastair, who entertained Philip Madoc at Morgans Hotel. It was a fitting end to the first year in the life of the Morriston Phoenix Choir.

26 - OVER TO ULSTER

Bookings in the summer of 2008 were coming thick and fast. At a happy occasion in Brecon, the choir sang at the Ruby Wedding party of baritone Derek Hills and his wife Jan. We also sang at the National Museum in Cardiff at a function for the Jaguar XK Club, followed by a wedding in Gorslas. After the wedding we felt obliged to visit 'The Phoenix' pub! Then it was the 'Sing the Nation' event at Castle Square in Swansea to celebrate the Olympic Games handover, followed by a performance at the National Conference of the U3A (University of The Third Age) at Swansea University.

In September, we gave the first concert for our new promoter at the Pavilion Theatre in Exmouth and enjoyed an overnight stay at this attractive seaside resort. We were also invited to sing at the launch of the NHS Bowel Cancer Screening programme. This was a high-profile affair at the Liberty Stadium, launching an important initiative by the NHS in Wales.

Although I was happy with the events we were doing, I was finding it difficult to retain commitment, particularly as I had embarked on an exciting project outside the choir. My mood wasn't helped by 'the concert that never was'. Our promoter had organised an ambitious event, headlining the Phoenix at the prestigious St George's Hall in Liverpool, billed as a 'Welsh Night for the City of Culture'. This would be our biggest show to date and Siân was putting a lot of effort into the preparation. In the event, the promoter pulled the show shortly before it was due to take place. This didn't help our confidence in the promoter, but we agreed to continue with him for the time being. The next engagement he arranged, at the Oakengates Theatre in Telford, went well.

We then gave a concert in Hay-on-Wye, reprising the Orpheus visit the previous year; this time we sang at the Hay Winter Festival. In December, events included a charity concert in Manselton, and we finished off 2008 with another Christmas show at Clyne Golf Club where we included *Mack the Knife* and *Delilah* in our programme. It was the 34th engagement of the year for the Morriston Phoenix Choir, a year that saw many positives.

There was, however, an issue that bothered some of us. We had enjoyed the services of two excellent accompanists since the choir's formation and they shared the rehearsals and concerts between them. They were both brilliant, but Siân decided she would prefer to have one main accompanist. It was proposed that the two accompanists would be auditioned and interviewed, and the upshot was that Rob Marshall refused as he found this unacceptable. He felt that both he and Richard had given loyal service to the Phoenix and that the loyalty was not being reciprocated. Siân had always publicly said how lucky the choir was to have two fine pianists to share the work and that if they wanted to continue down this road then he would make the decision for them and resign. Unfortunately, we lost a couple of choristers who felt strongly about this. At around the same time, Phil took a break from the choir, mainly for family reasons.

The new year started on a bright note, however, with an enjoyable concert at the Queens Hall in Narberth. We shared the stage with the local 'One Voice Choir' and it was great to see Orpheus member, Dudley Williams in the audience. Then, Siân conducted the choir at Castle Square in the 'Get Welsh' event organised by the *South Wales Evening Post*.

Next, it was off to Fareham in Hampshire for another theatre concert, this time on St David's Day. I was about to leave to catch the choir coach when Mari asked if I could help to move a grandfather clock. We were carefully moving the clock when the front window of the clock flew open and the heavy mechanism shot out, landing on Mari's foot and cutting it badly. It was bleeding profusely so I drove her straight to Singleton Hospital where they stitched it up. By this time the choir coach had long gone. After a discussion with Mari, we decided I should drive down to Fareham for the concert (which I'd organised with our promoter). I'd also arranged to meet our friends from Lee-on-the-Solent. I got there just in time for the performance at the Ferneham Hall. The afterglow was at the Royal Navy's training establishment at HMS Collingwood where we were entertained in the officers' mess. During this, my chorister friends gave a spirited rendering of *My Grandfather's Clock*! Fortunately, Mari's foot soon healed.

Our next engagement was at the Towngate Theatre in Basildon, a venue I'd visited thirty years before with the Cwmbran choir. Confusingly, the original theatre had been knocked down and rebuilt in a different place. Siân was absent due to illness, so our friend Mark Burstow from Bournemouth kindly conducted the show. In discussions with Mark, it was suggested that we should consider a visit to his homeland of Northern Ireland. The plan was to come to fruition later in the year.

Among our next gigs was a dream event: we were invited to sing at a brewery to launch a new beer! This was the Tomos Watkin Brewery in Llansamlet, and we entertained the invited guests celebrating the launch of '1879 Lager', named to recognise the anniversary of the heroic defence of Rorke's Drift during the Zulu War. Afterwards we enjoyed a generous buffet and as much beer as we wanted as well as receiving a handsome fee. Other engagements included a performance at the Grand Theatre Arts Wing which was my last concert as events manager. I had just signed contracts with my publisher to write a series of three books about a walk through Wales. The walk would follow my chosen route from the southernmost point to the northernmost point, some 370 miles in total, and would showcase the history and landscape

248

of Wales. The series would be entitled *Wales - A Walk Through Time*.

In May there was an enjoyable concert at the Frome Memorial Theatre in Somerset which was the last event arranged through our promoter. The series of theatre concerts had enabled us to travel the country and helped to establish the name of the choir. In June there were two concerts on consecutive days; the first was in Coventry at the lovely Warwick Road United Reform Church. The *Coventry Evening Telegraph* previewed the concert and highlighted the choir's mantra of 'no more singing with long faces'. The concert was organised by the Coventry branch of my family, and it was great to see my sister Peggy, with nephew Dan and cousins Jean and Liz. The audience included members of the City of Coventry Male Voice Choir. It was a special occasion for me as I'd been baptised at the church during World War Two (while my father was fighting in Normandy).

We rushed back to Wales for our second Annual Concert at the Taliesin Theatre. A lot of rehearsal time had gone into preparations, including choreography for the choir. We opened the concert with a lively version of *Rhythm of Life*, singing and moving at the same time. It was a refreshing change from standing to attention like tailor's dummies. We closed the first half with *Men of Harlech*, marching smartly on stage and our programme included the 'Take That' hit, *Rule the World*; Robbie Williams' *Angels*; Bonnie Tyler's *Total Eclipse of the Heart* as well as the 'Queen' hits we were well-known for. The guest artiste was Laura Collins, a rising star of British jazz, joined by her trio. We were buzzing coming off stage at the end after singing the Welsh hymns that would always be in our repertoire.

The summer continued with a civil partnership ceremony at the Brangwyn Hall followed by a concert at Pennard Carnival and a wedding party at the Stradey Park Hotel in Llanelli. I missed an event in Dorstone, Herefordshire (and the afterglow in Alastair's barn).

The choir was now all set for its first commercial CD, produced by Sain Records and recorded at the BBC Studios in Swansea under the expert guidance of sound engineer Peter Williams. The album was entitled *Having A Good Time* and it was decided to drop 'Morriston' from our title to avoid confusion and to emphasise our identity. The album contained many of our favourites and included the Michael Jackson hit *Heal The World*.

The next venture was the tour to Northern Ireland, arranged with the help of Ulsterman Mark Burstow and the Larne Concert Choir who arranged a couple of concerts for the Phoenix in County Antrim. Gaynor Fury took over the organisation of the tour from our end and did a great job. Sally Tarlton came along as our guest pianist, with Siân conducting.

We left Bristol Airport very early and were in Belfast city centre in time for an 'Ulster Fry' breakfast. This set us up for our prearranged Belfast city tour taking in the City Hall, Royal Courts of Justice, Waterfront Hall and the Titanic Quarter with the famous Harland & Wolff cranes and the dry dock where *Titanic* was built. We continued to the Stormont Parliament Buildings followed by the Crumlin Road Gaol! This led us to west Belfast and the divided areas well known from the Troubles. We drove along the Shankill Road with its Loyalist murals (Union Jacks and royalty) then crossed the so-called Peace Line to travel along the Falls Road with its Republican murals (Tricolours and IRA). The importance of flags and symbols was clear for all to see. We passed Queen's University and St Anne's Cathedral with its iconic Spire of Hope before heading north-east to our hotel in Carrickfergus, situated alongside the harbour with the imposing castle nearby. We soon discovered the Joymount Arms, one of the town's oldest pubs. It was great to be on tour again!

Next morning a few of us took a train into Belfast and visited St George's covered market, and St Malachy's Catholic Church, with its fan vaulted ceiling, and then the impressive Ulster Concert Hall. Our last port of call was the Crown Liquor Saloon, 'one of the great bars of the world' with its Victorian décor and carved mahogany booths. A pint of the black stuff completed our morning's taste of Belfast before we returned to 'Carrick' to prepare for our evening concert trip.

We travelled up the coast to Glenarm, one of the famous Glens of Antrim, in an area of outstanding natural beauty. We performed with Larne Concert Choir at St Patrick's (Church of Ireland) in Glenarm and received a warm welcome. The convivial afterglow was held at the Londonderry Arms in Carnlough where I engaged in a rather profound conversation with the Larne choir's conductor. He was a Presbyterian minister and we discussed predestination, among other things. The rest of my mates were drinking Bushmills in the other bar, but I was keen to learn something about the religious thinking of our new friends. We were able to continue the revelry when we returned to our hotel in Carrickfergus.

Next day, our pre-arranged coach tour of the Antrim coast took us to Glengariff and Cushendall and on to the attractive town of Ballycastle on the north-eastern coastal tip of Northern Ireland. Looking across to Rathlin Island and beyond, the coast of Scotland was surprisingly close across the water, just fourteen or so miles away. I was reminded of the close historical connections between the two countries. We carried on past the famous Carrick-a-Rede rope bridge on our way to the Giant's Causeway where we walked down to see the amazing stones, consisting of around 40,000 basalt columns that are uniformly hexagonal in shape; it's unbelievable that these are a work of nature. Afterwards, it was the Causeway Hotel for lunch, then a visit to the nearby Old Bushmills Irish whiskey distillery, before returning to Carrickfergus via Ballymoney and Ballymena.

251

In the evening, we were strolling along the harbourside in Carrickfergus when I noticed a prominent statue near the castle. I asked my companions who the statue was, when a little kid riding by on his bike overheard me and shouted proudly 'It's King Billy!' (King William III of Orange landed at Carrickfergus on 14 June 1690 prior to his victory at the Battle of the Boyne on 1 July). We spent the evening at the RAOB (Buffs) Club where we enjoyed the live band's performance. At the end, everyone stood to attention and sang 'God Save the Queen'.

On Sunday morning, the Phoenix sang at a service at the First Presbyterian Church in Carrickfergus. There were lots of families and children there as well as a live band and the service was very modern with videos projected onto a large screen. The church was packed full, and we received an enthusiastic welcome. After the service it was the Joymount Inn for lunch before we headed to Belfast Airport for our flight home.

It had been an enjoyable and thought-provoking visit to Northern Ireland and in just a few days I managed to get a sense of a place that I'd hitherto seen only on television, mostly for the wrong reasons. When I was initially planning the tour, I asked our hosts if we could sing in a Catholic church as well as a Protestant one. Perhaps this was a bit naïve on my part as we were visiting a mainly Protestant area. Our welcome throughout the tour was first class, and we marvelled at the city of Belfast and the scenery of the Antrim coast. I couldn't begin to understand the divisions between the people, although the Good Friday Agreement had clearly made a big difference, bringing a blessed peace to the province. At Belfast Airport I bought a book about the 'History of the Troubles' and read it as soon as I returned home.

We returned to our programme of concerts but personally, I was getting more and more involved with my walk project. There was a lot of research and planning to do and I realised I would have to commit more time to it, so I requested leave of absence from the choir. A few of my friends had left and joined other choirs, but there were still new members joining the Phoenix and the choir was in good shape. I attended about half a dozen more concerts leading up to Christmas, ending up with a concert at the Waterfront Church in Swansea's Maritime Quarter and finally, the Christmas Show at Clyne Golf Club. In the end, it was a relief to make the break and in my heart of hearts I knew I wouldn't be going back. After forty-three years of singing in three very different male-voice choirs, and performing on stages all around the world, my choir journey was over. Or so I thought.

27 - ENCORE A CAPPELLA

There was a sense of freedom after my break from the choir. I threw myself into preparations for my long walk, planning the route to reflect the history and landscape of Wales. I started at the southernmost point in Wales, on the island of Flat Holm in the Bristol Channel, after which I started walking on the mainland. The first leg took me to Brecon, which provided the basis for the first book in my 'Walk Through Time' series. Two further stages would follow: from Brecon to Harlech and from Harlech to Cemaes Bay in Anglesey (the northernmost point). I included three iconic mountains on my walk: Penyfan, Cadair Idris and Snowdon, and completed the 370-mile walk in stages, mostly walking on my own. There were lots of prior and subsequent visits to castles, museums, archives and libraries for research purposes. The walk itself took thirty days, but the whole project took several years to complete. I met many interesting people along the way and had some great experiences, but I can't remember doing any singing!

After the walk project I continued writing and had a couple more books about Mumbles and Gower published. I kept in touch with Bill Kenny and other friends from the Phoenix, and another good friend, Clive Williams, from the Orpheus. The Phoenix sang at several of my book launches, and it was great to see the boys still 'having a good time'. Siân moved on a couple of years after I left the Phoenix and was replaced as conductor by John Mills.

During the summer of 2019, someone mentioned that Mumbles A Cappella choir were rehearsing at our local church, St Peter's in Newton. Our vicar, Chris Darvill, and organist and choirmaster, Phil Orrin, had created a music ministry at St Peter's, and the A Cappella choir had been formed about a year earlier. Reports were glowing and I thought it may be something I would like to try. I was attracted because it would be a new challenge: I hadn't sung in a mixed choir before (apart from a few one-offs). It was almost ten years since I last sang with the Phoenix.

I turned up at rehearsal and had a chat with Phil and soon settled in the choir, singing first bass. I was impressed by the musical skills of the singers and the speed of learning. There were people of all ages and the choir had already given several successful concerts, including performances of the Mozart *Requiem* and the Allegri *Miserere*. They were about to embark on a tour to Belgium. I soon found myself singing at a concert at St David's Church in Neath where Mumbles A Cappella were the guests at a 'Valley Rock Voices' concert. We sang a short programme including *Northern Lights* by Ola Gjeilo. It was good to be on stage again, even as a supporting act to an almost 200-strong ladies' pop choir!

The A Cappella choir set off on their tour to Bruges and Ghent shortly afterwards (I'd joined too late to go on the trip). On their return, I was regaled with stories of their singing in great cathedrals (and sampling the Belgian beer!). There were plans to return to Ghent the following year.

In September 2019, we sang at Oystermouth with the Swansea Bay Symphony Orchestra, and I particularly enjoyed singing the Karl Jenkins *Benedictus*. In December we guested at a concert at the Brangwyn Hall and our Christmas concert at St Peter's followed. The demand for tickets was high so Phil and wife, Karen (choir administrator and one of our altos), decided to repeat the concert for a second night. My family was well-represented in the audience on the opening night, including four of my grandchildren. Our programme ranged from a Victorian madrigal to *Moon River* and *My Way*. We ended with *That's What I'd Like for Christmas* from 'Pickwick', which brought the house down!

In February 2020 we sang at the Maggie's Cancer Centre at Singleton Hospital which was to be our last public performance for a long while. The Coronavirus pandemic struck, and we were in lockdown from March onwards. Phil soon had the brilliant idea of creating recordings and videos by digitally combining our individual voices and pictures. The first such composite recording was of the Perosi *Ave maris stella*, and we recorded our individual parts at home and sent them electronically to Phil and Karen, who cleverly mixed them and produced a video which was posted on YouTube. The result was fantastic and received a high number of views. The process was repeated with further pieces which kept us singing during our enforced isolation. One of these was *Hey Jude* with an accompanying video showing the deserted promenade at Mumbles and locked up pubs and restaurants. A poignant scene. Phil also composed a motet called *Noli me tangere (Don't touch me)*, specially written for a masked choir, which we recorded and released on YouTube.

Our Easter concert for 2020 was cancelled and the return visit to Ghent was postponed. At least I could work on my latest book, and at various times I was able to get out and about in Gower. In early 2021, Phil offered music and singing lessons via Zoom, and a restricted choir practice resumed in May. By this time the Ghent visit had been postponed again, until 2022. Our first post-lockdown public engagement was in September 2021 at the Mumbles Fest, a major outdoor festival held at the spectacular setting of Oystermouth Castle.

My latest book 'A-Z of Mumbles & Gower' was now ready for publication and members of the A Cappella choir kindly agreed to sing at my book launch at Newton Village Hall, very much appreciated by everyone present. We were busy preparing for the Christmas 2021 concert, but when the event came around, I was unable to sing, having developed a nasty chest infection (not Covid!). I was sorry to miss singing the wide-ranging concert programme which included *Os Justi* by Bruckner and a medley from *Les Misérables*.

256

The year 2022 arrived with cautious optimism. Then on 24 February, Russia invaded Ukraine. There was an outpouring of support for Ukraine and Phil straight away arranged the Ukraine National Anthem for the choir. We recorded it less than a week after the invasion and posted it on YouTube. It had an immediate impact, with many thousands of views; it was even played in the bunkers of Kyiv! A week later the television cameras of HTV Wales descended on our choir practice to film us singing the anthem and to carry out interviews; this went out live on the 6 o'clock news. A few days later, we were singing the anthem again in Castle Square in Swansea in a fundraising event for Ukraine. Subsequently, several choir members welcomed refugees from Ukraine into their homes and we welcomed Ukrainian alto Svitlana Osiptsova into our choir.

Next up was our Easter concert with a programme that included the Perosi *Magnificat* and five sacred motets composed by Phil. The centrepiece of the concert was the *Stabat Mater* by Sebastien de Brossard, a magnificent but relatively unknown work of many moods and movements. The soloists were choir members, and the work was performed with harpsichord, played by Tom Howell (ex-chorister and brilliant organist). The concert closed with a rousing rendition of *The Heavens Are Telling* from Haydn's *Creation*. The following week, Mari and I tested positive for Covid, but we soon recovered.

Our summer concert was held at All Saints, Oystermouth, with the first half devoted to Beatles music. By contrast, the second half included music by Purcell and Boyce, with Phil performing a Handel organ concerto with a string quartet, followed by the choir's great finale, *Zadok the Priest*. We followed up with another performance at the Mumbles Fest, but thoughts were now turning to our forthcoming tour to Belgium, and another new repertoire.

In the hectic week before our departure for Belgium, we had two rehearsals and a lunchtime recital at All Saints, where we presented our full tour programme. We sang a cappella for an hour in very warm conditions and received a standing ovation at the end. The following day, we had a performance at Swansea's Grand Theatre just hours before our midnight departure. We sang at an evening of music, dance and drama to raise funds for Ukraine before meeting our tour coach at St Peter's where 'Chris the Vic' had open house in the vicarage before departure. It was a high-spirited group that boarded the coach and the party atmosphere continued on our overnight journey to Dover; there wasn't much sleep!

On arrival in Dover, our bleary-eyed party left the coach to pass through Passport Control. Soprano Tracy presented her passport for inspection, only to be informed by the unsmiling official that it was not her passport! It was her daughter's passport (packed for her by husband, Ian). Now, Tracy is very young-looking, but could hardly pass for a nine-year-old! After a terse encounter with the customs officer, a more senior official was summoned who point-blank refused to allow Tracy to travel. After desperate pleas, with Tracy supported by Phil and Karen, the official finally relented, but Tracy was sternly warned she would need her own passport to be allowed back into the UK. By now, poor Tracy was distraught, and the trauma would continue as she tried to somehow get her proper passport over to Ghent in time for our return (she didn't fancy trying to cross the Channel illegally in a rubber dinghy).

The ferry carried us to Calais without further problem and we arrived at the Ibis Hotel in Ghent around lunchtime. Our hotel was next to the magnificent St Bavo's Cathedral where we would be performing next day and after a short rehearsal in the hotel bar, we explored (and tasted) the delights of Ghent.

Next morning it was the market by the river followed by a boat trip on Ghent's waterways. Then it was back to the hotel to change into

258

our blacks. After a short warm-up, we headed across to the cathedral and took our places on the chancel steps. Our concert had been well-advertised, and the huge cathedral was full of concertgoers and tourists.

We started our recital with the beautiful *Jesu, dulcis memoria* by Victoria. I was a little nervous at the start, but soon settled down as we continued with the Caccini *Ave Maria*, performed (unusually) with a saxophone intro, splendidly played by Harry Hutchins. Our programme of sacred music carried on, including music by Palestrina and Ola Gjeilo, and three different settings of *Ave maris stella* by Grieg, Perosi and Hassler. We ended our concert with two famous Welsh hymns, *Cwm Rhondda* and *Calon Lân*, sung with *hwyl* and taking full advantage of the cathedral's acoustic. It was a privilege to sing with this choir in such a magnificent setting, and of all the cathedrals that I had sung in, this was one of the very best.

We were elated with our performance. Phil was delighted and the afterglow was soon in full swing. A group of us went for dinner to Bier Central (moules-frites and Fourchette beer) before joining the rest of the choir at a welcoming bar on the square; more Belgian beer-tasting (and singing) until late. But we were conscious of tomorrow's engagement at the Menin Gate in Ypres.

In the meantime, Tracy had been having frantic telephone calls to Ian in Mumbles, resulting in Ian sending the passport by express delivery. Tracy was making alternative plans but, happily, the precious passport arrived at our hotel the day before our return. Panic over (until Tracy got her hands on Ian!).

Next morning, I returned to the cathedral so I could appreciate it properly in my own time. I also ascended the nearby Belfort belfry tower and saw (and heard) the magnificent carillon and chime bells while enjoying great views over the city of Ghent.

We were soon on our way to Ypres, but first we visited the Yser

259

Tower that was built to honour the Flemish soldiers who died at the front in World War One. After the original tower was destroyed in an explosion, the present 22-storey tower was built in 1965 and houses an incredible museum. An elevator ascends to the top where a viewing platform affords panoramic views over the Flanders battlefields. The descent is then carried out by stairs through the 22 floors, each of which holds displays illustrating the Flemish aspects of the war. The chronology of the war is followed in a fascinating way, with many archive photographs, newspaper articles and artefacts, including many items recovered from the battlefields. Uniforms and weapons are displayed and the devastating effect of the war on the local population is brought to life. All this is revealed as you descend the tower, and the overall effect is quite profound, clearly showing the madness and folly of war. The lower floors consist of a maze of trenches, giving a sense of what it must have been like at the front.

We spent several hours at the museum, each of us leaving with our own thoughts. A choir photograph was taken in front of the museum before we boarded our coach, where a headcount revealed that one of our number was missing. There was no sign of Stewart. What had happened to him? Perhaps he was lost in the maze of trenches? A search party eventually found him, and when he boarded the bus, he was greeted with a chorus of *Guide Me O Thou Great Redeemer*! Stewart took it all in good part (but there was more to follow).

We carried on to Ypres for our performance at the Menin Gate war memorial. The 'Memorial to the Missing' bears the names of 54,000 British and Commonwealth service personnel who died in the Ypres salient during World War One, and whose graves are unknown. A solemn ceremony is held at 20.00 hours every evening at the Menin Gate, and this has taken place every evening since 1928, except during the German occupation of Ypres in World War Two. Large crowds gather to pay their respects when the buglers play the Last Post, and on this occasion, the Mumbles A Cappella choir had the honour of taking part in the ceremony.

260

After the Last Post and the immortal words 'At the going down of the sun, and in the morning, we will remember them', we sang *Cwm Rhondda* and *Calon Lân* while wreaths were being laid. The buglers then played the Reveille to end a very moving occasion. One of the wreaths was laid by Anthony Forwood, one of our party, on behalf of St Peter's Church. The ceremony had particular resonance for me as my daughter, Lucy, sang here a few years previously with Côr y Gleision, as did my friend, Des, with Pontnewydd Male Choir. I was proud to follow in their footsteps.

Before the ceremony, we changed into our blacks wherever we could. Many of us changed in restaurant toilets, and some changed on our bus, including Stewart. When he later changed back into his day clothes, he discovered he had an extra pair of trousers. They weren't his (and unfortunately didn't fit) so he dutifully looked after them and kept them overnight. In the meantime, we arrived back in Ghent determined to enjoy our last (late) night in Belgium. Phil suggested we all meet at a certain bar 'in a big square' where a convivial gathering was enjoyed by all, reflecting on a job well done.

We were up early for departure next morning and after breakfast were mustering to board the coach at 08.30 sharp; but Stewart was again missing. Then he suddenly appeared, cool as you like, having not woken up until 08.10! He'd managed to pack just in time, but still had the extra pair of trousers: he later joked that he'd spent the previous two hours walking the corridors of the hotel trying to find a man in his underpants! The trousers eventually turned out to belong to our illustrious conductor! More hilarity ensued.

Passport control and security checks at Calais went as smoothly as Brexit allows and we all boarded the ferry (including a much-relieved Tracy, who had luckily dodged the Rwanda bullet!). The long coach journey home was relieved by some funny memes circulated by Phil, followed by a hilarious quiz with questions such

261

as: 'which soprano asked the most inane questions'; 'who missed the choir photo'; 'which chorister had the trots after a dodgy moules-frites' etc. If you answered 'Stewart' to many of the questions, you scored high marks! We managed to get back to Mumbles without further incident.

A week later we were singing at the Grand Theatre Arts Wing on Ukraine Independence Day, performing with many of the refugees hosted in Swansea. It was uplifting to see the Ukrainians, particularly the children, singing and dancing in their national costume. The finale saw everyone joining together to sing *Calon Lân* and *Sospan Fach* in Welsh. Despite the celebration, we were all too aware of the shadow of the horrific war going on in Ukraine. I couldn't help reflecting on the ceremony at the Menin Gate a week earlier, when we remembered the terrible war of a century ago, and the way that history keeps repeating itself. When will they ever learn?

FINALE À PARIS

On 18 October 2014, I attended the Golden Jubilee Concert of the Cwmbran Male Choir at the Congress Theatre. I went with my old friend, Barry, and it was great to see the Cwmbran boys again, many of whom I hadn't seen for years. It was a smaller choir than in my day, but it was a memorable show. Afterwards, Barry and I met up with Des at the Greenhouse pub to share a few drinks and reminisce about old times. It was the last time I was to see Des: he has since sadly passed away and I feel that I've lost a soulmate. The choral world has certainly lost a great voice. I'll never forget our student days together when we were singing for our beer in the clubs of Cardiff! I have also recently lost my great friend, Bill, who was my roommate on many of our tours together. His singing and guitar-playing at many an afterglow will be sadly missed as well as his genial company.

Many other friends have also gone but the choirs carry on, albeit with reduced numbers these days. The flame of Welsh male-voice choral singing still burns, but perhaps not quite as brightly as in the 'golden' years that I was fortunate to enjoy. Many choir members are getting on in years and the Covid pandemic had its effect: the suspension of rehearsals for long periods certainly didn't help. The Cwmbran choir recently decided to join forces with the Pontypool Male Choir, the combined choir becoming known as the Torfaen Male Choir; I wish them all the luck in the world: one of their second tenors, Travis George, reached the final of 'Britain's Got Talent' in 2023. I recently met up with Barry, Ivor and Ken at the Queen Inn in Upper Cwmbran and it was great to remember the good times we enjoyed together.

It's difficult for male choirs to attract younger recruits these days, so the importance of moving with the times should be remembered. I'm sure this can be achieved without sacrificing the great traditions for which Welsh male-voice choirs are justifiably world-famous.

I've kept contact with my friends in the Phoenix Choir of Wales, and still feel proud to have been a founder member. They continue to enjoy themselves under their popular musical director, John Mills. I also maintain good contacts with Morriston Orpheus friends, particularly Clive Williams who has been a great help in the preparation of this book. It was an honour and a privilege to sing in this great choir for so many years.

In the meantime, I continue to enjoy my time in the Mumbles A Cappella choir, singing early polyphony and modern classic arrangements. We performed works by Schütz and Palestrina at our last Christmas concert, among other festive pieces, and there was a Schubert Mass for Easter.

Our 2023 summer tour was to Paris, with more great concert venues and experiences. We again travelled through the night and this time, there were no passport mishaps, and we arrived safely at our Paris hotel near the Place de la Bastille. The weather was beautiful, and we soon found some excellent restaurants (and bars) in this attractive part of Paris.

The following morning our popular driver, Charlie (who kept us all amused as well as expertly negotiating the Paris traffic) took us to the Eiffel Tower where we embarked on a Seine river cruise. We were now getting into the Paris mood, and it was suggested that I swim naked in the Seine, to add some spice to the final chapter of my book - I responded that it wouldn't be the first time!

But minds were soon turning to the serious business of singing. This would be my first time to sing in Paris, but I fondly recall the adventures I had when passing through the city with the Orpheus back in the 1980s. The A Cappella choir had been booked to sing at two magnificent Paris venues, at La Madeleine and Saint-Sulpice.

First up was the iconic Église de la Madeleine, the famous

neoclassical Paris landmark near the Place de la Concorde. I had always been in awe of this great building and to sing there was a particular thrill. Our recital included works in five languages (excluding English) with the French repertoire represented by the Gounod *Agnus Dei*. Our performance also included *Nu bede vi den Helligånd* by Pedersøn, the Welsh hymn *Melin Cwrt*, the beautiful *Tristis est anima mea* by Kuhnau and *Ave Regina Caelorum* by the young Polish composer, Marek Raczynski. There was a seven-second reverb in the great church, which was quite an experience!

Buoyed by our performance, there were welcome drinks back at the hotel bar after a short rush-hour Metro journey. Following a convivial dinner, a group of us went off to a Jazz Club on the Rue de Rivoli, urged on by my bass pal, Colin Cribb, a keen jazz enthusiast. The music was excellent and went on until the early hours. Sleep was becoming a luxury!

Happily, there was time for a lie-in next morning before Charlie conveyed us to our second concert at the beautiful Église Saint-Sulpice in the Latin Quarter. The acoustic here was perfect and there was a good audience to greet us. We ended our recital with the eight-part, double-choir, *Coelos Ascendit Hodie* by Stanford and the very lively *Salmo 150* by Ernani Aguiar and we were rewarded with an enthusiastic ovation for our performance.

Back at the hotel, the party started and continued long after dinner at a local restaurant. There was a great buzz among everyone, and conductor Phil was justifiably proud of the choir, as we were of him. The journey home was untroubled, with a very funny quiz to help pass the time. It had been a great tour of serious singing, Paris culture and much laughter. Here's to the next one!

So, my choir journey continues, although my book has finally reached its end. I'd like to pay a heartfelt tribute to all the choristers with whom I've shared the stage and to the brilliant musical directors and accompanists that made it all possible. My daughter, Lucy, carried on the tradition, singing with Côr y Gleision in

Cardiff, a fine mixed choir. My grand-daughters, Meg, Cari, Beth and Seren have all enjoyed singing in choirs and shows, performing at some notable venues. Meg was also accepted into the National Youth Choir of Wales, a proud moment. My son, Phil, who sang with me in the Orpheus and Phoenix choirs, is currently re-forming his band (he's the vocalist). I hope he will re-join the choir one day and, eventually, my grandson Ieuan as well.

Mari and I have been fortunate to travel widely and independently, but I would never have seen so many exciting places were it not for my choir journey. Singing in a choir is one of the most stimulating and rewarding things you can do. Please believe me.

Acknowledgements

I would like to thank the many people who have helped me to bring *My Choir Journey* to fruition. My particular thanks go to my good friend Clive G. Williams, Morriston Orpheus Choir member and my companion on many overseas tours. Clive has given freely of his wise counsel and helped me to circulate my draft manuscript for feedback. His love of good restaurants has enabled us to discuss the progress of the project over some excellent lunches!

I have been very grateful for supportive messages received from choir musical directors, Dr Alwyn Humphreys, Joy Amman Davies, Siân Pearce and Phil Orrin. Helpful comments have also been received from many others, including Keith Brown, Patrick Coghlan, Robert Gage, Jeff Harrison, Stewart Helm, Tracy Bowen, Alan Lewis, Ivor Maggs, Peter Richards, John A. Roberts, and W. John Roberts. The officers of the Welsh Association of Male Choirs including their secretary, Chris Evans, have also been most helpful and I'm very grateful to their president, Huw Tregelles Williams, for kindly contributing the foreword.

The images in the book mainly come from my own collection and permission to reproduce the official choir photographs has been gratefully received from the choirs concerned: Torfaen Male Choir, Morriston Orpheus Choir, the Phoenix Choir of Wales and Mumbles A Cappella. Thanks are also due to Catnic Limited and Cardiff Audi as well Pat Ward who took the Phoenix Choir photographs and to Sam Bevan for the Mumbles A Cappella pictures. Every reasonable effort has been made to trace copyright holders but, in some cases, I've been unable to make contact, or it is unclear who holds the copyright. I apologise for any unintentional infringement which will be corrected at the earliest opportunity. The informal photographs have been taken by me or my friends.

Finally, a big thank you to all the choristers that I've been fortunate to sing alongside over the years. There's nothing finer than a choir in harmony.

About the Author

Brian retired from the Electricity Supply Industry a number of years ago, after a career as an engineer and manager, having worked throughout South Wales. Originally from the Eastern Valley of Gwent, he moved to Mumbles some forty years ago. He was educated at West Mon Grammar School in Pontypool and completed his professional qualifications at the University of Wales, Institute of Science and Technology in Cardiff. He is a Member of the Institution of Engineering and Technology.

Brian is a keen singer and has sung in choirs all around the world having toured many times overseas with the Cwmbran, Morriston Orpheus and Phoenix Choirs. He currently sings with Mumbles A Cappella, with whom he recently toured Belgium and Paris. His memoir '*My Choir Journey*' relates his experiences travelling the world and singing in some memorable venues.

His interest in local history saw him publish his first successful book about Mumbles and Gower pubs in 2006, a subject he revisited in a new book in 2018. He has always been a keen walker and has ascended most of the main peaks in Wales and completed numerous long-distance trails. His idea of walking from the southernmost to the northernmost point in Wales saw the publication of '*Wales: A Walk Through Time*', an illustrated account of his journey in three volumes. Another recent book '*Mumbles and Gower Through Time*' explores the way a delightful corner of Wales has changed over the last century. His later book '*A-Z of Mumbles & Gower*' features a personal selection of Places, People and History associated with the locality. Brian enjoys giving talks about his books to many different organisations.

Brian is a Past President of the Probus Club of Mumbles and a Past Chairman of Oystermouth Historical Association. He and his wife, Mari, have a son and daughter and five very special grandchildren.

269

Back Cover images

Sian Pearce and the Phoenix Choir at the National Botanic Garden of Wales

Mumbles A Cappella Choir performing at the Eglise de la Madeleine in Paris

Milton Keynes UK
Ingram Content Group UK Ltd.
UKHW021941051123
432002UK00009B/30